MADHYAMAKALAMKARA VRITTI

Cool Grove Press, an imprint of
Cool Grove Publishing, Inc. New York.
512 Argyle Road, Brooklyn, NY 11218

www. coolgrove.com
For permissions and other inquiries write to info@coolgrove. com

ISBN: 978-1-887276-91-7
Library of Congress Control Number: 2022948637

with
Preface by Khenpo Tsewang Dongyal Rinpoche
Introduction by Marie Friquegnon

Translation Committee:
Marie Friquegnon, Arthur Mandelbaum and Pema Dondrub

Cool Grove Press is a member of
Community of Literary Magazines and Presses [CLMP]
and a past receipient of their Face Out Re-grant for marketing.

This book is distributed to the trade by Ingram Spark

Media alchemy by Kiku

Cool Grove Press

Dedicated to:

Khenchen Shantarakshita,

    Kamalashila,

        Mipham Rinpoche,

            Kyabje Dudjom Rinpoche,

                Khenchen Palden Sherab Rinpoche

and all great lineage masters of the past, the present and the future.

MADHYAMAKALAMKARA VRITTI

Shantarakshita's commentary
on his *Ornament of the Middle Way*

translated by

Khenchen Palden Sherab Rinpoche
and Khenpo Tsewang Dongyal Rinpoche
in collaboration with Geshe Lozang Jamspal

Preface by Khenpo Tsewang Dongyal Rinpoche
Introduction by Marie Friquegnon

Translation Committee:
Marie Friquegnon, Arthur Mandelbaum and Pema Dondrub

Cool Grove Press

Table of Contents

PREFACE
Khenpo Tsewang Dongyal Rinpoche ix

EDITOR'S INTRODUCTION
Marie Louise Friquegnon xiii

MADHYAMAKALAMKARA VRITTI
English Text. 1

MADHYAMAKALAMKARA VRITTI
Tibetan Text (from Tanjur), organized by
Geshe Lozang Jamspal 101

BIBLIOGRAPHY 162

GLOSSARY 166

APPENDIX 177

INDEX 214

THE TRANSLATION COMMITTEE
and BIOGRAPHIES: 216

Notes to the Reader

Following a commonly used system, Sanskrit words will be italicized the first time they are used. Sanskrit words are spelled phonetically except when they are within quotes.

Some members of the translation committee wanted every sentence to be translated literally. Others preferred to stress philosophical clarity. Our translation represents a balance between these two goals.

Acknowledgements

The translation group thanks Lama Drakpa of Padmasambhava Buddhist Center for his very helpful suggestions, and Lama Lorraine O'Rourke and Lama Laia for their assistance in finding a working space at Padma Samye Ling Buddhist Center during the Pandemic.

We thank Cynthia Friend and William Paterson University for their support during the early stages of this project. Most of all we thank our gifted and insightful copy editor Kathleen Miller for her hard work and philosophically eagle eye and our publisher Tej Hazarika, for his enthusiasm and patience with the editing process.

Preface

The great master Shantarakshita is widely known as an emanation of Buddha Vajrapani, and was the co-founder of Tibetan Buddhism along with Guru Padmasambhava and Dharma King Trisong Deutsen.

Shantarakshita was born as a prince in the east India kingdom of Zahor. In his childhood, Shantarakshita entered a Buddhist monastery and took ordination according the Sarvastivada school from the great Madhyamaka master Yeshe Nyingpo (Skt. Jnanagarbha). With him and other great masters, Shantarakshita studied and learned all of the Buddha's teachings, as well as all of the major and minor fields of knowledge. He became a renowned expert in all of these topics, and served as the head of Nalanda Monastic University.

According to the great master Mipham Rinpoche, Nagarjuna and his disciples founded the original Madhyamaka school, Acharya Bhavya founded the Svatantrika Madhyamaka school, Chandrakirti established Prasangika Madhyamaka school, and Shantarakshita founded the Yogachara Madhyamaka school which unified the two Buddhist philosophical systems of the "profound and vast teachings of the great masters Nagarjuna and Asanga." The omniscient lama Mipham Rinpoche said, "There is no Madhyamaka teacher who refutes mere conventional existence, nor is there a Madhyamaka teacher who claims that the nature truly exists."

The *Lankavatara Sutra*, the *Samadhiraja Sutra*, all the definitive meaning sutras, as well as all the Vajrayana teachings explain in one voice that on the relative level, everything is produced by the mind, including all appearances. This was clearly expounded by the great masters Asanga and Vasubandhu in the Mind Only school. The great master Nagarjuna taught the uncategorized absolute truth that is beyond all reference points.

To help beginning practitioners realize this, Shantarakshita and all the Svatantrika Madhyamaka school masters taught both categorized and uncategorized absolute truth. For average people with regimented duality, they skillfully taught them to first use conceptual, relative supports as direct opponents to solidity notions of true existence so that eventually they could completely break through the limitations of all conceptualization and directly experience and realize uncategorized absolute truth as it is taught in the Prasangika Madhyamaka school, as well as in Vajrayana and Dzogchen.

In his famous book *Adorment of Madhyamaka* (*Madhyamakalankara*), Shantarakshita perfectly united the profound Madhyamaka system of Nagarjuna and the vast philosophical system of Asanga, bringing together the Yogachara view of conventional reality and the Madhyamaka view of absolute truth into a single state of practice without any contradiction. In this way, Shantarakshita was the charioteer of the Yogachara Madhyamaka school just like the great master Mipham Rinpoche proclaimed. This book is truly the union of Madhyamaka and logic, which was praised by the great masters Tsongkhapa and Mipham Rinpoche, as well as so many other great scholars and logicians. They even said, "How fortunate we Tibetans are that such great masters were able to be invited to Tibet by King Trisong Deutsen!"

According to Tibetan Buddhist history, Shantarakshita purposely waited for many generations for Dharma King Trisong Deutsen to be born to establish Buddhism in Tibet. King Trisong Deutsen appointed his border guard Salnang to request Shantarakshita to come to Tibet. When Shantarakshita met Salnang he said, "For nine generations I've been going back and forth between different countries. Now that both you and the glorious king have taken birth and grown up, we have to start establishing the teaching." Just before King Trisong Deutsen and Shantarakshita were about to meet for the first time, the King told his ministers to ask Shantarakshita what was his religion. When he was asked this question, Shantarakshita replied, "My religion is that which is established by reason."

When Shantarakshita and King Trisong Deutsen met for the first time they held hands very intimately and Shantarakshita said, "I've waited a long time to see you. Do you remember me? In the past when we completed the Great Stupa, we made a commitment that in the future I would become a teacher, you would become a king where there was no Buddhism, and Salnang would be a messenger between us. Do you remember making that prayer?" King Trisong Deutsen replied, "I remember vaguely, but I don't see clearly because I haven't meditated enough."

Shantarakshita came to Tibet in the Tibetan Royal Era of the Iron Ox Year 888, which was 761 AD according to the western calendar. In 762, the great master Shantarakshita, Guru Padmasambhava, and Dharma King Trisong Deutsen came together to establish the full body of Buddhism in Tibet, which became one of the richest Buddhist countries in terms of practice, realization, and academic learning. Around 767, soon after they completed Samye Monastery, Shantarakshita ordained the first seven novice monks in addition to giving ordination vows to over 300 others.

King Trisong Deutsen and all of the great translators became students of Shantarakshita and Guru Padmasambhava. Shantarakshita composed about twenty-one different teachings that are currently available in the Tengyur, including *Madhyamakalankara* and its auto-commentary, as well as many others that were mostly translated by his students the great translator Yeshe De, along with the Indian scholars Surendrabodhi, Danashila, and others.

There were many great India masters who upheld Shantarakshita's teachings, including Kamalashila, Acharya Haribhadra, Dharmamitra, Arya Vimuktisena, and Abhayakara Gupta. In Tibet, all of the twenty-five disciples of Guru Padmasambhava and Shantarakshita also adhered to Shantarakshita's philosophy. Yogachara Madhyamaka was the principal philosophical system in early Tibetan Buddhism. Kamalashila came to Tibet and taught and wrote commentaries on *Madhyamakalankara*. Later, the Yogachara Madhyamaka school was continued by the great master Sakya Pandita, as well as by Chapa Chokyi Senge and many other great masters.

Over time the popularity of the Yogachara Madhyamaka school dimmed, but by the blessings and encouragement of the great master Jamyang Khyentse Wangpo, Mipham Rinpoche wrote a famous commentary on *Madhyamakalankara* known as the *Commentary That Will Please the Lama Manjushri*. Ever since, Shantarakshita's teachings on Yogachara Madhyamaka have once again become very popular both inside and outside of Tibet.

Just before Shantarakshita was about to enter mahaparinirvana he kindly gave many instructions for Tibetan Buddhist practitioners. He predicted that not long after his mahaparinirvana there would be turbulence within Buddhist philosophy. He told King Trisong Deutsen, "You should invite my student Kamalashila to Tibet," and he left a letter to give to Kamalashila. He also said, "As long as there is a memory of me, for that long Tibetan Buddhism will last." He went on to say, "Whenever practitioners experience low enthusiasm, they should pray to the Buddha as well as myself. Externally keep the vinaya vows, inwardly apply the bodhisattva vows, and secretly practice the Vajrayana, and you will reach enlightenment in the pure land of Vajrapani. If you visualize me in your heart center and maintain good conduct, you will fulfill your bodhichitta and also bring a state of peace and harmony to the monastery." Finally, Shantarakshita said, "If you follow the words of Guru Padmasambhava, King Trisong Deutsen, and myself you will never become lost." Those were his last words.

Shantarakshita was truly one of the greatest scholars, philosophers, logicians, debaters, and accomplished mahasiddhas of all time. I'm very happy that Professor Marie Friquegnon worked on this auto-commentary for many years with Arthur Mandelbaum and Acharya Geshe Lozang Jamspal, who also translated the auto-commentary back into Sanskrit with the encouragement of the great master Khunu Rinpoche. In addition, Ven. Khenchen Palden Sherab Rinpoche helped clarify many difficult points. I'm pleased that it's finally completed after all of their dedicated hard work, and hope that this new translation captures the exact meaning of the original teaching well.

In the Tibetan tradition, all the good scholars discovered the true meaning of profound philosophical points by studying and contemplating them for a long time. I hope that readers will understand at least a glimpse of this important book, and that this will inspire them to learn other profound philosophical texts by lineage scholars. May this work serve as an offering to honor the great mahasiddha Shantarakshita and all the lineage

masters. I pray this will benefit the Buddhadharma and all sentient beings.

Khenpo Tsewang Dongyal

Palden Padma Samye Ling

Chötrul Duchen
February 27, 2021

INTRODUCTION

"Scripture, without a logic that is based on
the evidence of things, will not satisfy even
faithful followers."

—Shantarakshita

With these words, Shantarakshita followed in the footsteps of Buddha Shakyamuni who stated that no one should accept his view without testing it as a goldsmith tests gold.

In the *Madhyamakalamkaravritti*, his commentary on his root text *The Adornment of the Middle Way,* Shantarakshita aims to completely clarify the position that, while ultimately reality eludes our comprehension, conventional knowledge is useful as a tool for navigating appearances all of which are no more real than the reflection of the moon in water.

His method of establishing this relies almost exclusively on one tool: To be real an entity must be one or many. If he can show that all the candidates for the real, such as atoms, matter, space, time, God, the soul, subject, object and causal relations fail this test, that if they cannot be said to be one, because the one is not substantial, then it cannot function to produce many.

Shantarakshita's motivation for this radical destruction of our basic and cherished beliefs, is to liberate us from anything that can cause us suffering. If we cling to our illusory world, it will fail us, because it is impermanent.

In *sloka* 16, Shantarakshita does make one positive assertion about reality, when he asserts self-awareness. But he is careful not to become trapped in the classic Buddhist model of subject, object and activity. Self-awareness, he argues, cannot be understood in this way. Subject and object are not distinct nor identical, not one, not many. Self-awareness has no substantial existence. Then what is it? Raziel Abelson, at a symposium with Jay Garfield, January 25, 2008, said that there is something about experience that makes you know it is yours. When I pick up a pen, I can always become aware that

I am picking up the pen and not someone else, although I do not usually reflect on this.[1] But I always have the potential to become self-aware. I suspect this is what Shantarakshita means to say. James Blumenthal quotes Paul Williams summing up of Shantarakshita's position: "What is meant by *svasamvedama* is that (i) consciousness does not depend on another thing to be known, and (ii) it is nevertheless known. Therefore it follows that it is self-known."[2]

Shantarakshita's Life and Works

Shantarakshita was born in East India in Sahor, a prince, the son of a king. A devout Buddhist from his earliest years, he renounced worldly life and became a monk. His root teacher was Jnanagharba, whose philosophy was sometimes characterized as Yogachara Madhyamaka, which became the view Shantarakshita highlighted. This position views ultimate reality to be beyond duality, but accepts relative reality as a construct of our minds.

Shantarakshita lived in an age of tolerance, where debates occurred freely between Hindus, Buddhists, Jains and materialist (Charvaka/Lokayada) scholars, as well as between the different schools of Buddhism. He lived and taught at Nalanda University monastery as professor of philosophy and head abbot of the school. Nalanda was beautiful, with gardens, fountains and lavishly decorated buildings and temples. There were faculties of philosophy, medicine and art. Students were only admitted by passing an entrance exam. Nalanda has been described as the Oxford of Ancient India. Surely every facility and comfort were available for their illustrious abbot.

In Tibet, under the reign of the sixth century monarch, Srongtsen Gampo, the minister Sambhota devised a phonetic alphabet for Tibetan from an archaic form of the Sanskrit alphabet. This made it possible for the first time, to learn, read and write Tibetan. Yet most Tibetans remained illiterate, and unaware of Indian Buddhist scholarship.

In the eighth century, King Trisong Detsen of Tibet, a powerful and enlightened ruler, was very interested in Buddhist philosophy, and even wrote a book on logic.[3] In the hope of educating his people, King Trisong Detsen asked his ministers to search throughout India for the greatest teacher and philosopher, who could set up a system of university monasteries in Tibet. They decided on Shantarakshita.

Although very advanced in years, Shantarakshita gave up his post at Nalanda University. After visiting Nepal, he made the arduous journey to

Tibet in 762 CE. Upon his arrival, when asked about his doctrine, he said it was "to accept what is in accordance with reason, and to reject what is not." He is famous for having said, "You cannot fault me, because I do not assert anything to be true" (ultimately).

Warmly greeted by King Trisong Detsen, he began to plan and construct Samye University Monastery.

Unfortunately, the construction coincided with some natural disasters, and the leaders of the indigenous religion blamed them on Buddhism. They interfered with the building of Samye, destroying whatever was constructed. Shantarakshita left for Nepal, and suggested that the king invite Guru Padmasambhava to control the hostile forces. Padmasambhava arrived quickly and solved the problem. The walls when built, now stayed up. Shantarakshita returned and Samye Monastery University was completed. Monks began their training and the Indian Buddhist philosophical tradition was established by Shantarakshita, Guru Padmasambhava, King Trisongdetsen (Trisong Detsen) who gathered together, and wrote and transcribed many texts.

Soon after Shantarakshita's death, a dispute began between his followers who believed in the gradual path and the followers of the Chinese monk Hoshang Mahayana, who believed in sudden enlightenment.

Kamalashila, Shantarakshita's student, came to Tibet and a great two year debate was held before the king (The Council of Lhasa, 792-794). When Hoshang Mahayana argued that all one had to do to reach enlightenment was to stop thinking, Kamalashila replied that one might as well call unconsciousness enlightenment, which is absurd. The king judged that Shantarakshita's side had won, and that the gradual path would be taught in Tibet.

Shantarakshita inherited the philosophical tradition of Shakyamuni Buddha. All of Buddhist philosophy begins with the realization of impermanence. On the commonsense level, this means that there is nothing permanent to which we can cling. We will lose our health, friends and family, possessions and our lives. All our happiness occurs in the context of this knowledge that it will end. Some try to find permanence in children, or artistic and literary creations, or even in a place in history. But in the vast cosmic picture, these flicker for only a moment.

Nor can we find permanence in our own self-identity. Our bodies, emotions and thoughts are constantly changing, and there is no aspect of our selves that endures throughout our lifetimes. This cycle of suffering and uncertainty is called samsara.

Buddha Shakyamuni taught that there is a way to find liberation from this endlessly challenged world. There is no suffering without consciousness. It would, of course, be pointless to try to get rid of consciousness. The aim has to be to get rid of that aspect of consciousness that produces suffering. As one text puts this point, if a barefoot man, afraid of injuring his feet, asked that a rocky road be covered with leather, people would tell him to put on some shoes. Similarly, one cannot remove all that causes suffering. But one can train one's mind in such a way as to transform one's responses, if you know the real nature of consciousness, because mind creates all the disturbances of our own environment.

The impermanence of selves, and the interconnectedness of all things as they rise and fall moment to moment, provides, for Buddhists, a solution to the problem of altruism. For if there is no separate enduring self, if one cares for oneself one should care for others. This provides a rational basis for universal compassion.

The heart of Buddhism was expressed by Buddha Shakyamuni in the following way. "Do good, avoid evil, purify your mind." This mental purification involves the overcoming of attachment, the subsequent overcoming of suffering, and the attainment of nirvana (enlightenment). Shantarakshita's way of achieving this involves a systematic process of pulling the rug from under us, time and time again, until we are 'standing' only in emptiness. In his root text *Madhyamakalamkara* and Shantarakshita's own auto-commentary on this text, *Madhyamakalamkaravritti,* he begins an onslaught on materialism and follows it with a critique of idealism. He demonstrates that idealism, the view that all we know is mental, is true on the relative level but not on the absolute level, which is emptiness beyond duality, beyond conception. In this way he unites the idealist and Madhyamaka (emptiness) schools and shows them not to be contradictory.

Here is a 'bird's eye' view of his argument:
1. The materialist, or atomist school which asserts that things are composed of atoms, which are ultimately real, is acceptable only on the gross ordinary level. It is not false to speak of material objects composed of parts, even the smallest parts, when we need to build houses. But on careful analysis, the idea of an atom can be shown to be seriously flawed.
Shantarakshita follows Vasubandhu's argument against materialism:
a. Atoms (according to the ancient view) are partless, and hence indivisible. The atomists claim that they are the building blocks of all material things. But there can be no extension (take up space) of a partless atom.

And particles that have no extension cannot add up to a table, chair or any other object.

b. A partless atom cannot have sides, or it would be divisible. But objects that have no sides cannot connect with other objects. Hence they cannot combine to form tables etc. Thus, Shantarakshita sides with the idealist (Chittamatra or Yogachara) schools in rejecting materialism.

2. Awareness cannot be denied without contradiction. One needs awareness to deny awareness. But attempts to understand awareness result in two types of difficulties:

A. To know the mind, one would need a different mind to know it. But what is the mind that knows the mind? This engenders an infinite regress (Cf. Kamalashila commentary to *Tattvasamgraha* 192)

B. What is the relation between mind and object? Are they one and the same, or different?

B.1. If they are held to be different, the following questions arise:

B.1.a. Can one mental state represent many objects or parts of an object? No, because the mental state would have to be compound if the object was compound. Since the subject must be affected by the awareness of an object, a subject that remained completely simple and unitary could not recognize distinct parts of the object. For example, the mental state that recognizes part of an object to be red cannot be exactly the same as that which perceives another part of it as blue.

B.1.b. Can many mental states each represent a part of an object in a single instant? No, because an object, even if mental, can have a vast number of aspects. It is absurd to think there could be so many separate mental states in a single instant of perception.

B.1.c. Can a series of quickly changing states of perception represent the object, as a firebrand, whirled about, produces a circle of fire? No, because we can only perceive the present moment, not a series of perceptions. Perception must be in the present.

B.2. Nor can the idealist school that holds that the subject and object of thought are the same be defended. For then the subject of awareness could not be caused to change in any way. Each change in awareness must depend on a distinct causal condition.

3. So on the ordinary level, speaking of thoughts is acceptable, as long as we do not analyze the relation of thought and object too closely. If we do, we come to realize that mind itself is beyond conception. On the absolute level, its nature is emptiness. For even the causally connected stream of experiences are subject to Nagarjuna's critique of the reality of causal relations.[4] Although we cannot describe emptiness, we can point to it and this is the proximate emptiness which is harmonious with ultimate emptiness.

Because of these difficulties inherent in the notion of mind, Shantarakshita only accepts the idealist view as true on the relative level. True, there must be awareness, but its real nature is beyond conception.

Shantarakshita sides with the Madhyamakas (the school that holds that all is empty of substantial existence) in viewing ultimate reality as beyond conception. And there is nothing whatever that has substantial existence. This includes self-awareness.

Shantarakshita is claiming that on the relative level everything rises and falls in accordance with cause and effect. Since, for him, relative reality is mental, mental events are also caused. Mental events are caused in such a way as to be earmarked as one's own. When I pick up a pen, I know that I am picking up the pen, rather than you. (One notable exception was pointed out by Jay Garfield. In an experiment many people can see their hand sticking out of holes and can become confused about which pair of hands is theirs. But this confusion was due to the special circumstances of the experiment.)[5]

Self-awareness is not the only type of earmarking that our brains do for us. We can see a pen, imagine an identical pen, dream about an identical pen and remember an identical pen, and know which is which. There are exceptions due to specific causal conditions. For example, a patient with Alzheimer's syndrome may think she is perceiving strangers in her living room, when they are a product of her imagination. Perhaps it is the plaque in the brain due to the disease that prevents the conventionally correct identification.

To conclude, according to the natural process of cause and effect, moment by moment, experiences arise, apprehended as my own, as perceived, as imagined etc. Nothing of this process need entail the existing of a substantially existing self-awareness.

To continue, using Nagarjuna's argument, cause and effect are either the s ame or different. If the same, nothing new could ever happen. If different, cause and effect would be at different moments of time and one could not bring about the other, because only one indivisible moment, the present, can exist at a time. Father (cause) and son (result) could never meet. It follows that even if events are mental and arise as if caused, on the ultimate level, mental events are ultimately beyond cause and effect. Their source is unknowable, beyond conception

One might ask why, if both matter and mind turn out to be equally unreal on the absolute level, Shantarakshita characterizes relative reality as mental and not material. Perhaps it is because atoms are imperceptible. Appearances however are undeniably experienced as objects of the senses, and so, on the relative level they can be said to exist phenomenologically.

Shantarakshita refused to assert anything as true on the absolute level, for this level is beyond propositional knowledge (beyond words). Yet at the same time, achieving non-conceptual awareness of this emptiness is the ultimate spiritual goal. This raises the following problem: What has emptiness to do with religion?

Shantarakshita's religious vision is best understood in relation to the co-founder of Tibetan philosophy, Guru Padmasambhava. Guru Padmasambhava focused on Dzogchen, the Great Perfection, which understands the highest form of Buddhism as a perspectival shift, where after appropriate spiritual training, the student is able to see all of reality in a new way. This view is experienced in such a way as to produce an all-encompassing experience of compassion and bliss. It also makes the student wiser, even in the ways of ordinary life.

Enlightenment for both Shantarakshita and Guru Padmasambhava consists in experiencing the world in a non-dualistic way. There is no sense of a separate subject and object. The interconnectedness of all sentient beings is also directly experienced. All seems bathed in the clear light of bliss.

Yet, just as a lover of art can see a painting, not only in terms of its beauty, but also in terms of its weight and height, sages who have experienced non-duality, and consequently, wisdom, compassion, loving kindness and equanimity, can still also understand how ordinary people experience reality, and have great compassion for their suffering.

—Marie Friquegnon

Notes to introduction

[1] Abelson, R. "Comments on Self-Awareness" in Studies in The Yogacara Madhyamaka of Santaraksita ed. Marie Friquegnon and Noe Dinnerstein. New York: Global Scholarly Publications, 2012.

[2] Blumenthal, James The Ornament of the Middle Way: A Study of the Madhyamaka Thought of Santaraksita. Ithaca: Snow Lion, 2004, p. 83

[3] King Trisrong Detsen's book on logic: Narthang Tengyur sgra sbyor ngo vol. 212 folios 636-996 or 63v-99v
Also: Shantarakshita advised the king to invite Guru Padmasambhava from the Swat valley (present day Pakistan) to help. The guru arrived, and quickly put a stop to this interference. Shantarakshita, who had left for Nepal, returned to Tibet and completed the monastery without further difficulty (810 CE). It was modeled after Odantpuri monastery in India, and its design formed a symbolic mandala of the universe.
The king decided to transmit many forms of Buddhism, and invited scholars to translate the entire canon from Sanskrit into Tibetan. Some of the famous scholars who came were Jinamitra, Sarvajnadeva, Danashila, Vimalamitra and Shantigarbha. Seven young men were ordained as novice monks and were carefully observed to see if they could keep the vinaya (discipline) vows. They were successful, and many more were ordained. Samye quickly became a great center for scholarship, philosophy and translation, as well as medicine and science.
Shantarakshita wrote five major philosophical works, Commentary on Jnanagarbha's "Distinction Between the Two Truths' (Jnanagarbha was his teacher), the Tattvasamgraha (Compendium of views),the Madhyamakalamkara (Ornament of the Middle Way), The Madhyamakalankaravritti, his own commentary on the Madhyamakalankara), Vipanci-tartha, a commentary on the logician Dharmakirti, the Tattvasiddhi (the Attainment of Reality), Paramarthaviniscaya (the Investigation of the Ultimate (which has been lost in both Sanskrit and Tibetan), as well as ritual texts and prayers. He died suddenly in Tibet.

[4] "Generally speaking he [Shantarakshita] argues as a Sautrantika when criticizing Vaibhashika views, as a Yogacarya when criticizing Sautrantika views, and as a Madhyamika when criticizing various Yogacarya positions While in the final analysis he maintains specific views and we can correctly say that he is a Madhyamika since he rejects the existence of an ultimate nature in phenomena, one might also be inclined to say he is a 'Yogacara-Madhyamika' in that he rejects the externality of objects conventionally. By the use of 'sliding scales of analysis,' I think Santaraksita's brand of Buddhist philosophy,

far from being exclusive, is much more inclusive of all systems of Buddhist thought. In fact...he utilizes multiple provisional views, not only that of Yogacara, in an attempt to lead followers to a Madhyamaka position realizing the lack of any inherent nature in phenomena." [Blumenthal, 2004 pp 167-168]

[5] "The Conventional Status of Conventional Awareness: What's at Stake in a Tibetan Debate?" in Studies on Santaraksita's Yogachara Madhyamaka ed. Marie -Louise Friquegnon and Noe Dinnerstein. New York: Global Scholarly Publications: New York, 2012. pp. 291-327

MADHYAMAKALAMKARA VRITTI
by Shantarakshita

To glorious Manjushri, I pay homage.

Those who possess a firm and pure mind,
and dwell in the high stages,

See from the transcendental shore the ocean-like profound dharma,

With a vast mind in every way completely accustomed to
high aspiration (*adi moksha*),

They ceaselessly bow down to those who dwell above.[6]

One who is not dependent on anything, will accomplish the benefit of self and others.

We know all things to be acceptable when not examined; they exist on the relative level like reflections. But on the absolute level things do not exist. When you examine in that way it will remove all the *kleshas* [afflictive and objective obscurations/ emotional and intellectual obscurations]. Therefore, through logic and scripture, one should make a great effort to understand the selflessness of things. Scripture, without a logic that is based on the evidence of things, will not satisfy even faithful followers.

Therefore, begin with the initial evidence.

§ 1. Whatever my [own] schools and others assert,
All things are completely free of
Inherent nature. Being neither one nor many,
They are like reflections.

---

[6](Kamalashila *Panjika* MAP) We cannot have omniscience because of external disturbances. That is subjective obscurations. Also, our knowledge is limited because things are limited. These are the objective obscurations. Thus, one should pay homage to *buddhas* who cultivate the mind of high devotion, and dwell above the great ones (non-Buddhists such as Vishnu), and who traverse the paths and stages, starting from devotion to 'no more learning.'

If inherent nature existed, it could not transcend the distinction between one and many. Thus, by abandoning one and then many, the characteristics of distinct categories are cleared away, such as the collections spoken of by Buddhists and others. For example, essential prakriti does not really exist. Thus, the absence of that which exists in itself should be clearly understood.

Do not think that the argument can be understood as unestablished.

§ 2. **Because results are brought about in succession,**
        There are no permanent single causes [like *prakriti*].
        If each result is different,
        Then causes cannot be permanent.

These things asserted by our own schools and others must fall into two opposite categories, permanent or otherwise. In the first case, if happiness, sorrow etc. are produced by the eternal [cause], it is not correct that they can both be successive, and also be one. They would not have the nature of one, because [if so] their [contradictory] results would arise simultaneously.

If the cause were not complete, the effect would be stopped. But when the power of the cause is not obstructed, how could one be able to stop the result? But if the cause is missing, then the result will be stopped, because of the process of exclusion and inclusion [forward pervasion and counter pervasion].[7] In particular, it is clear that there will be no change without the appropriate cause. And it is clear that change cannot depend on the auxiliary cause [if the primary cause, Ishvara, or prakriti does not change].

Others also claim that at the time of the effect, the primary cause [such as Ishvara] exists together with the result. But if the cause has this property, and if one asserts that the auxiliary causes are distinct, one from the other, because acting in succession, then these causal conditions must be linked to the primary cause [Ishvara], and are by its force continuing to exist, as if pulled by the neck by a rope. In that case, there would be no explanation of how the result would not be permanent. This answers those who talk about the power of the auxiliary cause and claim that by its stages the effect is successive.

---

[7] Example of pervasion and counter-pervasion: If there is smoke, there is burning. There is smoke. Therefore, there is burning; If there is no burning, there is no smoke. There is no burning. Therefore, there is no smoke. If there is a cause, there will be a result. There is a cause, therefore there will be a result; If there is no result, there would have been no cause. There is no result, therefore, there was no cause.

Some groups of our own schools [] claim that the object of knowledge rising from the power of meditation, is not harmonious with all the functioning of compounded things. Even the mind focusing itself [on uncompounded things like space, atoms] is not related to the uncompounded things [which are ultimate].

§ 3. That object of knowledge arising from meditation,
    Which some (the school) assert to
        be uncompounded,
    Even in their system, cannot be one,
    Because it is connected with successive cognitions.[8]

If subject and object are related to successive cognitions, then, anything that is related to successive cognitions would not have the nature of oneness, because successive cognitions are not one. Therefore:

§ 4. If one knew the former object of cognition
    Had the same nature as what followed after
    Then the former [cognition] would become the latter
    [cognition],
    And similarly, the latter would become the former.

[They say] similarly, that the unchangeable object to be understood by former consciousness exists at the time of the later consciousness but the former consciousness does not exist. This theory will lose. Similarly, [they say] the object to be known by later consciousness exists, but the former consciousness does not.

[But] your [] theory is mistaken, because the previous and latter cognition would each have to hold the object in a unique way, if the previous and latter cognition were different. But if you say that this knowledge does not exist in both the previous and later time, then in that case,

---

[8] "It is said [in the auto-commentary], 'When the uncompounded entity, that is, the analytic cessation (cognized by yogic perception acquired through meditation) which the s consider to be truly existent, is subject to rational inquiry, it is not found to be a truly existent, single entity. This is so because the same uncompounded object is related to a succession of cognitive instants in the manner of known and knower.'" Mipham Rinpoche in Padmakara p. 166. Labeled by Kamalashila MAP Ichigo's critical edition 1985,33 P5286 *Madhyamakalamkarapanjika*

§ 5. The uncompounded object
Which does not occur in previous or later times,
Should be known as knowledge
Momentarily arising.[9]

As consciousness arises, the former consciousness is dissolved [followed by the latter consciousness, as flowing]. Therefore, if that is so, the uncompounded object is also momentary. If consciousness is flowing, that is continually arising and dissolving, then it makes the former object dissolve and the latter object catch up. [That object is momentarily dissolving, so it cannot be uncompounded.] This includes the so-called uncompounded phenomena such as the wisdom arising from the meditation of an arhat. This must also be impermanent, arising and disappearing moment by moment.

Momentarily arising, awareness could not arise if each of the previous similar states had not perished. To describe this in any other way is demonstrably incoherent.[10]

§ 6. Each thing arises momentarily
By the power of the previous moment.
It cannot be uncompounded.
It is like mind and mental states [which are compounded because of being dependent on conditions.][11]

---

[9] Blumenthal's translation of sloka 5: "Since the nature of the [latter] object does not arise in the earlier [time] and [the earlier] object] does not arise at the latter time, uncompounded phenomena like consciousness must be objects known to arise momentarily." [Blumenthal, 2004 p. 68]

[10] "But, if the object observed by the present consciousness existed also in the past, (in the absence of the present knowing subject), and if it exists later, on (when the present moment of consciousness has ceased) why is the cognitive subject of those earlier and later moments not also present? For if the objects observed in distinct moments are unrelated to the observing consciousness, it is nonsense to speak of the perception of outer objects. The only truly existent, single entity is one that is not the object of different instants of consciousness. For if such an entity existed, it would follow that it is not the object of momentary consciousness. Accordingly, it should be understood that it is impossible to establish uncompounded cessation as one truly existent entity." (Mipham Padmakara Translation Group, 2005 p. 168)

[11] [Mipham Rinpoche, Padmakara, p. 176].
Also, Tsong Khapa points out that Shantarakshita's criticism applies equally to partless particles and space (as well as the meditative objects of the *arhat*) because since "they are also asserted to be known periodically by distinct consciousness, they would also be rejected in a similar way..." *dbU ma rgyan gyi zin bris* 58 [CF. Blumenthal, 2004, p. 70]

If it is said that subsequent objects arise by their own power, that would be impossible.

However:

§ 7. If one were to say that things occasionally
Arise by their own power,
Then since such things do not depend on another,
They should always be there or not be there.

Because arising periodically, mind and mental factors should be known clearly as dependently arising. [This is an attack on .]

All this is spoken in self-conceit. There is no purpose in intelligent people judging that which has no function.

§ 8. What benefit is there whatever
In investigating what is useless?
What benefit is there in lustful women investigating
Whether or not a eunuch is beautiful?[12]

Therefore, wise people assert functioning to be the characteristic of reality. All real things are like this [functioning]. Regarding this, the selflessness of persons and things, etc. can be demonstrated, and also the rejection of reification which is opposite to this can be demonstrated. The opposite of these, imputed entities, are refuted, because what people meaningfully assert about arising results [purusha artha, the four goals of life: dharma, love, wealth, and liberation] depends on efficacy.

Other than this we neither reject nor prove. It remains in the state of indifference. One should not think that the reality of things such as egolessness has not been demonstrated. All that one wants to say expresses the purposes of desire. Therefore, all the functioning things are instantaneous. Therefore, if it is functioning it is impermanent. (It is gradual, therefore the opposite of permanent.)

---

[12] Universals and generalities (Skt. *vishesha,* Tib. *khad pa*) are being compared to eunuchs because none of them, as Dignaga and Dharmakirti demonstrated can function. CF. [Blumenthal, 2004, p. 70]
See also:
> What benefit is there whatever
> In seeking meaning by investigating what is useless.
> What benefit is there in lustful women investigating
> Whether or not a eunuch is beautiful.
> *Pramanavartika.*211
> [*Svarthanumana,* VV. 211 CD, 212 ab]

Thus, [similarly] it makes no sense to say that a person exists at all, neither momentarily nor non-momentarily nor inexpressibly. It is proved without effort that it would be like a sky flower, etc.

§ 9. It cannot be properly demonstrated that a person
Is either momentary or non-momentary.
Therefore, it is clearly known
That it lacks the nature of one or many.

Regarding the person asserted by opponents (), the root evidence proving that it lacks the nature of one and many is easily demonstrated. If it is momentary, it should have many natures, because it arises instantaneously, one moment after another [every moment arising with a different nature].

If it were not momentary, it would be stable and would remain forever one in nature [which is absurd]. If it cannot be said to be either or both of these [one or many], it is not difficult to see that being neither one nor many, it is empty in nature.

Moreover, others accept things a different way, as either belonging to the two categories, pervading or non-pervading objects. Pervading objects are space etc. Non-pervading objects are gross [forms] and atoms.

Of all of these it can be demonstrated that it is contradictory to hold that they are one in nature:

Otherwise:

§ 10. Since they are connected in many directions,
How could pervading things be one?
And also since parts are covered or not covered,
Then gross things cannot be one.

[You say space is one. But if so,] Space etc. is related to different parts, [such as] trees and so forth. Whatever the nature of the relationship to the singularity of these, if it is also related to others, then because of the relationship of these, if it [space] has the nature of singularity, and then all of them [such as trees] will not become different. If the directions are different, then that singularity could not be related to others.

Body and so forth, asserted as a gross body, [is sometimes] covered or uncovered, moving or not moving, colored or not colored, burned or not burned etc., how could it have the nature of one logically? Since these qualities are discordant, it follows that the nature of the body in question cannot be undifferentiated. How could this be logical?

Atoms

If they say, covered and so forth [for example by clothing], belong to limbs and but not the possessor of the limbs, then would not this limb possessor, be combined with the limbs? If this is not like that, since covered and uncovered when combined are contradictory, it could not be true that the collection existed as a totality. Covered and uncovered would be true of the legs [i.e. the parts], and of the body. But they are differentiated (despite the fact that the body is claimed to be one). And if the leg and the body are two (distinct), then why would not the two (the total body and the part) both become objects of the eye?

And perceived separately they do not become the object of the eye, you should say.

If covered and so forth belongs to the parts but these do not belong to the part possessor, then if someone says these part possessors are not combined with the parts, then if this is true, how would the possessor not become the object of eye, as true of things such as covered, uncovered, mutually contradictory, like leg and body and so forth. Or if they have contradictory states, how would they be one in nature?

If this is claimed, how can the whole be separate from the parts, for otherwise gross objects could not be one? And this would produce many separate gross objects. And if there is another (single) gross object, it would have to be perceivable. Thus the whole is merely imputed by the imagination. Otherwise, one would have to begin by putting a name on every atom.

To begin, in order to form gross things, that subtle atom would have to have the nature of singleness as ultimate.

This will never be logically correct. If they are touching one another sticking together, as Kanada says, starting their activity or holding by mutual strength, circling each other, then since this combination is necessary to produce things, since they never touch [because of being partless], if not touching, how can the gross levels be constructed?

Thus, if some say:

> Many different atoms are in different directions
> If some of them are only circling
> These are mere words that atoms are this way.
> Because the central atom would not have the self-nature
>   of having parts.[13]
> [To circle or be circled there must be parts]

Some say the atoms do not touch, but nevertheless there is no space in between. Therefore, they look like they are touching. But this idea is also not correct. All these presentations are merely imagination.

If all of these atoms are connected, in a single natural body, then all of their substances will be mixed into one, because the nature of a single partless atom combined with others in a single direction could not become many. [A partless atom combined with others would occupy the same space.] If you touch it with one part it would have parts because atoms touch different atoms [in different directions].

If all of these are stuck together, they must have parts by which they are stuck to other atoms. If one atom is sticking, then it is stuck to another. And if it is stuck in any direction, then it must have parts. Then the so called partless atom would become one that has parts [which is absurd]. They would also combine, because they would be glued together in the intermediate space.[14]

[One might object that] these many (atoms) have no space between. How can these subtle atom even if not touching have no space between?

---

[13] (Shubha Gupta) [MF a 11th cent. logician mentioned in *Anekaan ta-jaya-pataakaa-tika* attributed to Haribhadra Suuri c. 1277 AD in Satis Chandra Vidyabhusana *A History of Indian Logic: Ancient, Mediaeval and Modern Schools*]

[14] See also: *Tattvasamgraha*, 1990:
> "Thus, seeing other atoms,
> If they are viewed to be in this way,
> Then how can extensive hills etc.
> Be formed by them?"

CF. also Kamalashila's commentary in *Tattvasamgraha* answering the opponent: p 945 (jha-commentary to 1990-1992)

Since there is no space then one understands they are connected. This statement is not correct. This point, as of all these points are just mentioned but they have no reality or essence.

If there is no gap, then this is no different from the theory that says the atoms touch. If there is no gap, then the so-called joining and colliding have no meaning [because they would occupy the same space]. This has already been taught in the path of the great chariot. Even so, we should examine it in brief.

If there is a space in between the atoms, [for them to contact] then it must be composed of either dark or light atoms. (Dark atoms make up the darkness of night and light atoms make up the lightness of day, according to Khenpo Tsewang Dongyal Rinpoche.) Because being either dark or light atoms, they would also combine, because they would be glued together in the intermediate space.

If there is no gap, then this is no different from the theory that says the atoms touch. If there is no gap, then the so-called joining and colliding have no meaning. This has already been taught in the path of the great chariot. Even so, we should examine it in brief.

§ 11. **[Even] if connected or else surrounded**
Or even completely [inseparable] with no gap,
A single partless atom is embedded in other atoms,
And faces another atom.

§ 12. **But if one says that they face one another and are partless,**
They would be the same.
In this case, would they not fail to
Become earth, water and so on?

[CF. *Tattvasamgraha* 1990]

According to the three schools, the subtle atom abides in the middle of atoms in the ten directions. If it faces an atom which is in the eastern direction, that part of it which faces the eastern direction would be the same as that which faces the other sides. [They would all occupy one space.] It would be as if a house which faced a house in the east were to have only one side. Such atoms could not form the globe or so forth [because all the atoms would be in one place.] The fault would be as follows:

§ 13. **Seeing that the partless atoms have sides,**
If one asserts they are different,
If this is like this,
How can the extremely subtle atom
Be considered partless and one?

Because those partless atoms abide in the ten directions, since the characteristics in themselves are distinct, the numbers must be distinct. Otherwise, they would have to be asserted to abide in the same place.

By having the characteristic of a manifold nature, they are diverse. From only partless atoms, how would there be a whole.[15]

Thus:

§ 14. **Each particle is thus proved to be without inherent nature.**
Therefore, the eye, substance, etc. [composed of atoms],
About which my own schools and others have much to say,
Should be understood as having no intrinsic nature.

When in our own school the existence of the partless atom is not accepted, then the parts of such things as the eye, forms, consciousness etc. which are held to be real, can be seen to be empty in nature. We can understand this without effort [twistings]. Are you atomists right because the king says so [a colloquial expression meaning it is written in stone].

§ 15. **Thus, the nature of the atoms which compose**
Such things as generalities and particulars,
If all of these are combined together like this,
How can they have intrinsic existence?

Our own [Hinayana/Foundation Buddhist] schools claim that the forms of the ten elements are composed of atoms etc. If atoms do not exist, this cannot be correct. Similarly [being composed of atoms] depending on the eye, forms etc. [sense organs, objects of consciousness, eighteen elements], the eye consciousness arises. If the external objects that are the objects of the

---

[15] See also *Tattvasamgraha* 1991

five sense consciousnesses relating to the five elements do not exist, how would the mind consciousness arise? If the five organs of consciousness that were formed by immediate causal conditions did not arise, how could one account for the arising of mind?

Thus, if the set of the six consciousnesses did not exist, the ever-changing mind could also not exist. Thus, the mind would have no intrinsic nature.[16] And similarly, if the nature of the mind is empty, that which is accomplished through it, those same abilities, feelings and mental derivatives etc. which are factors arising from mind, should be easily understood to be empty in nature.

Those adepts, heroes in examination, have already shattered those concepts of objects in a hundred replies. It is a dead issue, and there is no need to add anything. Thus, all forms etc., substances which are directly or indirectly related to those, from the beginning are unborn because of being non-existent.

s say that non-informative forms [e.g. monkhood, childhood] do not exist, because they do not arise from dominant elements [which are composed of atoms] to form large objects. And if this is so, objects have no intrinsic existence.

[Further, I also say] space etc., uncompounded things, have also been previously exhaustively eliminated. It is clear that the eighteen elements are clearly without intrinsic nature.

---

[16] Wikipedia (skandha article)
"The eighteen dhātus [ag] – the Six External Bases, the Six Internal Bases, and the Six Consciousnesses – function through the five aggregates. The eighteen dhātus can be arranged into six triads, where each triad is composed of a sense object, a sense organ, and sense consciousness. In regards to the aggregates: [23]
The first five sense organs (eye, ear, nose, tongue, body) are derivates of form.
The sixth sense organ (mind) is part of consciousness.
The first five sense objects (visible forms, sound, smell, taste, touch) are also derivatives of form.
The sixth sense object (mental object) includes form, feeling, perception and mental formations.
The six sense consciousness are the basis for consciousness."

The Eighteen Dhātus

Six External Bases (*bāhya-āyatana*)
Six Internal Bases (*adhyātma-āyatana*)
Six Consciousnesses (*vijñāna*)

Even two atoms have limbs [i.e. parts]. This is also true for single atoms. Thus, also the single atom which you assert to be single from the beginning, if atoms [in general] do not exist, this does not exist.

Form, taste and smell etc. and all qualities which mostly result from massing together, directly and indirectly, linking and composite, are like this.

Things like 'lifting up' etc. [the five actions of the Vaishesika: spreading, putting back, lifting, putting down, going] are also of this karmic nature. Having distinguished the particular and general, if all of these together, earth etc. close by or at a distance, rely [on atoms], even those that are asserted to be collections, all of them must be related, and can have no intrinsic existence. Eternal entities like space, time, direction, soul and the

---

16 continued

(1) Visual Objects (*rūpa-āyatana*)
(2) Eye Faculty (*cakṣur-indriya-āyatana*)
(3) Visual Consciousness (*cakṣur-vijñāna*)

(4) Auditory Objects (*śabda-āyatana*)
(5) Ear Faculty (*śrota-indriya-āyatana*)
(6) Aural Consciousness (*śrota-vijñāna*)

(7) Olfactory Objects (*gandha-āyatana*)
(8) Nose Faculty (*ghrāṇa-indriya-āyatana*)
(9) Olfactory Consciousness (ghrāṇa-vijñāna)

(10) Gustatory Objects (*rasa-āyatana*)
(11) Tongue Faculty (*jihvā-indriya-āyatana*)
(12) Gustatory Consciousness (*jihvā-vijñāna*)

(13) Tactile Objects (*spraṣṭavya-āyatana*)
(14) Body Faculty (*kaya-indriya-āyatana*)
(15) Touch Consciousness (*kaya-vijñāna*)

(16) Mental Objects (*dharma-āyatana*)
(17) Mental Faculty (*mano-indriya-āyatana*)
(18) Mental Consciousness (*mano-vijñāna*)

See also Kamalashila's commentary to Text 2000 *Tattvasamgraha Jha* p. 949-950:
"When Cognition is said to be 'self-cognisant", it is not meant that it is the *apprehender* or *cognizer* of itself; what is meant is that it shines, becomes manifested, by itself, by its very nature, just like the Light diffused in the atmosphere."

very subtle atom are thus dispelled. As has been taught before, they have no intrinsic nature. At the same time, having examined bodies and similarly the aggregate of consciousness, all of these are understood to be empty in nature.

The Dual and Non-Dual Teachings of Our and Other Schools

Now I should demonstrate directly the dual and non-dual teachings of ours and other's schools. As to the dual method there is an assertion about everything in terms of the grasper or grasped, and they assert they both really exist. [Concerning the non-dual method], proponents of this view assert that consciousness is like a pure crystal which they say does not grasp an aspect of an object. Those views should be examined.

---

16 continued

This is as the nature of self-reflection, because by nature it is illuminating. It is the opposite of a chariot etc. which by nature lacks understanding [Khenchen Palden Sherab Rinpoche]. When one knows the real nature of the self, one knows that blue, for example, does not depend on anyone other than oneself (Khenchen Palden Sherab Rinpoche). The so-called lack of the object of knowledge is asserted to be self-awareness. Thus, one asserts the object of self-awareness is not without awareness.

Also: The nature of objects which are not awareness would be different from knowledge. How could they be known because there is no relationship between object and knowledge? The awareness which is the characteristic of the nature of knowledge does not exist in the object. In that case then for what reason could the knowledge [of the object] be known by itself, and then, similarly and directly experienced and known? This is not possible because you assert of the object two things, that knowledge and that to be known are a different nature.

"Santaraksita follows this question in his autocommentary with a multi-layered argument aimed at convincing his opponents to accept that objects do not exist external to the consciousness which perceives them: for it would be impossible to know these objects directly if they are distinct entities. In addition, with regards to the neither-one-nor- many argument, if consciousness is truly singular, then it would be incoherent to assert that it could know objects from which it is different because it would have to be related to objects of a different nature. He is, of course, not arguing for a truly single nature of the mind, but merely as the truly single nature of consciousness and the ability to know objects distinct from itself. This is an excellent example of how Santaraksita pitches arguments to opponents on their own terms and aims to gradually lead them to what he considers to be the correct view (i.e. that of the Madhyamaka)]." [Blumenthal, p. 89]

Geshe Lozang Jamspal: The nature of the object is not luminous understanding because the object is different from knowledge.
"Since consciousness is luminous and aware, it is knowable to itself. But how is consciousness able to know things that are by nature different from itself and that lack these qualities of clarity and awareness? They are completely alien to it. Clear and knowing experience, the defining feature of consciousness, is wholly absent from the non-mental things that are foreign to it. How then can consciousness, which is self-cognizing, have

§ 16. Consciousness must arise
From what excludes non-sentience,
That is, [it must arise] from what
Has the nature of knowledge.

There are not two systems of appearance since [there is only one conscious-ness per person]. Consciousness projects the object without contact and there is only awareness. Otherwise there is no such experience of self and others. When establishing the nature of the self, awareness itself is self il-luminating nature.

Chariot etc. is the opposite of that which has awareness. Since self-awareness recognizes by its own self, when you perceive blue etc., you don't have to rely on others to know blue. One sees it is blue without hav-ing to rely on other means. Therefore, this is the meaning of [not seeing]. When one knows the real nature of the self, one knows that 'blue' for exam-ple, is not perceived. Thus, one asserts the object of awareness is not with-out awareness. [MLF after consultation with Rinpoche [double negations: not non-awareness is awareness. Cow is that which is not a non-cow.] No awareness not existing, means awareness is self-recognizing.

Thus said.

§ 17. Because its nature is unique [namely not all other things (Mipham Padmakara 202)] and partless,
It is impossible for it to have a threefold nature.
Therefore, self-awareness does not have
The property of subject and object.[17]

Consequently [some say] the object of self is able to establish its own as-pect. It is a cause and can elicit knowledge of its own form. And conscious-ness of the nature of the stipulated object is produced. Thus, the knower, the known, and the manner of knowing together are produced by the object which is said to be like this in its own nature. But self-awareness cannot be

---

[16 continued] a direct experience and knowledge of other things? For indeed those who af-firm the existence of external objects and the knowing mind do say that consciousness and the object to be cognized are two quite different natures. The so-called detection of the object (*yul yongs su gcod pa*) is an extraordinary feature of consciousness. This is like the mind's experience of happiness, and so on-which cannot be a feature of exter-nal objects. To the extent that something is experienced by consciousness or appears to consciousness, this same experience can only be due to the clarity and knowing of the

established as an object in this way, because this consciousness arises as partless (independent of everything else) in nature.

Because generating by itself a partless consciousness, it is not the producer, the producing, and what is produced. In this manner, the knower, the knowing and known are not different modes of awareness perceived in the threefold way. It is not perceived in this manner. Producing itself is a contradiction. Consciousness is able to establish on its own.

§ 18. This is the nature of consciousness.
Thus, self-understanding is possible.
But how could it know the nature of objects if
As you have asserted, the nature of objects is different
[from the mind]?

[CF. *Tattvasamgraha* 2078]

For example, self-awareness is by nature clarity. Likewise, one's nature is clarity. This we understand to be clarity. The nature of many experiences we believe to be self-awareness. We call it clarity, because it knows through self-awareness.

However as to consciousness of each distinct object, consciousness has the characteristic of recognizing objects. Thus, it has the nature of investigating the object. For this reason, to say we experience the reality of a self as an object is not correct.[18]

§ 19. Since its nature does not exist in [external] objects,
Because you have asserted

[16 continued] mind. How can there be an awareness of anything in the absence of clarity and knowing?" [Mipham Rinpoche, Padmakara, p. 204]

[17] TS 2079: Therefore that which is the subject of the dispute (i.e., self-cognizing cognition) is considered to be non-dual, since it is devoid of object and subject (*vedyakartrtvaviyogat*) because it is the nature of consciousness, like a reflection. [Trans by Blumenthal, 2004, p. 89]
See also TS 2080, 2081 and Kamalashila's commentaries on all three passages. [KTDR: "Consciousness is not mind, not matter, but it can know itself. Gyeltsan argues that if one claims self-cognition is productive, one must also claim that it has inherent existent. But this does not follow from Shantarakshita's view, because self-cognition is neither one nor many it cannot have inherent existence. I think the production is simply the result of interdependent co-origination." MLF] Refuting and Sautrantika because they say subject and object are different: [Since you are not accepting self-awareness, and believe subject and object are different, then how could the subject grasp the object if subject and object are distinct? This would not be logical]. (Khenpo Tsewang Dongyal Rinpoche)

That subject and object are different,
How could consciousness know that which is other
[than consciousness]?[19]

When one completely analyzes these properties, one can see that aware-ness is the extraordinary unique aspect of knowledge. Happiness and so forth, are as similar, and how could happiness [like cognition] exist in oth-ers [along with suffering]? What is this relationship? Arising from that, the self-privileged experience of the object is not attained, because one would have to say it would be a result of the contact of the eye organ etc.

[If] the object's nature is completely cut away from others (different), and if its nature is to be an object of consciousness, similarly, in that way, at that time, that object when completely analyzed is known not to be distinct from experience. [The Sautrantikas say] by the knowledge of conscious-ness, one will have knowledge of the [external] object (but a single, unified consciousness could not know diverse objects). But those intellectuals, who are attached to the existence of the external object, have spoiled minds. [Their view] is not possible.

Because knowledge and its object are distinctly two, then if the object is not intelligible, then so-called knowledge of the object would be inexpli-cable.

If there is knowledge, then if it illuminates, as it illuminates, it itself does not become illuminated. Because clarity cannot clarify clarity. So, one cannot perceive the other that you wish to perceive, because the cause that relates them is non-existent.

Furthermore, others take the view that the object of knowledge has aspects, but no relationships. This is an even worse explanation.

---

[18] It has the nature of experiencing objects but is not itself an object. "We find an explicit declaration of the non-dual nature of consciousness and its objects according to Shan-tarakshita in Tattvasamgraha when he says: 'Therefore, that which is the subject of the dispute (i.e.self-cognizing cognition) is considered to be non-dual, since it is devoid of subject and object (*vedyarkartrtyavivogat*) because it is the nature of consciousness, like a reflection'" TS 2078

[19] "Not relying on others to be illuminated, that which is self-illuminating, is called the self-cognizing of consciousness." [Blumenthal, p. 87]
Also:

"Since its nature does not exist in (external) objects,
Because you have asserted
That subject and object are different
Having this characteristic,
Ultimately [consciousness and its object] will remain separated."
[*Tattvasamgraha* 2002]

§ 20. The features [of subject and object] in your (Sautrantika) theory [of mental aspects]
Appear to be different in substance from each other.
But that reflection, and the object, are similar, being both aspects of mind.
And the distinction is, in a sense, experienced merely conventionally.

[CF. Padmakara p. 54 *Tattvasamgrah* 2004]

Thus established, the self-nature of awareness is explained as knowledge of the reflection of the [illusory] object of knowledge. If this is so, the reflection is explained as being a result of the object, and thus because of this experience of the object [as form], the name (label) is attached to this experience.[20]

Critique of and Others

§ 21. For those who do not assert that consciousness
Is transformed by the aspect of the object.
Then [for s], there would be no direct perception
Of the existence of the external object.

[CF. *Tattvasamgraha* 2005]

Because the object of knowledge is by nature unknowable, therefore one's object of awareness is distanced from the object which is by nature unknowing.

But it would be correct to attach a label if one accepts the reflection that is caused by the relationship.

But if this is not so, it is not correct to say that the object in itself can correlate with consciousness. This cannot be the case.

---

[20] "But since the object is akin to a reflection, It's by such means that things can be experienced." [Mipham Rinpoche, Padmakara, p. 54]
Also: [MLF: Clarity can clarify our unclear perceptions, it cannot clarify clarity which is beyond conception.]
Also: "Shantarakshita explains that according to this position, one directly experiences images of objects because the gross imputed object is like a mirror image of the gathered actual images of the external object....Shantarakshita states [in MAV] that the position of his opponent holds that the mirror-like image of the object which is known by the consciousness is in the nature of the object and that, therefore, the consciousness which knows the mirror-like image of the object also knows the object itself." [Blumenthal, 2004, p. 92]

Refuting the Sautrantika View

§ 22. [If you claim] one cognition is not many, then
There cannot be many images.
But then the view of mind as a unity,
Has no power to establish many objects.

[CF. *Tattvasamgraha* p. 203.][21]

In a single consciousness which perceives [in a single moment] a single painting unfurled and so forth, without doubt, representations originate equal to aspects, such as blue or yellow are gathered together within range. Undoubtedly, if so, a single cognition will not correspond to a plurality [diversity]. This could not be said to be logical.

If this view is so, it is not correct to hold that there are various objects. Because the single consciousness is not similar to a manifold, but is essentially self-awareness. Because of this, the cause of manifold objects such as so-called blue and yellow, and so forth, cannot be stipulated as manifold objects. However also clearly perceived, the variety of aspects must be accepted. Some the Sautrantika claim this the images of the object] because those images are not of a different substance.]

Even so:

§ 23. Without being free from diversity,
Consciousness would not be single
If this is not the case,
You must explain how these two [variety of aspects] are one.

[*Nam den pa*]

---

[21] "The gradual arising of thought
Is like a firebrand whirled around
Because of the speed
It appears in the mind simultaneously."
[*CF. Tattvasamgraha* 1246]

[CF. Blumenthal, p, 95] Gyel-tsab: "At the time that a multiplicity of images such as blue, yellow, white and red are known to a single consciousness, these images could not be substantially distinct from one another because they are all indistinct from the one partless consciousness. If you accept this, then having appeared as images of the object, it would be incoherent to accept the establishment of the object as substantially different from the [consciousness which apprehends the images of the object] because those images are not of a different substance.]

If consciousness is an entity that is not different from a diversity of its features, then it would become these features that are many. If consciousness is single, it can only have knowledge of a feature that is single in nature. If the feature were not this way, there would be a contradiction. If the features were manifold, this would contradict the concept of the mental state and its object being one.

Thus:

§ 24   **[You say] perception of white and so forth**
Have arisen gradually.
Because they arise quickly, foolish people
Think they know them simultaneously.

[CF. *Tattvasamgraha* 1246]

Similarly, [they say] as when piercing the one hundred petals of the utpala flower, one can say one knows a single object gradually but quickly, just as one 'sees' the circle of fire.

Because one sees it quickly, one says one sees a single circle of fire.

When a hundred petals of a blue lotus flower are pierced, because it happens so quickly although successively, [this opponent] still struggles to claim that people think it happens simultaneously. [Or] for example they say that it is like when one sees a wheel of fire, the sight of which is the result of rapidly [twirling] in a circle the burning end of a torch.

If this is so,

§ 25.   **[1/2 egg]**
The sound of the word 'vine' [*lata*]
Arises very quickly.
If [the syllables] were perceived simultaneously,
Then why would not [the syllables] be heard
simultaneously [as *tala*].

[Note from Geshe Lozang Jamspal: One line was missing from the Peking edition so he retranslated it from the Sanskrit *Tattvasamgraha* 1250.]

Lata [Skt: vine] and *tala* [Skt: palm tree], *sara* [Skt: lake] and *rasa* [Skt: flavor] etc., as they are called, when one investigates these objects, [or] these letters [syllables] one sees similarly that they arise very quickly. Thus, because they arise quickly, they cannot be known [veridically perceived], because how could they be simultaneous like a single unfurled picture? [We could not distinguish between *tala* and lata if they seemed to appear simultaneously. Similarly, with blue and yellow, if arising quickly and perceived as if simultaneous, the picture would be mixed up.

Similarly, if the cause and effect are distinct, the causal sequence would be obstructed. Similarly, if there is the same cause it cannot produce a different result. If so, the cause would not be the cause of the result.

§ 26. **[1/2 egg]**
The mind's understanding
Also cannot be known through successive [images].
Because [images] do not remain for long,
Thus, all mental states are similar because they
arise quickly.

[CF. *Tattvasamgraha* 1251]

Arguing and analyzing for a continuous mental state is not correct. For like the perception of the eye etc., mental states arise unmixed and uninterrupted, clearly and quickly dissolving. Why is it not known instantaneously? Even among non-Buddhists, it is accepted that, since they dissolve very quickly, aspects of mind, having arisen, cannot remain for a long time.[22]

§ 27. **Because of this, all the parts of an object of perception,**
Are not grasped gradually.
Yet for all the different aspects,
As they arise, they only appear to be grasped
simultaneously.

[If the cause is gradual, then the effect takes place in different moments of time and cannot be said to be simultaneous, and perception must be in

---

[22] THIS IS THE HALF EGG VIEW: Also B's explanation that terms such as ½ egg were introduced by Gyel-tsab and the Geluks and not used by Shantarakshita. [Blumenthal, p.121]
    [COMPARE WITH]:
    Through the aspect of the sound, the word 'vine'
    Similarly arises very quickly by the operation of the mind.
    By the precision of simultaneity
    How would not the reverse arise?
[*Tattvasamgraha* 1250]

the present.] You cannot say the cause of the experience is gradual and the experienced effect is simultaneous. You cannot say if the cause is the same, the experienced result is not the same.[23]

As previously conclusively explained, because the cause [no longer] exists, it is not correct that one sees the circle of fire.

§ 28. A firebrand whirled about once
Appears [deceptively] as a wheel.
Although it appears clearly,
It cannot be connected by perception.

[CF. *Tattvasamgraha* 1254.][24]

Are the clarity and boundaries a contradiction? [Yes?] If so:

§ 29. In that way [they say], the joining of the boundaries
Is done by memory [not perception].

[22 continued] Also: Blumenthal explains this last point in the following way:
[Shantarakshita argues] " ...[T]hat even a conceptualizing mind, which one could argue makes such mistakes out of ignorance, could not cognize in the way this opponent claims. This is the case because as with the way images arise and disintegrate moment-by-moment, so too does the conceptual consciousness perceiving them. If the consciousness does not abide for any duration of time, such a conceptual consciousness could not hold a direct perception of a succession of images arising over time in the mind and could not even erroneously consider them to exist simultaneously. It would only be possible if the images were enduring and thereby many could appear to a single consciousness. But then one falls back to the same fallacies as the NonPluralist, in addition to having to accept the true existence of images due to their enduring nature." [Blumenthal, 2004, p. 100]

"And even if the moments of consciousness [of sights and sound] do arise in a similarly rapid manner, since they do not result in the complete, instantaneous perception of the object, such an object cannot be posited as the cause of the apprehending consciousness. [Padmakara note 298: This belongs to the Sautrantika theory of perception. In the first moment, the object, sense organ, and the consciousness act as the cause; in the second moment, the mental aspect of the object is produced, (i.e. , the result, Khenchen Pema Sherab Rinpoche). For an effect is necessarily consequent upon a cause. Where there is no cause, there is no effect." [Mipham Rinpoche, Padmakara, 2010, p.211]

[23] "In other words, the opponent wants to claim that the consciousness is momentary like the images it perceives, yet must also make the contradictory claim that consciousness also abides for some duration of time in order to erroneously piece together the distinct consecutive images and to come to the incorrect conclusion that they are perceived simultaneously." [Blumenthal, 2004 p. 101]

Also: MLF's note: Perception must take place in the present which is instantaneous. Thus, if the mind unites the successive images, the resulting simultaneous experience cannot be considered perception, but only a kind of afterimage produced by the instantaneous states of the sense organs and the consciousness.

Because there is no perception of the past,
There is no perception of the object [the circle].

[They say] memory is what connects the boundaries which produces an object because perception does not apprehend [*zin*] it and has no ability to make connections. What is the consequence of this?[25, 26]

§ 30. **[I answer that] In this case the object perished**
And therefore cannot be clear.
Because of this it is reasonable that
The appearance of the wheel would not be clear.

[CF. *Tattvasamgraha* 1255]

[last sentence is different: 'Because it is not clearly grasped.']

Memory does not grasp very clearly even a substance which is in front of it. Understood in this way, similarly, it is correct to say that the circle made by the firebrand itself ought to be seen. The firebrand that appears so clearly, really appears clearly as grasped [apprehended?]. [It is not controlled by memory, because it is clear.]

---

[24] "Just through the manifesting of the torch
The circle arises appearing all at once.
Because each appears clearly,
The boundaries are mistaken."
[Tattvasamgraha 1254]

[25, 26] "The mistake of an eye consciousness and the mistake of a mental consciousness are two totally different types of mistakes. An eye consciousness can make a mistake by seeing something that is not there such as an hallucination…mental consciousness with its memory can join conceptual thoughts, but an eye consciousness cannot do that because an eye consciousness is only conscious of the present according to Santaraksita." [Blumenthal, p. 103]

Also: "That is to say, as long as there is a temporal sequence of appearance from the cognitive perspective, this will invalidate simultaneous appearance. And when the appearance is simultaneous, it cannot possibly be observed as occurring in temporal sequence. Therefore [the claim] that in the cognitive perspective the sequential appears simultaneously, it can never be established by direct perception. Moreover, since regardless of the objects of cognition one turns to, it will not be outside of the [above] condition no inference or example can be found [either]." [Doctor, p. 295] Blumenthal: "In other words, the opponent wants to claim that the consciousness is momentary like the images it perceives, yet must also make the contradictory claim that consciousness also abides for some duration of time in order to erroneously piece together the distinct consecutive images and to come to the incorrect conclusion that they are perceived simultaneously. According to Gyel-tsab's explanation of the argument Shantarakshita is making, if conceptual consciousness were momentary, it could not even erroneously piece together such images. This is because the previous momentary image known to a previous momentary consciousness would not be able to abide for any duration so as to be erroneously conceptualized as being known simultaneously with other related images." [2004, pp 101-102] Also: [Blumenthal, p. 101]

Some think that the piercing of the hundred petals of the utpala lotus happens simultaneously, and the simultaneity is not perceived clearly. Thinking this way is an error in logic. Therefore, in this case one ought to take the position that it is not simultaneous. One with one-pointed exactitude, with the eye of wisdom, ought to be sure that this happens gradually. The gradualness is inferred.

Many of these are pierced one by one, this happening gradually. For example, it is like copper sheets [pierced one by one]. The piercing of the many petals of the utpala lotus happens in this way.

Sautrantika Proponents of an Equal Number of Consciousnesses and Images.

Some have argued that when one knows objects there are many numbers of mental states [one for each aspect].

[Note: "…there are as many consciousnesses as there are images" Blumenthal, p.104] This is similar to the aspects on the surface of a painting that arise together, or forms, sound etc. which are not in the same categories.

§ 31. **If you say when one sees the surface of a drawing, since there are many aspects,**

   There are many thoughts [in a single moment] as there are parts to the painting.
   In what way could this happen through one [mental state] alone?
   This is how such mental states [would] arise together.

But then:

§ 32. **In that case, how could whiteness and so forth, which are known in a single way,**

   Have a great number of parts, such as a top, middle and bottom?
   Each of these would have to become distinct objects of knowledge,
   Which is impossible.

Thus similarly, blue and white, etc., are compound objects. They are asserted [by opponents] to be one, but they have opposite sides and a great number of parts. Thus, knowledge of this manifold must be diversified. Thus, having asserted a manifold, if in that case one claims to grasp only a small particle without branches [indivisible], then in that case, having distinguished with certainty the [postulated] divisions of each of the aspects of these branches of the object, this cannot be perceived even by those with very subtle insight.

This sort of perception cannot be experienced.

§ 33. A bit of white etc., atomic in nature,
In itself, single and partless,
Which appears to anyone's consciousness,
I do not feel exists.

Even bowing down [looking at details], I do not see a partless atom. But how can I, without seeing it, deceive myself by accepting it. The reason that intelligent people have for accepting something as existing is that they can perceive it. Since this [partless image] is not perceptible, it is not correct to assert its existence.

Just as [the colors of] many-colored butterflies are not one, so to designate [these bits of color for example] as one, is not correct. Without reifying (showing that) aspects of consciousness are one, one cannot say they are real.

Consciousness without variety would be one nature. Thus, the nature of a single aspect of mind is not a plurality. This view is not acceptable.

Therefore, there would be many objects. Now, about all views concerning these appearances of objects, I will now give my opinion in brief.

§ 34. Our own [Buddhist] group claims that the elements
of the five senses
Have features that are based on observing
compounded things.
The observations of mind and mental states are
established as
The sixth mental consciousness.

The objects of the five conscious elements which depend upon the organs endowed with form are collections. So, their representations are manifold, and therefore they are not free from multiplicity. Mind consciousness is also just the same as it is established in the same manner and substance.

[Thus], one could not see the elements of phenomena, because one does not see the uncompounded. Because of this I argue that the mind consciousness does not perceive [catch] mental events. Mind understands mind and mental events. Since everything is a reflection of the mind, then you cannot escape the manifold.

Having considered the perfect teaching of the Sugatas, [we will now turn to] that of non-Buddhists such as Kanada [Vaishesika] and Kapila [Samkhya] who believe as follows. The resulting objects are said to be known by means of a single unified conscious self. There is one mind which knows many objects. They think there is no contradiction in this.

Refutation of Some Non-Buddhist Schools

§ 35. **Even [some] non-Buddhists recognize**
That consciousness cannot be considered as a singularity
Because it perceives substances
Which have [a plurality] of qualities.[27]

Also (in non-Buddhist systems) many things such as forms, qualities, movements, actions, hands, one's own limbs, all components, as well as the whole body, and particles of the body are apprehended directly. In their systems the mind can be understood in many ways. Therefore, the mind cannot be understood as a single thing.

[Against Jainas and Mimamsaka:]

§ 36. **Like the nature of an agate**
Seeing all things like that
Then as to the mind which apprehends them,
It is not logical that the mind should appear as one.[27]

As they say:

About things having many forms,
The enumerators [Samkhyas] wish to assert
There are two possibilities. [Cognition] occurs all at once or
successively.
These are the only possibilities.
For example, a multi-colored object
Is called colored in accordance with peoples' [conventional]
assertions.

Objects [being perceived] as diverse,
Are given distinct names in accordance with these false and
imaginary distinctions.

It is not correct to say that a consciousness which is not a manifold is grasping diverse objects. This is because [the consciousness] would not be engaged with these objects in a consistent manner. Therefore, it cannot grasp
the object like the rays of a gem, nor can [a single] consciousness apprehend
an entire object, including its manifold images.

[The Charvakas say that]

§ 37. the accumulations of earth [and the four elements, five senses, five objects]
Are the basis of all objects and sense organs.
But this belief is not compatible
With a single means of apprehending

[CF. KTDR catching] entities. Blumenthal, p. 111]

[They say] there is only one truth [perception] and the accumulation of elements [are not perceived].[28]

Because aggregates are manifold, the cause of arranging these man-
ifolds [consciousness] must be manifold. Therefore it is inconsistent to
claim that manifold cognitions can be engaged consistently with a single
conscious state.

---

[27] Gyel-tsab quoted by Blumenthal in defense of Shantarakshita p. 104: "The subject, a
non-conceptual consciousness, could not join the boundaries of the former and later [imag-
es by means of memory] because it could not apprehend past objects. {For this position to
be coherent} there would first have to be [past] objects clearly appearing to the subject, and
a mind which joins the boundaries of the former and later [images] because it apprehends
past objects, [yet it is impossible for there to be clearly appearing past objects]."
Also: "...[T]here are as many consciousnesses as there are images "Blumenthal, p. 104]

Also: "Consciousness does not appear as one, for it is said to observe entities that
are endowed with sundry properties." [Mipham Rinpoche, Padmakara p. 217]
"The appearance of gross objects would not occur because its objects are substances which
have qualities [*guna, yontan* etc.]" [Blumenthal, p. 109]

Also: "If an aspect can be subdivided into a multiplicity of parts, it cannot be a single entity. It might be objected that the infinitesimal particle, which cannot be subdivided,
constitutes a single aspect that is observable. But, says Shantarakshita, however much he
has searched for it, and with painstaking effort, he has certainly never come across an infinitesimal particle of white and so forth, by nature isolated and unmixed with other things,
indivisible into its different directions and appearing to all cognitions. He says, in short,
that the infinitesimal, partless particle can never be the object of experience. [Mipham
Rinpoche, Padmakara, p. 16]

As is said regarding Kapila:

§ 38. **According to the position that it [prakriti]**
appears as a single object
Sattva [tamas] etc. which are the self-nature of sound etc.
[which are prakriti][29]
Cannot be understood in this way
Because they are said to have a three-fold nature
[the gunas].

The experience of many pleasures, pain and dread arise from contemplating even only one category, of sound, for example. How similarly does one validate those direct perceptions if one does not experience even a small bit of two qualities? They say the remaining [gunas] are not powerful, so they are not seen. This is also asserted not to be correct. [This cannot be established by direct perception.]

§ 39. **[If as the Samkhyas say] there are three aspects of**
a thing [the gunas],
But if there is a single aspect [of consciousness]
{or prakirti?}
They are inconsistent.
And how can it be characterized in this way?

[Cf. *Tattvasamgraha* 287-288][Geshe Lozang Jamspal includes this in the root text.]

[27 continued] Also: "Now the mental consciousness that observes mental phenomena does not apprehend mental factors alone; it observes the entire group of mind and mental factors together. Consequently, the object of that which is posited as the mental or sixth consciousness is considered to be an amalgam of main mind and mental factors." [Mipham Rinpoche, Padmakara, p. 21]

[28] "[Jains and Mimasakas] both say, for instance, that just as the nature of a many-colored onyx [*zi* stone] is one, so too is the nature of all the various aspects of different things. In other words, they bring together all the different aspects of different objects and simply assume that they form a single thing. But the different cognitions that apprehend a variety of different objects cannot be a single consciousness. If a variegated object is not apprehended as such by different apprehending objects of consciousness, how can consciousness be in accord with its object? And if there is a discrepancy between them, it is impossible to say that the object is known. These schools believe that all objects of knowledge form a single whole, and they use the onyx stone with its different colors as an illustration of what they mean. But if this were true, everyone would have the same knowledge." [Mipham Rinpoche, Padmakara, p. 223]

Also: "Gyel-tsab's explanation echoes Shantarakshita's argument by explaining by inference the argument in the thirty-sixth stanza. He argues quite simply that since entities

If the nature of the existence of the object is engaged consistently, then consciousness can grasp it. Otherwise, if the object is of a different nature, and if the consciousness which has a single nature engages it, then there cannot be a consistent matching, because [subject and object] do not match.

<u>According to the Tarthikas [followers of the *Upanishads*]:</u>
<u>[Refutation of the Vedantins]</u>

§ 40. **[They say] External objects do not exist,**
 But various appearances manifest to a permanent mind.
 But [Shantarakshita retorts,] whether arising all
  at once or gradually,
 Justifying this consciousness is very difficult.[30]

Even in the doctrine of those who speak in that way it is unavoidable to speak about a variety. Many aspects appear to consciousness, such as blue and yellow. Because consciousness is not different from the many aspects, consciousness would have to become many in accordance with the nature of the object.

The succession of forms and sounds that appear, [such as] the arising of sounds, is proven by both evidence [reasoning] and example. It cannot transcend the manifold. Otherwise you would have to say that two are one which is the same fault as before.

In the theory which affirms a succession this other fault also exists: asserting there is a single state of consciousness, since they are not separate consciousnesses by nature, former and latter representations would both exist. So, this is not correct.

[Vaibhashika] also assert that space, [atoms,] and individually analytic cessation etc. and whatever is said [not to be] relative, are said not to appear as a manifold. This should not be claimed.

[28 continued] have parts and emit manifold images, like the rays of a gem, and consciousness apprehends an entire object, including its manifold images, simultaneously, that the consciousness itself cannot be of a truly single nature by virtue of its relationship with manifold objects or images." [Blumenthal, p. 111]

[29] [Buddhist Text & Research Society – 1895 Journal - Volumes 3-5 - Page 15 - Google Books Result]
It is necessary to add here that according to Kapila the sense-organs have emanated from the Sattva qualities of the *Prakriti* ...
https://books.google.com/books?id=ubwoAAAAYAAJ

§ 41. Knowledge about space etc.
Appears mainly as names
Because of the appearance of many syllables,
It appears clearly as a manifold.

Apart from the reflection of conceptualization connected with names, no subtle, indivisible actuality is perceived.

§ 42. Some say there is a [truly existing] single mind
To which a diversity of objects do not appear.
Yet it is not correct to hold such a view
Because it has already been seen as faulty together with its characteristics.[31]

We see anything that has characteristics to be flawed. This characteristic is refuted, therefore [they] cannot take a breath of satisfaction.

§ 43. Therefore regarding all theories:
Because manifolds appear
All consciousnesses are clearly diverse
Therefore, to claim that consciousness appears diversely and is [also] truly one is not logical.

Thus, at this time it may be said:

Fingers are not different from the joint.

[In joints] there is nothing that exists that is not that [finger].

Otherwise one would not be able to establish joints etc.

Because the mere assembly also would not exist.

---

[30] Shantarakshita points out the same error in the Vedantins #330-331 in Tattvasamgraha. when they try to relate a single unchanging absolute to a diversity. [One should infer that the absolute which is beyond conception may not be said to be either permanent or impermanent.]

"The error in the view of these philosophers is a slight one, -due only to the assertion of eternality (of Cognition); as diversity is clearly perceived in the cognitions of Colour, Sound and other things, -If all these cognitions were one, then, Colour, Sound, Taste and other things would be cognizable all at once; as in an eternal entity there can be no different states."

Padmakara Mipham p.228: "The Samkhyas may say that the weak gunas do not appear, with the result that consciousness does not detect them. But to this we would answer that it is only a consciousness that perceives an object in conformity with the way it actually is that can be said to know its object. If the consciousness does not accord with an object, it is unsuitable to say it apprehends that object."

Accumulations of joints taken together:

As fingers etc. by these things,
Demonstrating that all things are non-existent,
Apart from assemblages, there are no subtle things.

Therefore, as knower of a single object,
How does one imagine such a mind?
The mental accumulations together with the mind,
How could they become a single mental state?

Critiquing Yogachara Views

Our own [Buddhist] school, relying on the Mind Only view, whose intellect is white [virtuous], holds that whatever objects are known by the mind are completely developed through maturation of one's habitual tendencies.

§ 44. **Similarly [Yogacarins say] continuously from**
beginningless time
Illusions are brought about by maturing habits.
All the parts appear to us erroneously
And are illusory by nature.[32]

Those ayatanas, the sense fields, [which are constituted by] the tiny atoms, substances, and material qualities etc. supreme and not supreme [or Buddhist and non-Buddhist] do not exist, as those skilled in this doctrine [that of Buddhist Shravaka and Kanada, Vashaishika (Hindu)] profess.

[Their views] are not logical because they lack the essential characteristics of experienced and experiencer, and is only like a fairy city and

---

[30 continued] "The Samkhyas say that the object of consciousness has the nature of three gunas; nevertheless consciousness itself manifests as a single entity. But do the Samkhyas then believe that the object is perceived in such a way that the knowing subject is not in accord with its object? In that case, how can they claim that this consciousness is the knowing subject, the apprehender of a threefold object? This is impossible." [Mipham Rinpoche, Padmakara, p.228]
[Sound would have to appear as the same thing to everyone. Geshe Lozang Jamspal.]
[See also Blumenthal, p. 113.]

[31] "It may be thought that since extramental objects like space and so forth are partless, the consciousness perceiving them must be a single entity. This however is not the case. In fact, a consciousness cognizing a nonthing (i.e. a privation) such as space never has the direct, naked, experience of an object. For these nonthings are nothing more than conceptual representations or reflections arising in connection with their names." [Mipham Rinpoche, Padmakara, p. 234]
See also: "If there is a truly existent single consciousness, It must be devoid of all capacity to function (as Shantarakshita explained when dealing with truly existent,

torches whirled about, emanations, dreams, magic and reflections of the moon on water. These images that they assert to be truly existent are moving images [objects] in your focus that have arisen since beginningless samsara. They appear simply through the power of ripened habitual tendencies due to clinging to substantiality.

§ 45. But although [the Yogacarin view] may seem good,
Is it really true?
One would agree
Only when one thinks on the unanalyzed level.

[Nevertheless] this [Chittamatra] system should be known through both valid reasoning and very clear scripture, and its virtuousness is also an antidote to great attachment/ obsession. It is also [to be valued] as a refutation to those [who have a belief in] partless atoms [Sautrantika]. Also, this method offers very clear proof explaining the contradiction [in the assertion] that there is an essential characteristic [differentiating] perceiver and perceived

Also, this method is endowed with scripture, such as the *Lankaravatara Sutra*, verse 137.

---

31 continued   permanent entities.) But this cannot be said of any consciousness." [Mipham Rinpoche, Padmakara, p. 235]

"One could claim *the existence of some consciousnesses that do not appear* individually *as a diversity* of objects. Such existence *may be allowed for*, or may be assumed. *Yet*, except for being mere imputations, *they cannot be posited authentically* as true singularities, *for* with respect to these consciousnesses, *their* possessing or *having such characteristics* of a true singularity, of a true singularity *is seen* by reasoning, *to be* hopelessly *flawed*. If there were some consciousness of a true singularity, it would, just as stated in [the section on] permanent entities, turn out to be entirely devoid of any ability to perform a function, and would therefore not be suited to be a cognition" [Mipham Rinpoche: Thomas Doctor p. 349.]

Shantarakshita points out the same error in the Vedantins folios 330-331 in *Tattvasamgraha*. when they try to relate a single unchanging absolute to a diversity. [One should infer that the absolute that is beyond conception may not be said to be either permanent or impermanent.]

"The Samkhyas say that the object of consciousness has the nature of three gunas; nevertheless, consciousness itself manifests as a single entity. But do the Samkhyas then believe that the object is perceived in such a way that the knowing subject is not in accord with its object? In that case, how can they claim that this consciousness is the knowing subject, the apprehender of a threefold object? This is impossible."

[Mipham Rinpoche, Padmakara, p. 228:] "The Samkhyas may say that the weak gunas do not appear, with the result that consciousness does not detect them. But to this we would answer that it is only a consciousness that perceives an object in conformity with the way it actually is that can be said to know its object. If the consciousness does not accord with an object, it is unsuitable to say it apprehends that object."

"From beginningless time by the sullied mind
   Forms are held in the mind as a reflection.
   The objects appear, but
   Their meaning is not seen as it really is.
   Continuities of persons, aggregates and
   Causal conditions, and similarly atoms and predominances [conditions, particles] and Ishvara,
   Are all imagined, only mind.
   No objects exist, only mind.
   To see external objects is an illusion.
   Looking at the forms by logic,
   Then subject and object will disappear."

Through this method [Chittamatra] learned scholars who rely on this system are able to reverse error and dispel ego and ego clinging and an extremely distinct subject and object. Even if so, this ought to be examined a little bit. Are the [mental forms] the true nature, or are they only satisfactory when unexamined, and similar to reflections?

§ 46. If the external aspects are real
    Consciousness would become a manifold,
    Or [these aspects] would become one [with the
       single consciousness].
    This [conclusion] is difficult to avoid.

The following view is also flawed [because] if the object is not completely distinct [from consciousness] and is the same in nature as consciousness, then, if the object is a manifold, consciousness must also be a manifold. Or if consciousness is one, then it would be difficult to avoid the conclusion that the objects of consciousness must also be a singularity [rather than a manifold.]. Since they are ultimately opposite in nature, ultimately, consciousness and its [mental] objects must really be different.

---

31 continued   things. Therefore how does one analyze a mind which is the knower of one object? How is a gathering of mental states the single object of a mind?" [MAV 58-59, Blumenthal, p. 117]

32 "Since these Chittamatrins have already said that the aspects [of an appearance] are not different, they cannot now say that they are different-that some aspects are moving and some are not. It is hard to sidestep such a consequence." [Mipham Rinpoche, Padmakara, p. 242]

Mentioning Further Mistakes

§ 47. If the aspects are not different
Then [concerning] moving and not moving [opposites] and so forth,
If one is moving, all would move
This would be an absurdity difficult to answer.

Not different, means it will be shown it is the very one. But if this is the case, then, if one grasps that if one object moves, then all would move. If one thing is yellow, everything would become yellow etc. This theory about aspects and their attributes similarly is shown to be absurd. [The rest would also be like that.][33]

§ 48. Also, in the case of any doctrine that objects exist externally,
If the aspects are not separate,
All phenomena would be one.
It's unavoidable.

[Refuting equal number of subjects and objects: *gzung 'dzin grangs mnyam pa*]

If those things which are remaining in the world are heterogeneous, then they certainly would be different and distinct. They assert that all things whatever such as happiness etc. [and] objects like blue which are only experience, belong to the same categories, but the knowledge which arises emerges as dissimilar. They say that two minds do not arise from both former and latter moments, but only a single [simultaneous] mental state. [But I argue] these are happening as opposite types. It is not logical that two [opposite] minds come together simultaneously, a contradiction difficult to remove.

---

[32] continued   And: "Yet their teaching says they are not different, that they are of that [single nature.] If that is the case, then if one image is engaged in the action of moving, etc. or if one is the nature of yellow etc. then all [related] remaining images will also be like that. If that is not the case, then they must definitely be of various natures (i.e. not one)." [Blumenthal, 2004. p. 123]

[33] Those who hold this view assert that happiness and so forth; as well as] the aspects blue and so forth have the nature of experience/knowledge. There are many, and also, they are homogeneous, but they occur as heterogeneous. According to their theory without previous and former states, according two minds do not arise, no chance for this.

If this is said: These are done by the power of ripening states of consciousness. If you say that two different minds are coming together, you are contradicting scripture. You cannot avoid this.[34]

"According to the great scholar of the past:
Because of their homogeneity [chain of similar experiences}
The ability to know with certainty
That thought constructions arise gradually.
Is understood well."

[Dharmakirti *Pramanavartika* 502 & 503]

This is contradictory for [this reason]. Having regarded the minds of the antidote [like light] and that of the adversary [like darkness] the view that two minds are occurring simultaneously is rejected. [As in a debate] It is very logically clear, I say.

A single sound is only one. There is no other particular singularity. Regarding this, the self, mine and grasping and grasped etc. and their existence as separate from mind, and yet [understood] to be the mind itself, will be shown to be not real. Other than this there will be shown there is nothing other than this. Is this system woundless? No.

To argue that the attainment of a completely matured body and mind in that [single] state will give rise to distinct representations, I argue is a harmful consequence. [If you say that consciousness is one, this is absurd because objects are varied.][35]

And is this system healthy? I say no.

And you asserted knowledge and what is to be known have a different nature.

§ 49. If according to the number of features,
One accepts states of consciousness
Then [states of] consciousness would be as numerous
as the atoms,
This analysis would be difficult to circumvent.

[Features like blue are accepted as atomic].

---

[34] "If we perceive as many, how can we call it a single object?" Mipham p.243 Also: the appearance would be infinitely divisible like the atom. Thus consciousness, like the agate [gzi], [is but one, but] appears variegated. This cannot be accepted in the way spoken of in this doubtful system [as atomic].

If the atom with no space in between, by nature is non-existent, then if all the many consciousnesses are similarly without anything in between at a time, then the same analysis we have performed in relation to the atoms will be true of these consciousnesses.

Similarly, if one asserts that aspects of consciousness are similar to partless particles surrounded by other particles, then what could be the nature of a partless aspect that faces one aspect and is to the other side of another?

Without consciousness holding many similar atoms without gap, then it will be mistaken as a single gross lump. What particulars are here? Blue and so forth appear without gap. If some people accept this as atomic, then it will not be beyond the same fault [as found with atoms].[36]

As with this [particle]. If we were to [hypothetically] claim that the consciousness is asserted to be [like the particle] in the center surrounded by other particles, then what is the nature of that [central consciousness] which is in front of one [image] and also in front of another?"

---

[35] "But even if we assume with the False Aspectarians that the aspects are non-existent, how is it possible that within consciousness, which the False Aspectarians consider to exist and to stand alone and unsupported like a pure crystal sphere, there manifest a variety of experienced features? If there are no aspects, is it feasible that consciousness should be generated in the likeness of what it observes? That is something for the False Aspectarians to think about." [Mipham Rinpoche, Padmakara, p. 249] "Gyel-tsab writes 'If one asserts that a variety of images would be truly in the nature of a singular consciousness [as the Non-Pluralists assert, it would be] like the system of the Vedantists and the Nirgranthas. If that truly singular consciousness to which various objects appear is asserted, then there is a pervasion, because if various objects appear [to it, it] would not be truly singular, like a heap of a variety of precious [gems]. There is also the appearance of various images to the consciousness. If you accept the singularity of images, then it would be impossible for many different images to appear, such as "visible" and "invisible" etc. and images of various sorts such as blue and yellow, etc. because the various images are truly singular.' Gyel-tsab echoes Shantarakshita's argument by pointing out that if the so-called Non-Pluralists wish to maintain, as they must, that the variety of images and the consciousnesses perceiving them are truly singular, then all the images perceived must have the same nature as the perceiving consciousness. Therefore, all the many images of an object must have the same nature since they are all singular and of one nature with the consciousness. For example, one object cannot be the nature of blue while another has the nature of yellow because that would require a perceiving consciousness with a manifold, not single, nature because it has parts (I.e. the part conscious of blue and the part conscious of yellow). Therefore, such a position entails internal contradictions." [Blumenthal, p. 126.]

[36] [CF. Mipham Rinpoche, Padmakara, p. 247]
Also [CF. Mipham Rinpoche, Doctor 383]

     Eight absurdums see Appendix. "[T]o demonstrate fallacies in the assertions of yogacharins who claim images are not real. [Blumenthal, p. 128]

§ 50. If variety is one
Is this the same as the sky-clad Jains?
But all the varieties cannot be as one, just as
A variety of jewels such as the many faceted dzi is not one.

[*Tattvasamgraha* 1733]

The assertion about things in the statement of their positions are as both instantaneous and gradual. There are no other words for this. Should you rely on it? If so, it is not logical.

This thus called variety of aspects are distinct features, if this is actually so, contradicts the nature of oneness. As much as there are features, there are that many natures. Having different characteristics means being different things.

§ 51. But if one [a Chittamatra] holds that a manifold's true nature is single
But appears to have a multiple nature
How could these many qualities appear
Such as veiled or unveiled and so forth?

If jewels like the agate had an intrinsic self-nature mixed into one, then this would contradict the variety of aspects that appear.] The self-nature of the objects [as they appear] would be no illusion. Otherwise the various aspects of the jewel would be identical. If one were hidden, all would be hidden. Similarly, one realization would become all realizations.

Criticism of False Aspectarians
(Yogachara-alikakaravada/ nal 'byor spyod pa'I rnam brdzun)
[Gyel-tsab's terms, not Shantarakshita's]

§ 52. If they believe the perception of forms is in error,
And that forms do not exist independently,
This is because forms do not exist on the ultimate level.
Therefore, the perception of forms is a mistake.
Since, they say, in consciousness itself
There are no mental aspects,
The mind, which in reality is aspectless,
Appears with aspects only through delusion.

[Mipham Rinpoche, Padmakara p. 247]

As to consciousness, from the ultimate point of view, [they say] it is like a pure crystal. Clearly, what they say is incorrect.

Thus, they say:

> If ultimately forms are consciousness like a pure crystal etc., distinct aspects such as blue would not exist. Likewise, from beginningless time under the power of ripening erroneous habitual tendencies, when the eye is confused by mantras etc. it sees pieces of clay as elephants and horses.[37]

§ 53. But how could it be that [forms] do not exist
When we clearly experience that they are different
from one another,
If this [appearance] is not existing how can all this
be clearly experienced.
And therefore there is no such [pure] consciousness
existing [apart] from aspects of appearance.

---

[37] If images are mere illusions, like flowers in the sky, direct perception of them, of something that does not actually exist, would be absurd. This is particularly true given that Yogacharas maintain direct perception based on the fact that consciousness and objects are of the same nature. Shantarakshita expresses this succinctly in the following manner in the fifty-fifth root text stanza. [Blumenthal, 2004 p. 129]
And Mipham Rinpoche's Padmakara [p. 247]:
"Indeed there is no consciousness
That from the aspects stands apart."
Also: "'Aspect' cannot be classified as anything other than a feature of the clarity and knowing of the consciousness that cognizes individual objects. This is why it is never possible for consciousness to be something that stands apart from the aspect. It is therefore important to reflect carefully on the consequence that if the aspect has no existence whatever it cannot appear. Otherwise, if one fails to do so and considers, without more ado, that the aspects just do not exist, this position will eventually turn against one and one will stray very far from the subtle position of the Madhyamaka path. Therefore, the authentic Chittamatra is the system of the True Aspectarians (who are authors of excellent treatises). On the other hand, in saying that the outer object in not even truly existent as the mind, the False Aspectarians are a little closer to the understanding that things are empty of true existence and thus provide in a manner of speaking, a bridge to the Madhyamaka. Although in the correct ordering of things the False Aspectarians are, as a result, placed higher on the scale of views, nevertheless, because the system exhibits many inconsistencies on the level of the conventional truth, the conventional should be expounded according to the system of the True Aspectarians. Once this key point is grasped, it will be easy to understand the refutations that follow." [Mipham Rinpoche, Padmakara, p. 249]

In reality those features are non-existent. [If you say consciousness and its objects are the same, you cannot say that one is existent and not the other.] Clearly, it is untenable to claim knowledge of them. Why is this said?[38]

§ 54. Since there are no things
There cannot be any knowledge of them.
Just as there is no happiness in suffering,
And no white in what is not white. [39]

Thus, there is an exclusion between what is to be proved and the proof. This is an inconsistent view and there will be no opportunity to doubt this. Thus said.

§ 55. The aspect cannot be a known directly [dngos su shepa].
This is not tenable
Because the aspect is other than consciousness.
[And] is like a sky [space] flower and so forth [impossible].

[According to them] consciousness does not have the nature of matter. Thus, if this is so, it cannot designate a single object of knowledge. Features such as blue etc. like the sky flower etc. similarly cannot result in a form of

---

[38] Khenchen Palden Sherab Rinpoche: Raising a doubt: Thus, what you established, and the proof are in contradiction. You must doubt this. Therefore, for you the object of knowledge and the aspect have no relationship, because both are your mind. CF. root text: If knowledge has no object, this is like a sky flower.

Also: [Blumenthal, p. 129] "...Yogacharas maintain direct knowledge of objects is possible, and since objects are considered to be of the same nature as consciousness, the claim for the unreality of images must in fact be faulty. This is the case because images do not actually exist in their view and so they must not be of the same substance as consciousness which is real."

[39] For a Yogacharin who denies the reality of images, it would be absurd for images and consciousness to have either of these two kinds of relationships, yet they are asserted nonetheless to be related according to this system. They cannot have a causal relationship, because if images do not actually exist, they cannot, by definition, have any causal efficacy. And images and consciousness cannot have a relationship of identity because, according to the Proponents of False Images, consciousness has a real nature while images do not. Shantarakshita explains this in the fifty-seventh MA stanza and the related auto commentary. [Blumenthal, 2004. p. 131]

consciousness. This is impossible because they have a nature distinct from consciousness and [therefore] non-existent.[40]

§ 56. Non-existent features have no power,
And cannot even be designated, like the horn of a horse,
Non-existent, they could not appear to consciousness
[as representations: btags pa'I tshul gyis shes pa]
One could not assert correctly that they had that power.[41]

The aspect cannot have the power to self-arise in consciousness. Just as a horned horse is not the cause of knowledge, because non-existent, knowledge which arises which is self-appearing would not produce consciousness and cannot be the cause of designating knowledge. [In the same way that

---

[40] Gyeltsab in commentating on Shantarakshita's sixtieth sloka: "Even if in reality there are no images, that since they are perceived, they still must be dependently arisen. And dependent phenomena are real, functional objects according to Yogacharas[/Chittamatras]. ' If one says that, although in reality there are no [images] of objects, images appear due to a mistake, then the subject, images, would be other-dependent because they depend on a mistake. This is the case because they (i.e. the images) arise from the force of a mistake.'" [Blumenthal, 2004, p. 134]
Also: Note [Mipham Rinpoche, Padmakara, p. 251]: "...non-existent things have no power to produce cognitions that resemble them."

[41] Kamilashila says that the hold that another form is in the mirror. Jaimini (Mimamsaka) says that the form itself is perceived that way. The Sautrantika's hold that what is seen in the mirror is not knowledge at all, only illusion. Shantarakshita says that all three are mistaken, because the example is misleading. The reflection does not exist [ultimately] (Mipham Rinpoche).

In this life and in another life
And at this time and another time
All objects are perceived as external
And as existing in themselves at separate times.

The analyzed object of dream-like knowledge,
This object and dissimilar objects,
Are like a paradoxical torch which is
Quickly whirled about.

Memories/visions of homes etc. are
Clouds of cities of gandharvas.
They are [the mind of] one who is tormented by thirst,
Perceiving a mirage of water caused by light in a desert wilderness.

a horned horse is non-existent and cannot appear to consciousness, a false image, which is also non-existent, does not have the causal efficacy to appear to consciousness.]

Similarly, the other aspects should be analyzed another way:

§ 57. **Because how would the experienced characteristic**
   Be related to knowledge?
   Being non-existent it is not knowledge,
   And knowledge cannot arise [be caused by] from the
      [non-existent] feature.

Thus, the aspect is not knowledge. [Thus, these features are not veridical.] If the features do not exist, consciousness would not exist since they are the same. The aspect cannot be produced from knowledge because they are the same. The aspect cannot be produced from knowledge because it is non-existent. It doesn't have the nature to be produced. [If images and consciousness are the same, then either images have to exist because consciousness exists, or consciousness cannot exist because images do not exist.]

Knowledge cannot arise from what is non-existent in nature, because the arising would be produced from what is non-existent in nature. If it arises it must exist from what is previous and then the result is subsequent. If so, it is not simultaneous and thus cannot be the same as knowledge. I'm not going over this again.

Also, knowledge at the same time would be of an imaginary object.

§ 58. **If there is no cause whatsoever, one cannot**
   Explain why [features] arise occasionally.
   If there is a cause,
   The feature cannot avoid being controlled by
      the power of an other.

Because [if as you say] the aspect/image does not exist, it is uncaused. If there is no cause, it is not possible [for changes] to arise occasionally. They could not be apprehended. If you proclaim this mistake about the arising of causes and conditions, then [this is to proclaim] the mistake that something comes from nothing. If one mistakenly accepts this, then if there is no inter-dependent origination, these features cannot arise from the power of another. If it does not rely on the power of another, it cannot come into existence. To exist is to arise from conditions. There is no other way.

If you do not accept features there is another fault:

§ 59. If you say the object does not exist, but only the mind
Without an image of an object, self-illuminating and
developing by itself then
Like a pure crystal glass,
The mind would not perceive at all.

If the nature of eye consciousness etc. is lacking the blue object etc. which is on a surface, [the object] if non-existent, like a pure crystal ball, would not be a representation. If the external and internal aspect does not exist, there is nothing else which would have the power to produce an image. It would not exist moreover just as illusions etc. do not exist. One must accept that this is a refutation.

§ 60. Then if you think all cognitions are illusory,
How is this illusion perceived?
If images arise in the mind by the power of this illusion,
Then it is still the power of another.[42]

For example, the eye when afflicted with disease [jaundice] sees what does not exist through seeing the object such as a white conch as yellow, and similarly knowledge through the force of habitual tendencies, mistakenly will assert clearly the truth of the yellowness. The mistaken perception occurs through habitual tendencies. Should one think this way?

If these arising characteristics are connected, they arise by interdependent co-origination, and therefore this is due to the power of another. Others say that the accumulation of habits from beginningless time produces deluded states. If so, this is the power of another. If they arise from habit-

---

[42] The Ten Sciences: "The arts, grammar, medicine, logic, inner science (i.e. religious theory and practice), astrology, poetics, prosody, synonymics, and drama." The *Nyingma School of Tibetan Buddhism* Dudjom Rinpoche, Vol. 2. Boston: Wisdom Publications, 1991, p. 167.

ual tendencies, they are connected with habitual tendencies. Or if the characteristics that arise are in combination, then that itself is interdependent co-origination. Therefore, it is dependent on another power. This would be hard to refute.

"Therefore, it is said, in a barren desert from far away small things appear as large." [Because of attachment, small things look large. Khenpo Tsewang Dongyal Rinpoche]

In the same way, [they claim] through attachment to/desire for external objects, non-existent objects appear clearly to the mind. But I have already argued that only the manifold impressions are directly apprehended by the mind and not knowledge of an object. For one who has an uncontrolled mind, even though the features are non-existent, they appear. The non-existent blue etc. are not separate from habitual patterns.

Therefore, some people say [such as Shubhagupta, Gesung Tibetan Sautrantika]:

"Consciousness is just knowledge by nature.
When there are erroneous habitual tendencies due to agitation
One will experience only
The aspect of blue etc.
This is the conception of blue and so forth.
The essential characteristics of blue etc. do not exist.
I have entered into delusion.
My mind considers the blue to be an external object."

I have already answered this objection. [The mind need not consider it an external object.] Features and aspects have no relation to what is mistaken and [to] habitual tendencies. And therefore, there is no possibility of removing either features or mistakes. Removing one gives no necessity of removing the other.

For example, when the cow goes away the horse need not be gone.

§ 61. [It becomes clear] that none has the nature of oneness.
[But] since no single thing exists by itself,
Then a collection of single things
Cannot exist either.

[from *Tattvasamgraha*, 1995]

"Thus, from every direction,
There is nothing that is essentially one.
And not being essentially one,
Similarly, it is impossible to be many."

When non-Buddhist schools or our own, following views which are accepted such as permanence and impermanence, and others such as the atom, coarse bodies that are perceived, objects of knowledge, knowledge etc., when each of these are investigated to see if it has the characteristics of one, at that time how can it bear the heavy burden of this very subtle investigation?

Since it is not correct to accept that anything has a single nature, it is not correct to accept that it is a manifold either. The manifold has the characteristic of an accumulation of many. If the one does not exist, neither does the many. Similarly, if there is no tree and so on, there is no forest, and so on. Therefore:

"Any characteristic being analyzed,
There is nothing found which is singular.
If no 'one' exists,
No manifold exists either."
[Aryadeva *Catuhshataka* 14:19]

As is said in the *Lankavatara Sutra,*

"If one investigates [anything] through mind
One cannot grasp the essence.
Therefore, it is inexpressible
And also, it is shown to be essenceless."
[Chap. 2, Verse 173]

"When the mind investigates the object [correctly],
There is no imagination and relativity
(i.e. no dependent or imputed [natures], Doctor, p.409).
If there are no substantially existing things,

How will the mind correctly envision the object?"
[Chap. 2, Verse 196]

"No inherent nature, no thought,
No things, no alaya,
But childish, lifeless, logicians,
Imagine these things".
[Chap. 3, Verse 48]

"Science, things and thought,
All the waverings of the mind,
My children have thoroughly transcended,
And they conduct practice in the non-conceptual."
[Chap. 3, Verse 53]

Thus said. Thus, the meaning is stated here and there by those who have correct knowledge:

"Having examined these things definitively,
Ultimately there are no entities.
Similarly, there is no intrinsic nature.
Of single things or pluralities."
[Dharmakirti, *Pramanavartika* (Chap. 2 on perception) Verse 360]

"For all the different things,
If it is not logical that they are one,
Then these diverse mental states which appear,
[Similarly] how can they be one?"
[Verse 208]

"By the sayings of sages,
Which are clear,
Like that, like through ultimate awareness
Like that, like that, the concept is destroyed."
[Verse 209]

"Subject and object when understood
Have no external existence.

Thus because all characteristics are empty
Their lack of intrinsic existence has been clearly explained."
[Dharmakirti, *Pramanavartika* (chapter on perception) Verse 215]

In that way when one examines with wisdom infused with logic and scripture, all these things are crushed into one hundred parts. This establishes that they lack plurality and oneness.

[They claim] their reason is established, but is there an example which combines both [probandum and probans]? How would this be? [Jaimini says] a ray of light [eyesight] impinging from the eye onto a mirror, reversing, produces a perception which is one's own form/or the cause of holding the same relation to one's own face. Otherwise another form arising in the mirror would be seen clearly. But [Shantarakshita asserts] the energy of mere consciousness appears that way by the force of the inconceivable energy of things.

If this is the case for all that I have investigated, to bring this up again is illogical.[43]

Branches of the topmost trees on a mountain by the side of a clear lake/water, if reflected, are perceived incorrectly as facing downward. If this is the case, because the reflected object that is known is not like what appears, what is grasped is not its own intrinsic nature. One can draw inferences in the same way from sound/echoes etc.

Others claim, the ray of light from the eye that impinges on the surface in the mirror etc., returning again, will become the cause of holding the relationship to one's own face etc. But however, in that case, when the reflection on the surface faces north, one looks from the south. Your large face reflected will look small on the surface of the mirror. This is not logical. Thus, it is not logical to say one's own face is in the mirror.

---

[43] One should pay attention to the illusory experiences of beings as one would pay attention to a child's nightmare.
"...entities have no nature like a reflected image. He {Shantarakshita} explains that the erroneous assessment of entities as having a truly existent nature is similar to the way we cognize an image of water in the desert due to the intense rays of the sun on a dry surface. Although there is cause for cognizing in this way, it is not correct to say that the conclusion which we tend to draw, that there is water, is correct. (see MAV 81) Similarly, it is not correct to draw the conclusion that objects which appear to us to have a truly established nature actually do. They are also like the images in mirrors: they do not actually exist in the way that they appear to exist." [Blumenthal, p. 136]
Note: [Blumenthal, p. 117]: There are no subtle entities which are not included among the accumulated things. Therefore how does one analyze a mind which is the knower of one object? How is a gathering of mental states the single object of a mind? [MAV 58-59]

That another form arises is itself not logical. Because forms do not remain simultaneously, reflected forms on the surface of the mirror would have to be perceived in the same place. Things having form can never occupy the same space because they would have become one. Thus, merely knowledge of appearances arises. If there are no distinctions, why would one not assert they are the same? Therefore, the tiniest atoms and their parts are not logical. Because almost all would agree that these essential pervasive attributes are contradictory.

By this, examples of magic, dream, mirage, fairy city, a torch whirled about etc. are explained. When a piece of clay etc., is grasped, one does not speak of this as an illusion etc. For example, a [clay] elephant etc. is similarly perceived but does not exist. Consciousness, together with the non-existence of the object in both theories, and the essence of anything whatsoever appearing, and the mere cause of the perception of seeing itself, [all] are non-existent. Then when one perceives it in the form of an elephant, the lump of clay etc. is not perceived. The non-existent object appears in both ways. What one sees in the perception is only mind. [Khenpo Tsewang Rinpoche: But also that mind is not really existing ultimately There is only the cause of the appearance due to consciousness, but not the existence [of the object]. If this were so, the eye etc. [sense organs] would be consciousness, which is absurd/unwanted.

> "This arises as what is dissimilar from the perceiver
> And at this time and at another time
> All objects are perceived as external."

> Dream objects of knowledge also function, and [in that dream] the subject of the dream mind and the object of the dream are different.
> Similarly, the fire ring movement [appears] because it is spinning so fast
> And similarly, the city of the dhatura clouds, and
> The mirage perceived as water, all this is all perceived because of the dense beams of the sunlight
> When you are tormented by the heat of the desert.

These so styled entities remain non-existent. Although they exist as the cause, it is not correct to say one perceives them. It is not necessary to go over what already has been thoroughly explained. How could this view as well as similar views be consistent with the true nature of things? By excluding this, doubts and fallacious thoughts will not arise in this deceitful manner. In this way, this is claimed:

§ 62. Things must be classified as one or many,
Nor can they have another classification
That includes both aspects,
Because these are mutually exclusive.

The mutually exclusive characteristics of one and many exhaust all possible categories. So, one must dispel the existence of an object, which is neither the thing nor its contrary. There is no non-exclusiveness of this exclusiveness. [There is nothing that can have another classification other than one or many.] Hence there is nothing left that exists or fails to exist. Because of this reasoning, from these premises, by this view, oneness does not exist.

As for knowing the object through the actual characteristics, for example the dewlap of an ox etc., because they have the (apparent) self-nature of collected features, similarly there can be agreement about the words used to describe the object. Similarly, these can be understood as lacking the nature of one and many.

Whoever from beginningless samsara continually has only false views about one and many, having increasing attachment to material things, which is difficult to remove, is not skilled in removing this through proper attitudes. Pervasively, on the absolute level, all phenomena lack self-nature. This is certain. One never thinks or talks about this. Others are certain that on the conventional level, one can understand that sound and word establish the object. On the conventional level, mind perceives and there are characteristics. Other than this perception there is nothing that knows the word for [objects] and the designation of an object. If it is perceived, it exists. If it is not perceived, it does not exist [as mistaken people believe].

All of this was said by the Lord himself. In the *Meeting of Father and Son Sutra* it is said:

"Similarly, in a very clear mirror,
That which has no intrinsic existence
Appears as a reflected form.

Oh Druma, you should know all phenomena in this way."
[Chap. 10, Verse 709]

"Thus, by this very nature of emptiness
Phenomena are explained as empty.
But for those childish people with erroneous views
Their empty nature is not known.
In order to show them
The nature of emptiness was taught by the Tathagata.
Conceptions produce thought constructions
And they [the childish people] are bound by imperfect thoughts."

Thus, it is said. And in the *Lankaravatara Sutra*:

"Excluding all thoughts of one and others,
As forms as in a mirror,
Although appearing, do not exist.
This is similar to the nature of things."
[p. 13 file ///CI/WarriorX/*The Lankarvatara Sutra* htm (130f 38) (15/02/2001
10. 02. 35 am)]

This being shown, then because of this, similarly:

§ 63. Therefore these objects,
Have only conventional characteristics.
If someone asserts they are, in their essence, true,
Then what use is my labor?

Through the logic of my explanation, because all entities cannot bear close examination, their reality is only acceptable when not examined, just as a magician's elephant, a horse, a man etc. when unexamined, seem real. If these phenomena therefore are not created by others, and they wish to hold them as real, then I cannot refute them. If existing and not existing are like this, is their own nature owned by themselves? [But] There is no iron hook by which their nature can be grasped. Thus, it is explained in *Collecting All Dharmas* [*chos thams ced yang dag par sdud pa*].

Similarly, the bodhisattvas, arhats and the tathagatas, the fully purified enlightened buddhas, who are expert in explaining such things, must teach conventionally concerning the skandhas, the elements, the inner sense organs, sentient beings, karma, birth, old age, death, rebirth, and the supreme pure transcendence of suffering.

Therefore from the *Precious Cloud*: "Son of noble family, a bodhisattva with ten forms of knowledge,[44] is skillful in conventional truths, but is not attached to their reality, and does not perceive these forms, or similarly, feelings, conceptions, volitions, and consciousness," as Buddha explained in detail.

Therefore, it is said in the *Inexhaustible Noble Knowledge*: "Thus, in the correct manner, all things are without inherent nature. Thus similarly [when] all these are viewed logically, just as sentient beings are similarly without inherent nature, one should know through logic that all phenomena are like that." *The Mother of the Conqueror* says, "Because the characteristics [self-nature] are empty, one knows everything starting with form up to consciousness, that things are also empty in nature."

If thus it is said under examination that the nature of reality is emptiness, this truth of the ultimate nature of reality (*yang dag pa*) is only [understood through] relative reality. If ultimate reality itself is attained by the power of another, by the two truths/duality etc., then as has already been said, a mistake in logic will not be made. [By 'power of another' Shantarakshita means cause and effect, the examination of which leads to an understanding of their emptiness. He uses the same argument in his refutation of the Chittamatra.]

---

[44] Cessation: Kalupahana p. 339: "We state that whatever is dependently arising, that is emptiness. That is dependent upon convention. That itself is the middle path.

Jay Garfield's Nagarjuna's Root Text *Madhyamakacarika* [Chap. 24, Verse 18, p. 305]:
"Whatever is dependently co-arisen, This is explained to be emptiness. That being a dependent designation, That itself is the Middle Way."
Thus said. If like that: Are similarly heuristically/intentionally spoken about:
"Santaraksita does not explicitly delineate a distinction between real and unreal conventional truths as Kamalasila does in MAP. Kamalasila clearly distinguishes between dependently arisen functional entities which can be considered as real conventional truths, and mere conventional constructs, such as the creator God" asserted by the Samkhyas which are unreal conventional truths." [Blumenthal, p. 141]

From the *Skillful Elephant Sutra*: Buddha asked Shariputra, "What do you think? Does that consciousness which knows the nature of phenomena exist or not?" he asked. Shariputra responded, "Oh Lord, whoever understands the nature of all things understands the nature of illusion. Oh Lord, it is not existing. It is not existing at all. Why? Because nothing is perceived."

The nature of all things is to be non-existent, not to exist at all. Why? Well, if someone asks, "What is the reason for this?" the Buddha taught that all relative phenomena are non-substantial by nature. If it is the case that these characteristics are non-existent, then would what we see, and wish and do, be in contradiction? This has been explained not to be the case.

> **§ 64. That which is agreeable when unexamined—**
> **Phenomena—both arises and decays, and**
> **All things have the ability to function.**
> **Thus one should understand the conventional form of**
> **all things.**

Mere conventionality of sounds/symbols by the usage of sound does not establish self-nature. Things seen and wished are dependently arising and do not bear examination. They are conventional. This is perfect functioning.[45]

It is said in *Arya-Aksyamati Nirdesa, Teachings of the Noble Inexhaustible Intelligence*:

> "What is the relative truth? One designates samsara
> Through convention with letters and words and showing symbols.
> On the ultimate level, there is not even movement of mind.
> Needless to say, it is needless to discuss letters."

In this statement the meaning is: The world is comprised of a habitat and its inhabitants. The way of experiencing here is intended as a worldly convention, justified because it is functional. Thinking about the way characteristics are expressed on the relative level, when completely understood, it is said that things do not exist. Because letters, etc., are used functionally, just in this way, the meaning is taught. Because in this way by knowing without

---

[45] See Mipham Doctor p. 479; Gyel-tsab Blumenthal, p. 144; See Nagarjuna's Establishment of the Conventional [*Vyaviharasiddhi tha snyad grub pa*]

thought, through examining the intrinsic nature of forms, etc., and happiness, etc., one does go beyond the relative truth, expressed by letters, etc.

Because of this, something is mentioned in scripture and is happening in the world. It [can be] mental or oral. For example, Buddha taught Indra the Abhidharma mentally. Similarly, in this way, he answered in the form of mental verses. [Verses transmitted mind to mind without words. Khenpo Tsewang Dongyal Rinpoche]

Lacking the heap of elaborations, free from this, there is no movement even of mind, when speaking of the absolute truth. [But] it is unfitting to have a non-cause on the relative level. Is it the case that upon examination neither the cart nor the person exists [Cf. *Questions of King Malindaphani*]?

The Protector also said:

"For example, in the accumulation of the branches (parts),
One asserts that the chariot is made.
Similarly, because of this production of the skandhas,
On the relative level one speaks of sentient beings."

Thus said. If like that:

§ 65. **That which is agreeable when unexamined,**
Relies for its cause on an antecedent cause,
And thus, the next result happens
All results are similarly brought about.

§ 66. **Because of that, is not correct to hold**
There is an ultimate cause on the level of conventional
appearance.
But if you claim this proximate cause is ultimately real,
You should explain it.

Through this, one explains in this way: Those entities which are unable to stand up to close examination, but which nevertheless have the ability to function, are relatively correct. Similarly, persons, beings etc. should not be considered merely words. Similarly, if it is said in this way [since] those things unable to endure close investigation arise dependent on their own cause, how can they be uncaused? Wisdom and intelligent analysis of the nature of the cause will lead the wise to say there is a cause [conventionally]. Chariots etc. also in their nature do not transcend the way of all things [dharmata] which has already been explained/applied.

> "If one syllable of a mantra is missing,
> Then likewise a multitude if other syllables do not exist.
> The blocked syllables being non-existent,
> That on which they depend must be non-existent."

[Nagarjuna's *Establishment of the Convention*, Vyavaharasiddhi Tib. tha snyad grub pa]

> "Thus, similarly apart from its own branches (parts),
> Medicine definitely does not appear.
> [As well as] The appearance of an illusory elephant,
> These also are not otherwise than non-existent."[46]

> "Arising through interdependent co-origination[tendril],
> Who can say they do or do not exist?
> In this way, perceptions are made
> Arising through the eye consciousness."

> "Propelled by power of karma [arising through becoming] and afflictions,
> Things arise together through grasping and karma

> Other than that, as forms arise,
> Who would assert this as existent or non-existent?"

---

[46] This is similar to the modern notion (Wittgenstein) of non-vacuous contrast. Because on the conventional level, the meaning of hot (for example) must be in contrast to cold, otherwise we could not make sense of these terms at all, and clearly, we do.

[47] "To the minds of immature beginners, emptiness and appearance or existence and non-existence inevitably seem as if they were mutually exclusive, with one being the negation of the other. It is hard to realize how these form a union. Nevertheless, when the vase placed in front [of us] is investigated with the reasoning of the absence of one and many, it is seen to be, in essence, devoid of even a particle of established nature. That emptiness is not something that did not exist before and has only now occurred at the time of investigating. Therefore, although it appears to arise, cease, and disintegrate, the vase has not moved in the slightest from the state empty of nature. While being empty, it appears as it does, and so one must develop certainty that the actual condition is one of appearance and emptiness united." [Mipham Rinpoche, Doctor p. 481]

"In this way all the existent branches,
Are designated conventionally
Cessation etc.[47]
Are similarly heuristically/intentionally spoken about."

"Just as mantra is not mantra,
Just as medicine is not medicine,
They are similarly spoken of as relying on that [conventional level]
And neither can be established as real."
[Nagarjuna]

In the case of all things that are without intrinsic nature, all samsara would be like a sky flower. Therefore, if seeing, hearing, distinguishing particulars, and consciousness, etc. are non-existent, then how can nobility and the ignoble, etc., the conventional stipulations which are not contradictory to the doctrine be applied? If you say so, this dispute is without essence.[48]

§ 67. The nature of all things
   Follows after the path of logic,
   Dispelling the assertions of others.
   Thus, inferior challengers have no place.

§ 68. Those who do not assert anything to be existent or
      non-existent
   Nor both existent and non-existent,
   Not even very diligent opponents
   Can successfully criticize.[49]

---

[48] Aryadeva *Four Hundred Verses* Chap. 16, Verse ??

[49] Khenchen Palden Sherab Rinpoche's suggested changes:
"From the childish to buddhas their experience is different. Whatever their experience is, it is their own perception, and I do not object. On the absolute level contrary to Kapila etc. [Nyaya-s, exists], [Charvakas, do not exist]-[Jains, things both exist and do not exist], and all of this is exaggeration. The buddhas [the speaker], do not see wrongly the nature of emptiness. These do not exist on the absolute level. Thus, seeing the nature of everything as emptiness is not incorrect."

From the childish in manner up to omniscience experiencing all that, when nature is unexamined, is agreeable to the mind. That nature I am not refuting, and I do not reject it.[50]

In the ultimate level the result is already existing, not existing, and both, and neither. Those who are speaking like Kapila, what they say [exists] is not existing.

"Concerning those views about existence
Non-existence, existence, both and neither,
It would be a long time
Before you could challenge this position [one who has no position]."
[Aryadeva, *Four Hundred Verses*, Chap. 16, Verse 25]

**§ 69. Therefore, on the absolute level
Nothing can be established as existing.
Thus, it was said by the Tathagatas,
"All phenomena are unoriginated."**

From the absolute point of view, we do not accept that there are any subtle things [like atoms] that are completely established, because of the manner of teaching that they lack the nature of one and many. Because of this they do not arise nor previously exist. They are impermanent, and what dependent phenomena could exist in any other way?

---

[50] Santaraksita clearly wants to emphasize that he does not merely talk about the past and future when speaking of a lack of inherent existence of production, but also of the present, of the "time of arising." This eliminates any potential ambiguity about the lack of inherent existence necessitating a relationship to a specific time other that the present, because the lack of inherent existence is the same in all of the three times." [Blumenthal, 2004 p. 14]
On the ultimate level, things and nothing, birth and non-birth, emptiness and non-emptiness, etc., are all abandoned like a complex net of elaborations. Though nothing arises etc., since entering into [accepting] this is harmonious with the ultimate, it is designated as ultimate.
Without the staircase of perfect conventionality,
One should not go
To the roof of the house of the ultimate.
It is not suitable for the wise.
[Madhyamakohrdaya by Bhavaviveka Chap. 3, v. 12 legs ldan 'gyed]

Thus *[The Sutra of] the Ocean of Intelligent Teachings* states:

> "Those which dependently arise
> Are not actual things at all.
> By not having any self-essence
> Therefore, they do not come into existence [ultimately]."

From the *Skillful Elephant Sutra*:

> "The coming into existence
> Of phenomena has never been observed.
> Of those dharmas which do not arise
> Childish people assert they do arise."

And this is also said In the *Sutra of the Source of Jewels/The Abiding and Arising of the Jewel Sutra* [Blumenthal, 2004 p. 147]:

> "Of that which has no intrinsic nature
> How could there be any causal conditions from another?
> How could it be produced by another that has no self-nature?
> This is the Sugata's teaching of the cause."[51]

---

[51] [
Blumenthal, 2004, p. 148]
Also: Nagarjuna The Dispeller of Disputes:

> If objects are not established,
> Then non-existent objects will not be established.
> When the object changes into something else,
> People say, "It does not exist."

Thus said
> "In milk, yogurt etc. does not exist.
> It does not exist previously [in the milk].
> In yogurt, milk does not exist.
> It has the characteristic of non-existence, being destroyed.

> The protrusion of the head
> Lacks any solid existence.
> The characteristics of the horn of a rabbit etc.
> Are said to be absolutely non-existent.
> As to the cow, there is no horse.
> They are mutually exclusive."

Therefore, it is also said in the *Meeting of the Father and Son Sutra*:

Because one engages in interdependent origination, it is shown that one enters into the sphere of reality [dharmadatu/ultimate truth]. "What is the reason", Oh Lord? Regarding this, Oh Lord, ignorance in itself does not exist. Why? Because no dharmas have intrinsic nature. What is the reason? Because ignorance is free from intrinsic nature. And anything that has no self-nature, is not a thing and is not established.

Whatever is completely unproduced, is unborn. If there is no birth, there is no cessation, and cannot be designated as past. Nor can you give a name to the future and the present. What is not perceived in the three times is nameless.

The characteristic does not exist, the designation (mtshan ma) does not exist. There is no other. There are just characteristics, signs on the relative level, just words, just merely designations.

For the sake of all sentient beings, that in the future they may understand, Buddha showed the path. But on the absolute level, nothing exists.

---

51 continued

Thus trivially, the meaning is, none of these things exist. They are certainly non-existent. They are all brought together by association. The non-existence of things is the enemy of certainty.

Certainly, one can now establish that a barren woman having a son etc. is not certain [cannot happen]. If one considers the matter, it cannot exist. In this way from the Ocean of Intelligence Sutra it has been taught: "Brahma, that phenomenon which is completely [presumably] established as self-existent, has been well explained as non-existent. " In the Lankavatara Sutra, Chap. 3, Verse 14 [MLF: Since things don't exist, we can't be certain about anything.]

Also: "Mere existence is the counterpart, the simple negation, of true existence. It definitely belongs to the conventional or relative level. It is not the ultimate or natural condition of phenomena. Since, however, it is in agreement with ultimate truth (that is the authentic ultimate state of things), this mere absence of true existence, the conceptual opposite of true existence, is called 'ultimate truth', in much the same way that the name of result is given to its cause. This is the approximate or conceptual (btags pa ba) ultimate." [Mipham Rinpoche, Padmakara, p. 296]

Khenpo Tsewang Dongyal Rinpoche taught that the Svabhavakaya was completely beyond words. The Dharmakaya was the intelligence or wisdom aspect of the Svabhavakaya and could be indicated by words. Online retreat April 20, 2020. This is similar to the true ultimate and the proximate ultimate.

Ultimately any phenomenon which is perceived does not exist, the designation does not exist, and thus it is said that it does not exist even as a characteristic. And cannot be expressed. Thus in reply to a questioner, Buddha said that from characteristics up to mere designations, and on and on, are not real.

> "As the wheel of dharma turns
> From beginningless time, [all phenomena] are peacefully free, peaceful from the outset, unborn.
> Thus, the nature of phenomena is Nirvana,
> This doctrine was shown by the Protector."

[*Wheel of Dharma Sutra*]

The above sentences explain this verse very well. By this verse, all in the three times are completely equal. Past present and future can be pacified, because they have no intrinsic nature.

In *The Meeting of the Father and Son Sutra* it is also said that all phenomena in the three times are shown to be completely equal [because none exist]. In the past all things are free from intrinsic nature. In the present and in the future all things are free from intrinsic nature. Making clearer, all phenomena are empty by intrinsic nature. Any phenomenon not having intrinsic nature are not past present or future. Why? Not having intrinsic nature, they should not be designated as past, present, and future as it is stated. If in the past time all phenomena do not exist then nothing comes into existence because nothing can arise. How could this be otherwise? Even non-production and the like have been classified as conventional realities.

Even in the past these are lacking in intrinsic nature because these are not future, not present. [Why?" Since nothing exists, you cannot designate past, present and future". (Khenchen Palden Sherab Rinpoche)]

As for non-arising, etc., it is classified as the right conventional truth.[52]

---

[52] "...Consequently, even a nonthing (absence) is posited in dependence on its counterpart: a causally efficient thing. If there were no certainty that barren women and children existed, it would be impossible to derive any meaning from the expression 'a barren woman's child'. It is through the understanding that this expression evokes that one uses it as an example of nonexistence.

Conversely, existence depends on its counterpart, nonexistence. One speaks for example of the birth, or coming into being, of something because this did not exist in the past.

Proximate Ultimate Truth.

§ 70. This is harmonious with ultimate truth,
And thus, it has been called "ultimate truth."
Truly it is free from all
The accumulations of mental fabrications.

On the ultimate level, things and nothing, birth and non-birth, emptiness and non-emptiness, etc., are all abandoned like a complex net of elaborations. Though nothing arises etc., since entering into [accepting] this is harmonious with the ultimate, it is designated as ultimate.

"Without the staircase of perfect conventionality,
One should not go
To the roof of the house of the ultimate.
It is not suitable for the wise."
[*Madhyamakohrdaya* by Bhavaviveka
Chap. 3, Vol. 12 legs ldan 'gyed]

[52 continued] If it existed already, its present existence would render impossible any ulterior entry into existence. If something that was already existent could come into being, it would never stop coming into existence (which is absurd). Therefore, existence and nonexistence, truth and falsity, emptiness and nonemptiness—all such things are only the positings of thought. None of these categories correctly corresponds to the ultimate nature, for the latter is beyond all conceptual elaborations." (Zhonumalen/ Kumarila, in [Mipham Rinpoche, Padmakara, p. 304-305])

"The counterpart of existence is non-existence.
The counterpart of non-existence is existence.
Thus, one should not think of existence,
Nor should one think of non-existence.

Where nothing whatever arises,
Nothing whatsoever will cease.
Seen without imagining,
Nothing is, and nothing is not."

It is said along with this: The meaning of this is that regarding existence, you can establish non-existence: Before something existed. Now it is destroyed. And one that is born, did not exist before.

For example, when viewing destruction, three aspects of non-existence can be shown. (1. Some things are mutually non-existent; 2. Before something is born, it does not exist; 3. When something is destroyed, it no longer exists; 4. Some things are mutually non-existent, like a cow and a horse. As the companion of existence, there is nonexistence

Why did (Lord Buddha) teach the non-existence of things on the absolute level?

§ 71. The notion of birth is refuted.
The notion of non-birth is equally refuted.
Because the reality of both is refuted,
Not even the sound of their names can really exist.

§ 72. [Others say] since that which you are trying to refute
does not exist,
Reasoning about it cannot be correct.[53]
But relying on discursive thought,
It will all be true on the relative, not the absolute level.

If birth etc. does not exist, then the sound of the word is not correct [does not designate anything]. If this is the case, there is no cessation of the object [if it was never born it cannot cease]. Therefore, if there is no object, then because of the refutation of existence, then even birth does not exist. Neither non-birth. Thus, non-arising is impossible. None the less,

---

52 continued

[non-vacuous contrast]. For example, birth is previously non-existent. Similarly, if the previously existent were born, then that past being will again become.
If this is the case, as Nagarjuna said.
[Mulamadhyamakakarika, Chap. 15, Verse 6]:

> "Those persons who concerning things and other than things,
> Perceive neither objects nor the non-existence of objects.
> By these the essence of Buddha's teaching,
> Is not perfectly perceived."

[See Doctor 517 Padmakara 309: CF. Mipham Rinpoche Padmakara p. 296 on proximate ultimate.]

[53] "Consequently the explanatory methods of the Prasangikas and the Svatantrika converge. As far as the ultimate view, the absence of all conceptual constructs, is concerned, they are the same. But when distinctions are made in the postmeditation period, it is easier to divide the ultimate truth into two categories as the Svatantrikas do. When in meditative equipoise, one penetrates nonconceptual primordial wisdom, there will be no further need to divide it, and a great freedom from all conceptual constructs will be accomplished. If one understands this, one will grasp the vital point of the Madhyamaka. It is difficult to do so otherwise." [Mipham Rinpoche, Padmakara, p. 302] 53 continued next page

the self-characteristic is not the object of these sounds Therefore, also non-birth etc. is not existing. But however, from beginningless time the habitual patterns of discursive thinking have arisen and have the nature of appearance. And they are produced as if it were the object itself.

Birth, etc., when examined in this way, need not be abandoned, because they arise from mind and are united with words.

Discursive thought is the nature of consciousness. Therefore, what is grasped should be eliminated. We should rely on discursive thought on the conventional level, not on the ultimate. This is true of the meaning of the word / sound for tree etc. By this consideration regarding this, ultimately there is no existing self-nature of anything

Thus it is said (defense of relative level).[54]

"The counterpart of existence is non-existence.
The counterpart of non-existence is existence.
Thus, one should not think of existence,
Nor should one think of non-existence.
Where nothing whatever arises,
Nothing whatsoever will cease.
Seen without imagining,
Nothing is, and nothing is not."

---

53 continued

"...Yogacharas [who claim subject and object are the same and images are unreal] maintain direct knowledge of objects is possible, and since objects are considered to be of the same nature as consciousness, the claim for the unreality of images must in fact be faulty. This is the case because images do not actually exist in their view and so they must not be of the same substance as consciousness which is real." [Blumenthal, p. 129]

[54] "In the present context, this 'seeing' may be expressed negatively as when one says, "I did not see anything." or positively, as when one says, "I saw nothing." There is, however, no difference in meaning, because even the latter statement does not indicate that there is something (a nothing) to see. Likewise, there is no difference in meaning between the statements "The ultimate is beyond the reach of intellect," "The ultimate is not the object of the intellect," and "The ultimate is the object of no-thought." Since the state of no-thought is identified as the halting of all concepts and the absence of all duality between the perceiver and the perceived, it does not mean that the ultimate can be "detected" as the object of no-thought. [Mipham Rinpoche, Padmakara, pp. 300-301]'

It is said along with this: The meaning of this is that regarding existence, you can establish non-existence: Before something existed. Now it is destroyed. And one that is born, did not exist before.

[On the absolute level, there is no birth. Birth is interdependent co-originated/caused by consciousness and male and female elements. There is nothing on the absolute level, so on the absolute level, birth and no birth do not exist. Not even the name of birth or no birth exists. Even the words are not correct. Khenpo Tsewang Dongyal Rinpoche][55]

For example, when viewing destruction, different aspects of non-existence can be shown. Some things are mutually non-existent. Before something is born, it does not exist. When something is destroyed, it no longer exists. Some things are mutually non-existent, like a cow and a horse. As the companion of existence, there is nonexistence [MLF non-vacuous contrast]. For example, birth is previously non-existent. Similarly, if the previously existent were born, then that past being will again become.

If this is the case, as Nagarjuna said:

[Mulamadhyamakalankara, Chap. 15, Verse 6]:

"Those persons who mistakenly view things as objects that exist or don't exist,
Perceive neither objects nor the non-existence of objects.
By these the essence of Buddha's teaching,
Is not perfectly perceived.

"Those who see entities in the form of self and other,
And who see entities and non-entities
All such people fail to see aright
The teaching that the Buddha has set forth."[56]

---

[55] "All is real; all is unreal
All is both unreal and real;
All is neither real nor yet unreal;
Thus by steps the Buddha taught."
[Mipham Rinpoche, Padmakara, p. 309;

[56] "Those who say that things arise dependently
And like the moon reflected in a pool
Do not exist and are not non-existent,
Can never be assailed by other views."
[Mipham Rinpoche, Padmakara, p. 309]

"Those who depend on entities,
Are like the moon reflected in water,
Imperfect, but not mistaken
In asserting these views, they are not robbed."[57]

"Those who say that things arise dependently,
And like the moon reflected in a pool
Do not exist and are not non-existent,
Can never be assailed by other views."[58]

"All dependent entities
Are like the moon in water:
Not authentic and not wrong.
Those who so assert will not be harmed by views."

"All apparent permanence is impermanent.
What does not exist is similarly impermanent."
[Chap. 24, Verse 14 Mula*madhyamakakarika*]

How Could These Permanent and Impermanent Objects Come into Existence?[59]

---

[57] "Phenomena are not real, yet nevertheless appear, and this is the union of the two truths and is a great wonder." [Mipham Rinpoche, Padmakara, p. 312]

[58] Or Doctor p. 519 And 304-305 Padmakara (Mipham Rinpoche): "...[C]onsequently, even a nonthing (absence) is posited in dependence on its counterpart: a causally efficient thing. If there were no certainty that barren women and children existed, it would be impossible to derive any meaning from the expression 'a barren woman's child'. It is through the understanding that this expression evokes that one uses it as an example of nonexistence.

Conversely, existence depends on its counterpart, nonexistence. One speaks for example of the birth, or coming into being, of something because this did not exist in the past. If it existed already, its present existence would render impossible any ulterior entry into existence. If something that was already existent could come into being, it would never stop coming into existence (which is absurd). Therefore, existence and nonexistence, truth and falsity, emptiness and nonemptiness—all such things are only the positings of thought. None of these categories correctly corresponds to the ultimate nature, for the latter is beyond all conceptual elaborations."

[59] Quote from Nagarjuna, Mipham Rinpoche, Doctor p. 119.

"Thus, everything which is explained
Is itself empty by its own nature.
The 'so-called' empty is also empty.
Therefore, nothing exists which is not empty.
For whom emptiness is not fitting.
For him, nothing is fitting ."[60]
"Nothing is permanent and likewise,
Nothing whatsoever is impermanent,
If permanent, entities that were permanent and impermanent
would exist [non-vacuous contrast argument? MLF],
And how could that ever be the case?
To whom emptiness itself does not arise,
To them also, how would the non-existent arise?"

This was well said.

From the Great Questions of the Ocean of Naga Kings:
"The preceding state and the future state are both empty.

Arising, perishing and remaining things are empty.
Thus, there is no reality to either existing or not existing things."[61]

Thus, it is said:

§ 73. Now having realized this (the solidity of these arguments). [What if an opponent were to object] that if The nature of reality is perceptible. Then do not even simple/lowly people Recognize the nature of things?

---

[60] "The reasoning of the intrinsic nature is beyond bias, and from that perspective, none of the objects apprehended by those fond of characteristics are posited. When the ship of attachment to entity is crushed in the ocean of emptiness beyond extremes, the merchants of the mind of [the realm of] existence, obsessed with the net of the characteristics of various observations, may, shocked and confounded with fear, try to grasp for the support of some object. Yet the support itself is unsupported—this is the intrinsic nature." [Doctor, p. 501]

[61] [CF. Padmakara p. 314:] "But the false theories of Kapila and Kanada are far stranger. For when they clearly see the shapes of objects, such as cows or pots-objects that are themselves empty of universals (spyi) such as "cowhood" or "pothood" -they consider to be real not the thing seen, but the unseen universal instead! See also Dreyfus' *Recognizing Reality* pp. 52-59)

If thus perceived, [they say] it would not be correct that its own nature would not be perceived.

If one perceives the earth without a jar, then similarly one perceives it as lacking the nature of the jar. As each thing arises, those with the wrong view, who are inferior will impute things as existent. If all are said to be completely non-existent, why do not people perceive them as non-existent?

Lacking reification, why do not people accept them in this way?[62]

§ 74. This is because from time without beginning,
   ### The mind stream of beings has been burdened
   ### By being controlled by reification.
   ### For this reason, all sentient beings lack direct knowledge
   ### [of reality].

Born from beginningless samsara, having disturbed mind, by the poison of great attachment to things, stirred up by this poison, they are not able to understand through direct perception. For those who perceive similar things as a continuum, one after another, momentariness is not realized. This is not surprising. Thus, of the jar and the ox etc., one sees the shape of the ox by itself clearly, but not its nature. Kapila's (Samkhya) and Kanada's (Nyaya) doctrines have similar mistakes and failures of realization.[63]

§ 75. Some come to know through
   ### Cutting reification [as well as through] evidence and
   ###   reasoning.
   ### The lord of the yogis
   ### Perceives directly and clearly.[64]

---

[62] "He [Shantarakshita} explains in MAV that the difference between the perception of those of low intellect who are unenlightened and the perception of unenlightened ones is that in addition to valid cognition of gross objects, those of low intellect also impute inherent existence onto the objects they perceive. Thus they impute an extreme perspective onto objects which do not abide in either of the two extremes." [Blumenthal, 2004 p. 152]

[63] *Samadhiraj Sutra*, Chap. 9, Verse 23: "This is not ordinary perception but non-dualistic." trans. Joshua Cutler *Great Treatise on the Stages of the Path to Enlightenment* by Tsongkhapa: *King of Concentration Sutra*

[64] Shantarakshita means valid perception as non-dualistic.

The eye, ear, and nose consciousnesses are not valid cognitions.
The tongue, body, and mental consciousnesses are also not valid
cognitions. If these sensory consciousnesses were valid cognitions,
Of what use to anyone would the noble beings' path be?[65]

With regard to dispelling the superimpositions imposed on entities, that
which is shown to be the establishment of part of a view through logic,
produces from the accumulation of phenomena arising from mind, great
certainty about phenomena [defense of autonomous inferences/*svatan-
tranumana/rang gyud kyi rjes dpag*]. From pondering, the very exact accumulation (i.e. the arguments given), removing reification becomes certain.

For the yogic king, all phenomena arise as equal in meditation, and
completely lacking all stain of thought construction. By this wisdom, things
appear harmoniously without essence. For all just like the emptiness of the
plantain, when examined by beings, one should realize that similarly the
seed of reification will not arise thereafter.

Thus, it is like the stalk of the wet plantain. From the *Mahakarunava-
tara Sutra*:

> "Just as with the living plantain tree-
> We may dissect it, seeking for its core,
> Yet fail to find it, outside, or within.
> Tis thus that we should know that all things are."[66]

And it also said likewise as even in the *Udanavarga*:

> "Like the *Udanavarga* lotus flower [flower with no fruit]
> One who contemplates the essencelessness of samsara,
>
> That monk abandoning the hither side [samsara]
> Attains the farther side [nirvana] like an old snake changing
> its skin."[67]

---

[65] The center of the plantain plant is not hard, but edible.

[66] [Cf. Blumenthal, 2004 pp 154-156]: "...Shantarakshita responds by arguing that a common subject can be established since there are validly established entities known by all
beings." Sloka 76.

[67] Shantarakshita wants to refute the view that if all conventionalities are unreal then
inference has to be unreal and invalid. But he would argue that relative to the system of
convention, inference is valid.

Thus, it is said [by the opponent]:

If one accepts that all things have no intrinsic existence, since the evidence is not established by oneself by the convention of inference, then is it not the case that inference on the relative level is not established? Thus similarly, the inferer, in establishing a thesis, that all dharmas are without inherent existence, cannot assert a valid argument. And if there is no reason for this non-establishment [of intrinsic nature] then one cannot establish a meaningful hypothesis. If one asserts this, and there is no valid reason, then the meaning of your assertions is not established. You need a reason. But if its nature is non-existent, you cannot establish it. This would be pointless.[68]

Nevertheless, then:

§ 76. By giving up all the different conceptions
Without being proclaimed as doctrines,
And accepting those things
Well known by the learned, women and children, all
Will be able to recognize what is really provably true.

You are not going to have a problem because you have given up all perceptions. Thus said.[69]

---

[68] [Mipham Rinpoche, Padmakara, p.327]: "This is a trashy argument."

[McClintock/Blumenthal, 2004 p.367 note 211]: "... Sara McClintock (2003) has argued that Shantarakshita is using "sliding scales of analysis" in which he utilizes autonomous inferences (*svatantranumana*) when analyzing lower views from a Yogachara perspective, and when analyzing the Sautrantika position from a Yogachara perspective, yet in his final shift (when finally analyzing Yogachara views from a Madhyamaka perspective he no longer uses autonomous inferences. If this is the case, and Shantarakshita is only using such a form of reasoning when it is acceptable from the perspective of the tenets whose acceptance he is in a sense feigning, then use in such a circumstance should not be problematic.

Possible similarity to the use and mention distinction in contemporary philosophy. The criterion used, inference, is not the sort of thing that exists or doesn't exist. It is a technique that is used, but it is not validly considered as an object. [MLF]

[69] [Blumenthal, 2004 p. 156] and Khenchen Palden Sherab Rinpoche: Mipham: "Appearances are there, but empty. If there is no appearance there is no emptiness and visa versa."

This then, is how one should understand that phenomena appear, even though they do not truly exist.

If one upholds the essencelessness of all dharmas,

§ 77. **The mode of proof and what is proved**
Must all be perfectly established.
If not the basic ground of agreement would not exist.
And how could you respond to that?

§ 78. **As for myself, I never rejected,**
Those things having appearances.
Therefore, having established this view of things,
One will not be confused about establishing premise
and conclusion.

Following this inference, what is proposed by the various philosophical theories which are mutually in disagreement have been shown Thus for sages, women and children, what appears through eye, nose consciousness etc., logic, the sound of theory [dependent on the logical subject] is shown to be inconsistent and must be given up completely. But what is accepted by sages and ordinary people, like women and children, through sense observation, I am not rejecting [on the conventional level][70].

Some say that all inferential reasoning and the conventional objects [of knowledge] inferred by such reasoning must be given up completely [since they depend on] different subjects generated by incompatible tenets.

Eye, ear and nose consciousness, etc. of everyone from masters to women to children (i.e. come to know) [in subjects for autonomous inferences] by relying on subjects which [correspond with] the sound [of the words pointing to] that which possesses the taste of appearances.

If this is the case, that is, if there is no common ground of argument, then, there will be no basis for establishing reasons such as that smoke is evidence for the existence of fire etc., and there will be no evidence for impermanence, etc. because one will not be able to establish the qualities

---

[70] [CF. Blumenthal, 2004, p. 158]

of the subjects under consideration. The qualities of space etc. will not be established.[71]

Thus because of being possessed of two elements, things and the properties of things, the example of phenomena is not established as intrinsically existent. If this kind of convention of establishing and not establishing is widely used and well-known when disputing with scholars, then similarly from our own (Buddhist) point of view, unlike that of others, the mistakes of the errors of other views has been mentioned [refuted] exhaustively.

We also do not reject things which appear to the eye consciousness and so forth. When we analyze with wisdom knowledge, like the plantain tree, a single essence does not appear. We don't assert things as ultimate truth. If this is the case, through non-attachment, appearances are not a hindrance to the ultimate meaning. Engaging like this in the relative level, one says that all phenomena have no intrinsic nature. How could this be harmful? [Thus because the relative is not ultimately real that does not mean we can't use the relative. Ven. Lodro]

---

[71] Shantarakshita offers a detailed explanation of his argument in the *MAV*. He argues that these imputed notions of entities and entitylessness which even exist in newborn babies do not arise as a result of external entities. This is verified by the fact that such entities have already been rejected in this text. Likewise, they are not sudden and are not permanent since there is nothing that is permanent. Since the consciousness of even newborn infants are already accustomed to common modes of consciousness, such as perceiving entities and entitylessness, they must arise from a previous instance of a similar type of consciousness, and thus from one of a previous life." [Blumenthal, 2004 p. 160] [Cf. Gyel-tsab Blumenthal. P. 161]

Shunyasaptati [70 *Stanzas on Emptiness*, stanza 21, Nagarjuna]:

"If existent, an entity will be permanent.
If non-existent, an object will certainly be eliminated.
If there would be an entity that existed, it should be both.
Therefore, entities cannot be accepted.
Entities evidently arise,
And because of that, this is not nihilism.
Because entities are changing [reversed]
This is not eternalism.
Those who rely on enlightenment
Do not assert non-existence on the ultimate level.
Those not thinking and not acting,
How could they be nihilistic?"
["Pramanasiddhi" Chap. of *Pramanavartika*]

Thus, it is said.

> "Without depending on heavy grasping
> Conventions will be thoroughly established.
> If one skillfully establishes conventions,
> The meaning of the scriptures will not be obscured."

[*Lankavatara Sutra*, p. 25]

Those who have become controlled by hatred towards the system of absolute meaning, and reject the view that all phenomena lack inherent existence, they see Madhyamaka as the king of nihilism.

In this way, cause and effect are slandered [or deprecated]. By that wrong view the white side of phenomena will be uprooted. This hailstorm of harvested sky flowers menacing the holy dharma should be left far away by those who are benevolent.

These verses are expressed regarding those adversaries:

§ 79. Therefore continuously from beginningless time
All thought constructions etc. of existing and non-existing things
Come only from the conformative seeds [of thought construction] harmonious in their class [its own kind]
And are known as the objects of inference.

§ 80. By the strength of entities,
Nothing arises, because they are non-existent.
The self-nature of things,
I have refuted extensively.

§ 81. Because if arising gradually and therefore not suddenly
And not always present, and thus not permanent
Because of like habitual patterns,
Things are born from the first of their own kind.[72]

---

[72] "If a phenomena were to exist inherently it should be permanent. If a phenomenon were to disintegrate completely then you must accept the nihilistic view. If a phenomenon were to exist inherently it would either exist permanently or else undergo complete disintegration: it cannot occur in a way which is different from these two. Therefore, one should not

Thus, from an ultimate point of view, all these entities are free from elaboration, yet for those of good intellect, these entities do not exist. Thought constructions arise about existing and non-existing things etc. and arise from no other cause than conformative seeds. This is not happening through the force of perception. Since there are no entities and non-entities etc., the existence and non-existence of things in themselves I have extensively refuted.

Because of this if one grasps that there is no cause of a seed of its own conformative class (own type), what else is left to exist? There is no permanent cause of birth, no permanently existing self. Similarly, if it is said that things arise, this could be adventitiously, or if one believes in causes like Ishvara etc., or similarly accepting a permanent mind, this would be inconsistent, since events are successive in nature. (1) That which does not depend on a cause, as well as (2) anything which is permanent and always connects with [successive things], are both inconsistent with the successive origination of things.

Thus, elements in life are due to thought constructions that arise for the first time, [as well as] those that follow, and are similar to the habits to which we have become accustomed. For beings born of lesser, medium or great ability, etc., these habitual tendencies will arise in distinctly different ways, similar to their thought constructions. There is no beginning to samsara.

Thus, the existence of a future has been already explained by inference. Similarly, the dying one who is not free from attachment, will have a mind that is connected by habitual tendencies/erroneous connections with I and mine. It is clearly established that the reborn mind will be similar to the one before. This point is clear.

§ 82. Therefore the views of eternalism and nihilism
Are very far from the view of this doctrine [the middle way].
Perishing and arising [engaging and avoiding] also continue
Like the seed, sprout and shoot, and so forth.[73]

[72 continued] assert that a phenomenon has inherent existence." *Nagarjuna's Seventy Stanzas: A Buddhist Psychology of Emptiness*. ed. David Komito. Trans. and commentary Geshe Sonam Rinchen, Tenzin Dorjee and David Ross. Ithaca: Snow Lion, 1987 p. 128

The system of Madhyamaka does not have the faults of permanence or nihilism. There is no fault of permanence because after the cause is eliminated (ldog) the subsequent effect ceases (log), and there is no fault of nihilism because fruits arise from causes as sprouts arise from seeds.

Ultimately, there are no extremes of eternalism and nihilism. They rely on things. If there are no things, how could that be? Having relied on the relative truth, the former moment is instantaneously removed by the next moment as it arises from other moments. Therefore, entities do not have a beginning or an end. Similarly, to the views of some non-Buddhists, these two [past and future moments] are altogether non-existent. Thus said:

> "If existent, an entity will be permanent.
> If non-existent, an object will certainly be eliminated.
> If there would be an entity that existed, it should be both.
> Therefore, entities cannot be accepted.
> Entities evidently arise,
> And because of that, this is not nihilism.
> Because entities are changing [reversed]
> This is not eternalism.
> Those who rely on enlightenment
> Do not assert non-existence on the ultimate level.
> Those not thinking and not acting,
> How could they be nihilistic?"

[*Sunyasaptati* Nagarjuna, *Seventy Stanzas on Emptiness*, Stanza 21]

---

[73] *Vyavarharasiddhi* [accomplishment of usage] probably Nagarjuna [only in Chinese].

And: "Gyal-tsab's commentary refers to the cause of the afflictive emotions as the grasping at true existence (*bten 'dzin*) and eliminates Shantarakshita's use of the term "lack of inherent existence" (*rang bzhin med*) later in the stanza in favor of the more general "emptiness" (*stong nyid*). Geluk critics say that Shantarakshita accepts inherent existence). These changes again lend themselves in subtle ways towards reading Shantarakshita's text through a framework which will contribute to later Geluk critiques in other philosophical materials." [Blumenthal, 2004 p. 162-163]

And it is also said in the *Candrapradipasamadhirajasutra Royal Meditation of the Moon Lamp Sutra:* "This attachment and to that to which there is attachment and the one who is attached are not seen on the ultimate level."

Also nb CF. Mipham Rinpoche, Padmakara, p. 337 on primordial wisdom.

18. "If things are not empty
There would be no cessation, no arising
If they are intrinsically empty,
Where do they cease or arise?

19. Without existence there is no non-existence
A non-entity without entity is not possible

20. Without entity there is no non-entity
Not from self, not from others.
Therefore there is no entity
Also there is no non-entity

21. If there is entity it is eternal[74]
If there is none there is nihilism
If there is an entity there should be [one of] these two.
Therefore, do not accept either."
[Dharmakirti, Pramanasiddhi Chap. of *Pramanavartika*]

"If there would be an entity that existed, it should be both,
Therefore, things cannot be accepted.
Because of this, entities evidently arise.
And because of that, this is not nihilism.
Because entities are changing [removing].
Thus, there is no eternalism.
Those who rely on enlightenment
Do not assert non-existence on the ultimate level.

---

[74] "Pramanasiddhi" chapter of *Pramanvartika* [Blumenthal, 2004, p. 162]: "Santaraksi-ta's treatment of this topic here is explained in the context of demonstrating how 'libera-tion' is easier [if one understands the meaning of] this text. 'understanding the meaning of this text' means understanding the lack of inherent existence of all persons and phenomena, which Shantarakshita has gone to great lengths to logically establish here. It seems as though his argument claims that by cultivating a realization of emptiness, knowledge of the selflessness of (persons and) phenomena, such an *arya* eventually attains liberation from cyclic existence through the abandonment of afflictive emotion obstacles (*klesavarana*; *nyon sgrib*) and contrived erroneous views. This is a result of a process of deepening one's understanding of emptiness through meditation and familiarity. (Sloka 83)

Those not thinking and not acting,
How would they be nihilist?"
[Nagarjuna's *Seventy Stanzas*, Stanza 21]

Thus, it is also said in the *Ratnamegha Sutra*:

"If someone were to ask, 'How are the Bodhisattvas skillful on the Mahayana?' They do all the practices, but they do not perceive the subject, object or activity [path] of training. Because of the cause, conditions and ground [accepted conventionally], Buddha said they would not be nihilistic. It is stated that way."
[Also in Mipham Rinpoche, Padmakara, p. 336]

And it [The *Ratnamegha*] also says:

"Child of noble lineage, the bodhisattva investigates forms with perfect wisdom. Similarly, when he/she examines, feelings, perceptions, volitions (applications) consciousness, forms, concerning the generation of forms, he/she does not perceive the origination of forms/suffering. For all of them, their arising and cessation are not perceived. The arising of feelings, discriminations, volitions [applications] and consciousness is not perceived. No arising is perceived. No cessation is perceived. There is no arising which is not the nature of the conventional. Liberation in this doctrine is easy."
[Also in Mipham Rinpoche, Padmakara, p. 336]

§ 83. The expert in the selflessness of things,
By meditating on that which is without self-nature—emptiness,
By this all emotions will naturally dissolve [Khenpo Palden Sherab Rinpoche]
Which come from mistaken views.

As mentioned in *The Moonlight of Samadhi Sutra*, "That individual who is attached to phenomena is never going to see clearly." [Khenpo Tsewang Dongyal Rinpoche: (Those who see clearly) won't see subject, object or activity because of their realization."]

47. "[Ego] is the cause of all these views,
If you know things to be non-existent, defilements will not arise.
Thus, if this is completely understood,
Then this view and the defilements will completely purify."[75]

48. By this, if realization is achieved,
By seeing dependent arising
"The dependent arising is not arising."
This is said by he who is the perfect knower (Buddha)."[76]

[Pramanasiddhi chapter of *Pramanavartika* by Dharmakirti (tshad ma rnam 'grel)]

It is also said:

49. "If there is acceptance of the reality of things,
There will be no end to horrible hatred and attachment.
When one is thoroughly attached to an unsuitable view,
Disputes arising from this will occur."[77]

[Nagarjuna's *Yuctishastrika, Sixty Verses*, Verse 46]

Moreover, if as you say nothing is existing then one might disagree and ask then what is affliction, karma, the arising of extreme affliction? What is purification? What is the relation of cause and effect, of inference, what is inferred through conventions, ignorance, formations, and the limbs of existence [twelve links]? When one becomes familiar with the antidote one

---

[75] [*Sixty Verses, Yuctishastrika*, 47-49]
[Mipham Rinpoche Tib Doctor p. 422]:
Moreover, if as you say nothing is existing then one might disagree and ask then what is affliction, karma, the arising of extreme affliction? What is purification? What is the relation of cause and effect, of inference, what is inferred through conventions, ignorance, formations, and the limbs of existence [twelve links]? When one becomes familiar with the antidote one is able to experience that which is not harmonious and without defilements, beloved and non-beloved, [all of] which is the maturing of virtuous and unvirtuous karma, and that is itself the antidote.

[76] "The two truths make one another clear. How could they be contradictory? Ripened virtuous and non-virtuous actions arise and result in what is beautiful and not beautiful. Everything arises completely like this." [*Pramanavartika*, Chap. 2, 81, 80].

[77] "Since the mind is purely determined By the actions of the [earlier minds,] [The subsequent] minds cannot arise without the [previous moments of the mind.] Therefore [the mind] is dependent on the [preceding] minds [and not the body.]
[bodhiwisdom.org/wpcontent/uploads/2018/05Pramanavartika-root of Pramanavartika]

is able to experience that which is not harmonious and without defilements, beloved and non-beloved, [all of] which is the maturing of virtuous and unvirtuous karma, and that is itself the antidote.[78]

[The characteristics of a person resulting from karma, are incorporated with respect to the virtues and non-virtues ripening [smin] from karma, [those] pleasing [sdugpa] and not pleasing. Khenpo Tsewang Dongyal Rinpoche]

Everything arises completely like this.

When you have become expert in egolessness, [and accepting] no solid existence [the antidote,] then all the opposite incorrect ideas such as the two egos of emotions (to self and phenomena) will not arise and it will naturally not be incorporated with the emotions. For that reason, all the virtues good and bad karma will not come.

> "Since the mind is purely determined
> By the actions of the [earlier minds,]
> [The subsequent] minds cannot arise without the [previous moments of the mind.]
> Therefore [the mind] is dependent on the [preceding] minds [and not the body.]"
>
> [*Pramanavartika*, Chap. 2, 78]

---

[78] "Santaraksita proceeds from here to establish the argument by positing a logical connection between the correct view of emptiness and right moral action. The link is to be argued that, if one does not see all phenomena as lacking true existence, then ultimately valid cognition is harmed because one knows objects as truly existent when they actually are not. As a result, strong grasping becomes prevalent, serving as a basis for all sorts of inappropriate actions and intentions." [Blumenthal, 2004 p. 165]

Also: "When Santaraksita speaks of 'masters who know selflessness of phenomena,' it is interesting to note that Gyel-tsab refers to them more specifically as 'arya bodhisattvas.' This is as opposed to Hinayana arhats who, according to the Geluk presentation of Svatantrika-Madhyamaka, only know the selflessness of persons. This is worth knowing because for Gelukpas both Hinayana arhats and bodhisattvas realize the selflessness of persons and phenomena. This subtle shift presents Santaraksita's views in accordance with the way they will be later be presented and criticized in other Gelukpa philosophical materials. Neither in MA nor in his autocommentary on this stanza does Santaraksita refer to such persons or imply that such persons are necessarily arya bodhisattvas.

"The second interesting shift worth pointing out here concerns the technical terms used to describe emptiness. Gyel-tsab's commentary refers to the cause of afflictive emotions as the grasping at true existence (bden 'dzin) and eliminates Santaraksita's use of the term 'lack of inherent existence' (rang bzhin med) later in the stanza in favor of the more general 'emptiness' (stong nyid)." (Geluk critics say that Shantarakshita accepts inherent existence.) [Blumenthal, pp 162-163]

Rejecting the mind to be dependent on the body on the ground that it is of the nature of the body:

> "Just as anything is perfectly known
> By the mind through signs/evidence.
> Similarly, things through causes
> Are arising in the mind through [as] signs."

What is produced, producing and the result of what is produced are they not gathered together (simultaneously?) This statement is a mistake. Although conventionally like that, there is a whole bunch [or mother and son] [ma bu] of problems to which I am responding. Otherwise it is like a mother and son disputing all at once, trying to answer all criticisms.

§ 84. The status of cause and effect is
Not rejected on the relative level on which
All afflictions and purification
Are not confusing to maintain.

If constructing the ultimate meaning with great effort, at that time one must establish from those subtle atoms on up to consciousness proving that they are completely one or many in nature. To do this one must respond to the statements I have expressed previously. If so, one must show similarly that this without exception is true and not false. Undeceiving phenomena is accepted in that way with certainty.

Thus, it was also said [by Nagarjuna]:

> "Those who, without knowing the meaning of solitude [emptiness],
> And those who only study,
> Not making merit,
> Those inferior people will be lost.
> The existence of karmic effects
> On migrations [in the six realms] is widely proclaimed.
> Likewise, the complete knowledge of the self-nature of these,
> And their absence of origination has been taught.
> Just as the Victorious One, with power over the world,
> Has said 'I' and 'mine'"

Similarly, the aggregates, elements and sense fields
Have been taught due to necessary [skillful] means."
[Sixty Verses, 32-34]

Furthermore, those who assert objects would ask "How would the accumulation of merit and wisdom be agreeable [consistent with there being no object, activity, or agent?"] When you purify the three circles [no subject, no object, no activity], the Madhyamaka would say the fulfillment of merit and wisdom is appropriate. How? When you worship you need an object of worship. Also, who benefits? However, in one with devotion, with offering and beneficial wisdom, faith similarly arises. But not by the way of perceiving the three circles, the giver, the giving and the receiver. Without this how can you fulfill?

Also, because nothing exists subjectively for you, how can there be any objective activity of giving, etc. Or if the object is non-existent, would it not fail to be perceived? If the first, he who does not give anything to anyone will not be without merit. By the non-existence of giving there would be no merit. The effort of the bodhisattva for sentient beings would have no purpose for non-existent sentient beings.

[One might ask] [Sautrantika objection]) If the giver, the object to be given, and the receivers are beheld by the Thus Gone Ones, therefore if the object did not exist, it would not be perceived [by them] and the statement [not perceived], not be established. Furthermore, if like the object of giving a son, etc., by one's own mind and mental derivatives, are recognized by oneself, how could the object not exist?

To be given, on and so forth, receiver and giver mind and mental pictures self-realizing how would they not be objects?

"It is said further in reply by the opponent:
Each who gives wisely benefits and worships,
The offering has been given by one who
Has acted very devotedly.
You cannot do this if you cannot perceive the object.
Now then, because of its complete non-existence,
If the object does not exist for you, there is no merit.
If there is no object, then the merit would be destroyed.
There would be no purpose to effort.

Since seeing the three by Buddha,
By this, there is no non-existent object.
[And there is also] one's own mind and the arising of mental factors,
By this, one is self-aware.

Thus, to all these disputes etc., which are not clear knowledge, in order to see reality, I offer an argument in response.

[Great bodhisattvas give away very dear ones if someone asks for the sake of others. These bodhisattvas have realization of the absolute truth because they give that [their dear ones] beyond subject and object and action. Therefore on the ultimate level there is nothing lost or gained. Khenpo Tsewang Rinpoche, 2/6/21]

§ 85. **In this way, since cause and effect have been maintained,**
Then since this dharma is established,
The stainless accumulations
Are suitable in this doctrine.

§ 86. **Through a completely pure cause**
There will arise a completely pure effect.
Similarly, from a perfect view, morality
And all its pure branches will arise.

§ 87. **Similarly, from an impure cause,**
An impure effect arises. Just as
From the force of wrong views,
Sexual misconduct, and so forth, arises.

Since all effects follow from their respective causes, arising exclusively and harmoniously, completely pure and impure arise from what is completely pure and impure. For example, from both good action and evil action, results completely mature like that deriving from what is named existent and not existent. These completely mistaken views previously enumerated in this manner, are the source of the branches of immorality, [as well as] the ways/branches of attending to existence etc. and similarly the mistaken desire to act wrongfully. What is established by this? It shows:

§ 88. Perception of objects is
Destroyed by valid arguments,
Therefore, they [objects] should be considered erroneous
Like a mirage, and so forth.[79]

In reality, it is not appropriate to maintain that all objects do have the nature of one or many and have not been disproved logically, which was explained previously. The essential characteristic of the knower and that which is known, and the object itself, has also been invalidated by means of the previous explanation. Thus, the existence of the object is clearly a matter of attachment. This is like taking many mirages to be water. Because of this such views arise.

§ 89. If one's practice of all the six paramitas,
Arises under the power which objectifies objects
Like practices arising through the false notion of I and mine,
They will be weak.

---

[79] [*Vajracchedika Sutra* P. 81). In *Mahayana-Sutra-Samgraha* Part 1 in Sanskrit Learning, Darbhanga, 1961 Buddhist Sanskrit Texts #17. Ed. By Dr. P. L. Vaidya. Pub. By the Mithila Institute of Post-Graduate Studies and Research] [Cf. Kamalashila, *Panjika* Derge folio 127b]

Also: "While in many cases, Santararsita's text has been quite dynamic in his utilization of an assortment of both Buddhist and non-Buddhist views to help illuminate his own view, at this point in the text he is explicit in incorporation of a Yogachara framework for understanding conventional truth. I think it is important to reflect on what has happened in the text up to this point in order to fully understand his Yogachara Madhyamaka synthesis. Santaraksita is engaged in a dynamic philosophical enterprise in this text in which the perspective of his philosophical analysis shifts depending on the perspective of his opponents. Generally speaking, he argues as a Sautrantika when criticizing Vaibhashika views, as a Yogachara when criticizing Sautrantika view, and as a Madhyamaka when criticizing various Yogachara positions, While in the final analysis he maintains specific views and we can correctly say he is a Madhyamika since he rejects the existence of an ultimate nature in phenomena, one might also be inclined to say he is a 'Yogachara-Madhyamika' in that he rejects the externality of objects conventionally...By use of 'sliding scales of analysis', I think Santaraksita's brand of Buddhist philosophy, far from being excusive, is much more inclusive of all systems of Buddhist thought....he uses multiple provisional views, not only that of Yogachara, in an attempt to lead followers to a Madhyamaka position realizing the lack of any inherent nature in phenomena."

Just as when Buddhists and opponents carefully practice generosity and morality etc. from an ego-centered point of view, or a view that accepts objects as real, immediately they [these practices] do not become aids to the branches of enlightenment since they are weak. They are no different [from ordinary activities] because they arise from an erroneous view. Their concentration is weak. They are without power because they are acting erroneously.

§ 90. From not perceiving things as real,
A great result, [giving and so forth] can arise,
Because it arises from a nourishing cause,
Like a sprout coming from a healthy seed.

[This is] because, in reality, existence and the knowledge of it are [really] not appropriate. As to the absolute, that which is to be known is not perceptible. The nourished cause is not mistaken because not involved with grasping at perceptions as real. [If one has] the view of the selflessness of persons, by this the arising of generosity etc. is brought forth from the previous powerful cause. Similarly, a very vast result is accomplished, as the sprout arises from the seed.

Thus it is said in the *Dharmasangiti Sutra*, considering ultimate dharma being considered together, all dharmas are not perceived. Thus, consciousness is not engaged. [There is no focus, therefore there is no conception. Khenpo Tsewang Dongyal Rinpoche, 2/6/21].

Also, from the same text: "Lord Buddha, when all phenomena are not seen, one sees them perfectly." (*Dharmasangiti Sutra*). Thus said.

From The Mother of all the Conquerors: [Prajnaparamita]:
"Consider Subhuti. What do you think? Can one grasp easily the measure of the eastern direction of the sky?" Subhuti responded," Oh, Buddha, it is not so."… "Similarly, Subhuti, the heap of the accumulation of the merit, due to generosity of the bodhisattva, who does not dwell in the dualistic view of things, is not easily measurable." Consider that to be the giving of the bodhisattva.[80]

---

[80] "Without consciousness there can be no appearance of things." /Mipham Rinpoche, Padmakara, p. 362]

[If you infer another form which is external to the mind which produces knowledge, then this is different from the result. Khenchen Palden Sherab Rinpoche].

For example, one who has fallen into darkness does not see anything. This is like a bodhisattva who has fallen into existence [duality], having given gifts.

Subhuti, for example, when the sun has risen, a sighted man sees various forms, and is said to be like the bodhisattva who perceiving perfectly, does not while giving fall into [the view that like ghosts, there exist] objects."

Whoever wishes to revere the wise ones, and has interest in giving benefit, giving through the purified three circles, [giver, giving, and receiving] remains very faithful. Therefore, generosity involving the non-perception of the object is not erroneous. Thus, the root of virtue does not exist in ignorance.

The destruction of merit and the uselessness of effort are not unwanted consequences that follow, because the two states of cause and effect are not removed conventionally. Also, the seeing of the three [giving, giver and gifts] is thus also only relative. Self-awareness is also included in conventional truth because on examination of being one or many, this is said to be [correctly] understood. Because of this, I will not go through the arguments again. Those who propose existents as conditioned by cause and effect conventionally and wish to give all the wrong debaters an answer, should judge [in this way].

One may ask whether things [arising interdependently through cause and effect], are only mind and mental factors, or are existing as entities external to the mind. [The view of those who think that things have inherent existence.]

Thus, only relying on the former position, they oppose the agent and enjoyer teaching, and that there is only mind. In the scripture it is stated thus in order to reject creator and user [Heart of the Madhyamaka].

Others [Yogachara] think:

§ 91. Cause and effect
Are also only consciousness.
Whatever is established by the self,
Remains consciousness.[81]

---

[81] Bhavaviveka argued against this. [Khenchen Palden Sherab Rinpoche].

After examination, having given up that self-nature can be self-established, there is no [veridical] realization of any other nature. Thus [if you infer existence of the cause which is separate from the result] then forms are like dreams and illusions. If one wishes to assert that one knows forms and external objects as remaining existing separately [from cognition], as with the eye consciousness etc., there is no gradual cause at the same time or at a different time, and knowledge [of such a cause] is not established as knowledge. Similarly experience [perception] of blue objects etc. is not justified.[82] Similarly the experience of them is like dreams and illusions etc.[83]

If another object produces the object of knowledge, if it exists separately, then the fruit/result would not be proved through perception, but only by inference.

In that case proof doesn't exist because the existence of the immediate conditions and atoms are already refuted. And this is harmonious with everything that comes from the Gandavyuha and the Sandhinirmocana.

From the *Lankavatara Sutra*:
    "External forms do not exist
    External appearances are our own mind.
    But our own minds appear as external objects.
    [Due to habitual patterns]."
[Chap. 10, Verse 489][84]

This teaching [the Yogacharas] consider as an excellent explanation. [But] those able minds that are not small, having great diligence, similarly with

---

[82] Mipham Rinpoche, Padmakara, 2005, p. 362]: "It may be objected that, even granted that the experience of a mental aspect is necessarily consciousness, it can be inferred nevertheless that there must be a mental object that is casting its aspect on the mind. But because the subtle particles and so forth do not exist (even though they have been inferred), this is untenable. Even in those systems where the particle is considered to exist, the latter is not established by perception. It is hidden and that it exists is no more than an inference. Now the fact that the non-existent hidden object is (only) inferred, whereas one experiences things clearly (in the mind) lends considerable force to the argument that phenomena are merely established by the mind itself. Indeed, this position cannot be invalidated by any other view."

Also: Nagarjuna's argument about causality is applied here, because causality is mental, and is only habitual patterns which arise in the mind like magic. There is no creation. [Khenchen Palden Sherab Rinpoche]

[83] What we see as real is a projection of our minds

skill examine the mind as one or many. Ultimately they see no essence. They do not assert it as really absolute truth.
Because:

§ 92. In relying on Mind Only,
One knows that external objects do not exist.
Relying on this doctrine [Madhyamaka],
One will know as well [the highest state], the selflessness of all things.

By relying on the system of only mind and mental factors, similarly to [what we understand about] the mind, those things associated with mind which are asserted to be external, and to have a self or to be owned by a self, and grasped by a self, after examination, are understood without difficulty to be without inherent existence. According to this system, since nothing arises independently, after investigation, the mind also has no self-nature. One who realizes the central path, abandoning all extremes, then since things are neither one nor many, then nothing [including mind] has substantial existence.

Lokatitaparivarta: "Oh sons of the Conqueror, the three realms when realized are only mind. The three times are also only mind."[85]

Mind should be understood to be without circumference or center. This teaching is explained very well. Because [all things are] beyond the extreme of birth, destruction, and remaining, there is no limit or center.

---

[84] [Reference not found]. Mentioned in p. 49 in *Vijnaptimatratasiddhi*, Vasubandhu, Gaganathajha-Granthamala series, pub director Research Institute Varanasi 1972.

Mind should be understood to be without circumference or center. This teaching is explained very well. Because [all things are] beyond the extreme of birth destruction, and remaining, there is no limit or center. In the *Dharmasangiti* it is said, "Oh Buddha, all elements have an imagined essence. The totality of things is mental, insubstantial, and like illusions, rooted in non-existence." *Lankavatara*: 10, 256---p. 246-247 Suzuki:

[85] There are no external things
Also, the mind is not grasped.
Because of giving up all views
This is the characteristic of birthlessness.

Thus, it is said. Because of this it is also said:
There is not any birth.
There are no blockages.
Arising and cessation,
Are only mind.

In the *Dharmasangiti* it is said, "Oh Buddha, all elements have an imagined essence. The totality of things is mental, insubstantial, and like illusions, rooted in non-existence."

In *Lankavatara* [10, 256---p. 246-247 Suzuki]:

"By relying on mind
One does not imagine external objects.
Staying completely within perfect perceptions,
One even goes beyond mind only.
Going beyond even mind only,
Even to the view of the non-existence of appearances,
The yogi who abides in non-appearance,
Sees the great vehicle.
Without accomplishing by peacefully spontaneous engaging,
And completely purified by pure aspiration,
Without the excellent wisdom of selflessness
Reality cannot be seen.
Removing cause and conditions,
Even the remaining cause [mind] is an obstruction,
In the stipulation of Mind Only [things] arise unborn
As I have taught."
[*Lankavatara Sutra*, Verse 16][86]

§ 93. By riding the chariot of the two systems,
Grasping the reins of logic,
This is how the genuine meaning
Is attained by the followers of the Mahayana.

---

85 continued

Explaining the primary elements etc.,
As included in consciousness,
By knowing that, they are dispersed.
Are they not just wrongly imagined?

[86] There are no external things
Also, the mind is not grasped.
Because of giving up all views

Those who are engaged with the force of conventional reality, relying on inference, are grouped together, condensed, in speaking of the two methods. The great vehicle into which all the buddhas have gone has brought them into enlightenment from the depths of no intrinsic nature. By the great vehicle of the 'will be gone tathagatas' all things should be understood from the depths to be lacking self-nature.[87] This is like one who riding on the great chariot, grasping the reins and bridle very well, has completely obtained the purpose of the Mahayana.[88]

> "The five dharmas, intrinsic existence
> And the eight consciousnesses themselves,
> Are entities with two selflessness [of dharma and persons] nature,
> All included in the Mahayana."

Thus said.

The two views as discussed by Brahma, Vishnu and Shiva are explained in many ways. In the *Guhya Amrita Bindu* [*Secret Drops of Nectar*] it is stated: What is special in the great vehicle? [Even non-Buddhists say]:

---

[87] All the tathagatas are gone, going, will be gone. [De bzhen gshags pa rnams gshegs pa 'gyur pa.]

[88] From the *Lankavatara Sutra*: The Mahayana which is combined into two systems is the only concise teaching of the essence of the Mahayana sutras. [88] From the *Lankavatara Sutra*: The Mahayana which is combined into two systems is the only concise teaching of the essence of the Mahayana sutras.

> "The five dharmas, intrinsic existence
> And the eight consciousnesses themselves,
> Are entities with two selflessness [of dharma and persons] nature,
> All included in the Mahayana."

Thus said. The two views as discussed by Brahma, Vishnu and Shiva are explained in many ways.

In the *Guhya Amrita Bindu* [*Secret Drops of Nectar*] it is stated: What is special in the great vehicle? [Even non-Buddhists say]:

> "As to only mind which is completely pure,
> One who is enlightened is permanently liberated.
> Imagined without accepting and rejecting,
> Brahma always remains without sorrow."

"As to only mind which is completely pure,
One who is enlightened is permanently liberated.
Imagined without accepting and rejecting,
Brahma always remains without sorrow."

[Even in the *Upanishads* they say that Buddha is always pure, always liberated. Geshe Lozang Jamspal] From *Five Days* by Vishnu [Hindu work—they are saying we have no need for Madhyamaka because we already have these ideas.]:

"Having completely transcended mere names,
Having abandoned entity and non entity,[89]
Thus free from evolving and dissolution,[90]
This is the so-called son of the wealth deity. [Vishnu]

---

[89] All the tathagatas are gone, going, will be gone. [De bzhen gshags pa rnams gshegs pa 'gyur pa].

Name, reason, conceptualization (controlled by others), suchness and perfect knowledge.

[Even in the *Upanishads* they say that Buddha is always pure, always liberated LJ]

From *Five Days* by Vishnu [Hindu work-they are saying we have no need for Madhyamaka because we already have these ideas.]:
"Having completely transcended mere names,
Having abandoned entity and non entity,
Thus free from evolving and dissolution,
This is the so-called son of the wealth deity. [Vishnu]"

[90] Therefore, the King of the Sages, taught only the beautiful vast complete teaching of emptiness of no short duration, which was not common to the heretics. It is said in the Chandrapradipasamadhi:

All entities are always empty in nature.
Thus also it is similarly said: here stated:

"Also, similarly for the subtle entity
One is not wise because one
Will not see the arising
Of objects through cause and conditions."
[Nagarjuna, *Yuktishastika*, #13]

"So, if even one object were to exist,
Would it not have intrinsic nature?

In things, substantiality does not exist.
Substantiality and non-substantiality do not exist in things.
Completely free from substantiality and non-substantiality,
By that knowing that one understands the Vedas."

In the *Santiparve* [*Beauty of Peacefulness*] [Beautiful Arrangement] [prayoga]:

"Only son, Brahman is the absolute truth,
The lord of knowledge.
It is said that only Brahman exists
All else is well explained as completely destroyed/non-existent."
[*Upanishads*.]

In the *Pitaputrasamyoga* it is said by the great Sri Kapila [Samkhya]. [Kapila said one cannot see the true nature of the gunas.]

"The excellent self-nature of the gunas,
Does not become the path of seeing.
The path of seeing becomes
A collection like an illusory image/a hollow straw."

If thus, what is the nature of the extraordinary effort of the Tathagata which is consistent with non-existence? It is not like that [their theories]. It is demonstrated by the teaching of the empty nature of all phenomena. This is the lion's roar of the Tathagata that alone strikes fear into the herds of heretics as with the elephant and the herd of deer.

In this way, these views of the outsiders, all of the heterodox extremists etc. only understand a small bit of what is explained as emptiness. For example, that view which is that of the followers of the secret *Upanishads* [Vedanta], holds that which has the intrinsic being of only consciousness, is the pure self which alone exists. They say it is like great space. Thus the accomplished yogi meditating is free from ignorance, both innately born and learned through study, as when the jar etc. is broken, the space within it combines with great space and also the quality of life [atman] combines with this, that great soul, which is expressed by philosophers to be infinite

things, which are imagined etc. The world has the nature of a magical illusion, like dreams appearing in various forms. Things are [really] non qualified/non-dual. Vedanta View

Thus, it is said:

"When a jar etc. is broken,
It is combined with space.
Similarly, when one's life combines with Self,
It is called form and result.
Even though there is a difference between this and that,
There are no distinctions in space.
Similarly, this is true of life [is like this and that].
Just as for the childish,
Space becomes stained with stains [The sky becomes covered with clouds.]
As with those without knowledge,
The Self becomes stained with stains.
Just as in the darkness, not understood,
A rope is imagined as a snake.
Entities are similarly imagined
The self is also similarly imagined.
Similarly, if a rope is known with certainty,
Because completely understood [the snake is] a thought construction.
The nature of one rope is not two,
Just as the Self, when known with certainty.
For life etc. being infinite,
Entities are completely imagined,
By this these things [are known to be] illusory,
That's the illusion of the gods.
It is fitting to life, therefore it is called life,
Thus, this is the source of the elements.
The classification of qualities is due to thought
These things are real.
Mind is non-dual, but [as] in a dream
In this manner, the dual appears without doubt.

Similarly, when not sleeping,
The non-dual appears as dual without doubt.
What would be moving and not moving?
The appearance as two is only mind.
If the mind is not existent,
The perception of duality will not occur.
When one realizes the Self is true
There is no thought construction.
Therefore, at the time there is no mind,
Because there is no grasping, there is no grasper."

Critique of Vedanta

[Shantarakshita replies]: Thus, in this view the Self is proclaimed as permanent and non-dual. As previously discussed, I refuted this. Otherwise, if one were liberated, all would be liberated. Or in another way, if all were not liberated, the one would not be liberated. Because there would be no difference, they would be inconsistent with phenomena.

By practicing yoga, for the [Hindu] yogi
Whatever is accomplished, that is only reversed
For it is false in itself,
And there would be no ability to abandon [the wrong nature of this].
This knowledge is not producible,
Because it abides permanently.
Therefore, the yogi's meditation will be fruitless.
The result cannot develop.

These [above] are the verses of digression.

The non-dual view of the adibhavas [Vedanta], as proclaimed before, that existence is permanent and single is refuted. And thus because of the previous statements, [this view) does not succeed through the example of the jar and space. If one is gathered, all will be gathered. Or if this is not the case, then what you wish will not be demonstrated, because they are not different. Disputation and analysis are suitable for this.

By getting accustomed to seeing suchness free from sporadic afflictions, in this clear light, one will see that in this system [Madhyamaka] it is appropriate that the mind is destroyed in each moment. Otherwise [if permanent] in previous and subsequent moments there would be neither pure nor impure, because there are no differences. It would be both confused and unconfused, erroneous and non-erroneous, and all stipulations would be logical for those who rely on impermanence. [Views] are illogical, which are not derived from momentariness. That permanent person [purusha] that by nature is permanent and unitary, no one on any occasion can defend.

Regarding purusha [the super spirit], which is permanent and lone, it is illogical to characterize it as being in the condition of returning to sleep [reality] or not returning to sleep [because nothing could change it]:

> We [the Vedantists] say through the Vedanta,
> How like a dream, an illusion,
> Seen as a fairy city,
> But all things whatever in the world are seen [in this way, correctly in our theory].
> [Again the Vedanta view]: No ceasing, no arising,
> There are no fetters, no liberator.
> There exists no desire for freedom, there exists no freedom.
> This itself is the ultimate.
> Free from desire, fear and anger,
> By being able to realize the extreme state of the Vedanta,
> Pacifying the elaborations, through non-duality,
> One sees all non-conceptually.

No matter what is expressed in this way by them, [when they talk that way] it is beautiful for the Buddhist relying on the ultimate truth [because it is about emptiness], but not [completely] for them, because by eliminating the all-pervasive permanent Self, space etc. the view of the *ye srit pa* is already eliminated. The *ye srit pa* view of [the permanent and unitary Self of Vishnu/ system of Upendra/Vedanta] [or primordially existent; Arthur Mandelbaum] by refuting pervasion, permanence, and entities asserted as ultimate by the Samkhya, has already been eliminated.

What Kapila said, about the power of brightness, atoms and darkness/mass remaining equally balanced, which are signs of the chief nature [*prakrti*], which is proclaimed to be pervasive and permanent, has been clearly refuted.

Whoever in our own school, when they explain all phenomena existing and the meaning of the sutra [med pa] the non-existent entities words of the sutras [Hinayana- in terms of the three baskets] and entities in this lower way, these inferior explanations have little meaning, and affirm erroneous views, because they are not steady in the center and with present conditions, because they do not rest firmly on the middle and the present. [Not stuck in the past, present and future because they are changing.] They say Buddha said this because of what he meant by empty-inferior [because changing, Khenchen Palden Sherab Rinpoche.] In another way [Buddha said] of all things, non-existent things are more, because previous and future (ages) are not born and remain without nature. [When Buddha said phenomena are not existing he was using hyperbole. Compared to the enormity of the past and the future which do not exist, present phenomena are practically non-existent. [Khenpo Tsewang Dongyal Rinpoche] Since this explanation also has been previously abandoned because of past explanations given and rejected, therefore if one by this establishes control of others, my own mind will be delighted. Thus, those of the way of the rule of Vaibhashika and the Vasyaputrias (pudgalists), and the Samkhyas [with their] hindering entities, are refuted effortlessly. How can they have any force? So also, this explanation is used to refute fearful disciples whose minds are rough.

This is finished, so I won't think more about it.

Therefore, the King of the Sages, taught only the beautiful vast complete teaching of emptiness of no short duration, which was not common to the heretics. It is said in the Chandrapradipasamadhi:

"All entities are always empty in nature."
Thus also it is similarly said: here stated:
{Not in Derge, but in Peking. Inserted by Mipham Rinpoche.]
" Also similarly for the subtle entity
One is not wise because one
Will not see the arising
Of objects through cause and conditions."
[Nagarjuna, *Yuktishastika*, #13]

"So, if even one object were to exist,
Would it not have intrinsic nature?

If so, it would contradict many of the scriptures,
And in itself, it would be incompatible with the world."
[Precious Garland (*Ratnamala*) by Nagarjuna]

§ 94. Even those such as Vishnu and Shiva never experience
The cause of remaining in the limitless/infinite state.
Even those who are crowned in the world [Shravakas and
Pratyekabuddhas],
Absolutely never can taste this.

§ 95. This perfectly pure nectar [enlightenment],
The cause of pure compassion
Is experienced only by Buddha,
And enjoyed by no others.

Like the pure light of the moon, this nectar is not ephemeral but made of
the selflessness of persons and things. This is tasted only by the Protector,
impartially. Because Buddha is the embodiment of the wisdom which
possesses all aspects of excellences, he is the embodiment of the totality
of atoms of compassion. He is entirely free from all the heaps of the objective and emotional defilements, the most excellent, and will remain as
long as there is samsara.

In this way, this is not the territory of even those pure minds such as
the Shravakas and Pratyekabuddhas, because they have merely realized
the first selflessness of persons. Needless to say, it is not the territory of
gods such as Vishnu, Brahma, and Mahadeva (Shiva) etc., who are attached to a wrong view of the self.

§ 96. Because of relying on mistaken teachings,
Those that have minds which trust in mistaken tenets,
[For these], in the minds of those who follow the system
[of the bodhisattvas].
Arouse great compassion.

For the bodies of ourselves and all others, many kalpas of suffering are
continuously caused and connected. For those disciples that teach erro-

neous views, those who follow along with the knowledge of suchness by searching for the view of the Sugata and having decided on this and are accepted in the household of the family of the Compassionate One, they accept the heavy burden of these people. Those compassionate ones having realization do not mix even a small part which is disharmonious with the position. This great compassion is the wish to free others from suffering.

And for those that suffer, the cause of their suffering arises and increases, [this] arouses great compassion as adding fuel augments a spark that is ignited.

Those who are angered by the ultimate meaning are suffering, and they remain in the great cause of suffering. Thus, what is to be done? Those who perform [harmful] actions therefore are not an enemy of self or other because their actions are impermanent as bubbles of water that arise in the wind. Their bodies cannot perform even a small benefit because they are as powerless and swollen with pus. [It is as if] the body is killing itself. [But the [Buddha's] body will remain in samsara, beautified by the perfection of self and others.[91]

Countless conquerors reach the ability of the Dharmakaya. If one stays in the state of harming devotion to the dharmic seed of ultimate reality, there will be a complete terrible consequence due to the abandonment of the pure dharma in this way, as was similarly said in many sutras. So said:

> "The non-enthusiastic who are not studied in
> That which is vast and profound,
> Through their ignorance, enemies coming from ours and other's
> schools,

---

[91] [Kamalashila *Panjika* Derge Folio 130b]:
"Free from intrinsic nature of forms or non-forms."
　　[Kamalashila *Panjika*. Derge Folio 130b]:
"Having abandoned arising and perishing."
　　Kamalasila identifies Brahman with "nature of self."
　　[CF. Kamalashila, *Panjika*, 31a et al.]
　　[CF. Mipham Rinpoche, Padmakara, p. 273]
Also: [Kamalashila *Panjika* Derge Folio 130b]:
"Free from intrinsic nature of forms or non-forms."

Blame the Mahayana."
[Nagarjuna's Ratnavali]
It is better to lose morality
Than to lose your view.
With morality, one goes to heaven.
With the view, one goes to the excellent state.
[Aryadeva's *Four Hundred Verses*, 12, 11]

"By the power of ignorance one becomes obscured.
Whoever makes obstacles to the ultimate,
In this way, does not become virtuous.
Needless to say there is no liberation."
[Aryadeva's *Four Hundred Verses*, 12, 10]

"When many the heretics
Sow seeds of harm,
For those who wish for the dharma.
Who would not be compassionate?"
[Aryadeva's *Four Hundred Verses*, 12, 293]

Quoted in the Chandrapradipasamadhisutra it is stated in the seventh chapter, verses 1-8, on the first kind of patience[92]:

"Thus if one examines the system of others, like very bright rays of sunlight hitting the snow of many mountains and melting them, so similarly other doctrines cannot endure. If one wishes to increase one's own good, one should not be attached [to those doctrines."

Furthermore, the thorough examination of the vast teachings of ours and others, free from all the fabrications of the elaborations of inter-dependent arising, has already been done in the *Tattvasamgraha* and the Paramarthanirnaya [which has been lost in every language] etc. Those who want to understand this in more detail should study these.

---

[92] Three kinds of patience: (1) Accepting suffering, (2) Realizing the nature of dharma, and (3) Seeing the nature of things [that we are in samsara].

§ 97. Those who possess the treasure of knowledge
See no essential truth in the doctrine of others.
Thus, the utmost respect arises in them
For the Protector.

I see the mistake of other doctrines which are well known, by foolish and inferior people who accept coarse objects. The Sugata's words are virtuous in the beginning, the middle, and the end, like good gold, burnished, cut, rubbed, and not contradicted by direct perception, inference and its own words, not confused about deep reality, and is the wisdom which is not mixed with samsara. And Buddha, his two feet beautified by rows of crowns of men and gods, will generate great certainty and devotion without attachment, which will arise through the essence of the practice in those who have for themselves known the guru of the world. Therefore:

> Having in the past searched for perfect knowledge,
> And having ascertained the ultimate meaning,
> For all the world remaining in the darkness of wrong views,
> All compassion is generated for them.

> Those who have been benefactors of beings,
> Learned through the mind of enlightenment,
> Adorned with intellect and compassion,
> Hold the vows of the sage [Shakyamuni].

> Following with perfect faith,
> Having generated the mind of complete enlightenment
> Having adopted the vows of the sage,
> They endeavor to search for perfect knowledge.

> Possessing the intelligence of the subtle wisdom eye,
> Enter the high path.
> Endowed with the clarity of scripture and reasoning,
> It is the teaching of a single theory.[93]

---

[93] Madhyamaka

Like the pure moon, by all the merit I obtain,
May all in the world, happy in the system of the supreme Buddha,
Dispelling well many nets of dark wrong views,
Completely dispelling very strong worldly passions, achieve en-
lightenment.

By having experienced the object of truth, may I dispel the dark-
ness into which I have fallen.
May I know the supreme state, and associate with good people
Only for the sake of others, alighting at the feet of Manjughosa,
May I, very respectfully, rely on this pure lotus.

Whatever is expressed here by the light of scripture and logic,
As a pure great lamp held by the supreme leader,
By illuminating on earth the nature of things,
May all these teachings remain as long as possible.

I bow down continually
To those conquerors who spoke of interdependent arising,
And liberate us from the terrible net
Of thought constructions.

In this manner through the system of Madhyamaka
I have made this ornament
Beautified by the precious array
Of the collection of various sutras and logic.

Those who by knowing with subtle intellect,
The depths of the Candrapradipa, etc.
That person having a wealth of intellect who is firm in this
Should fearlessly cultivate.

May the steady ones grasping this,
Rely on the sage,
Pervadingly delightful for self and others,
And rejoice very completely.

Having dispelled the arrogance,
Of those who dare to have any object
Those, who through their eloquence and discriminating awareness,
Will be elevated to look down [on them] with high spirit.

The fame of the great sage
Demonstrating the reality
Of profound truth,
Spreads infinitely in all directions.

The proof of the selflessness of phenomena,
Due to the discovery of thousands of teachers,
Composing all proofs,
Seems not to be spread widely.

For those who are completely wise,
Those who have knowledge,
Combined with stainless devotion,
May it be completely certain.

For those who blame this doctrine
May I eliminate this blame without difficulty.
Through the logic of successive pervasiveness[94] and reversing pervasiveness.
May all be without difficulties.

---

[94] Successive pervasive (Skt. anvaya; Tib. dogs khyab):
"What is created, is impermanent."
Reversing pervasive (Skt. vayavyapanti; Tib. rjes khyab):
"What is impermanent is not created."

The ornament of the middle way, I, Lopon Shiwatso, having crossed the ocean of limitations of what others have proved, put my head at the anthers of the stainless lotus feet of Manjushri Lord of Speech, and have finished.

The Indian Khenpo Shilendra Bodhi and the great translator and editor Bande Yeshe De having been requested, decided to do this.

The Madhyamaklankara was translated by (older brother) Chang chub od in the early aspect of Buddhism (7th-8th centuries)

The *Tattvasamgraha* was translated later by (younger brother) Zhi wa od.

Tibetan Text

of

MADHYAMAKALAMKARA VRITTI

(From Tengyur)

organized by

Geshe Lozang Jamspal

སློབ་དཔོན་ཞི་བ་འཚོས་མཛད་པའི་དབུ་མ་རྒྱན་བོད་དའི་དང་སྣར་ལེགས་སྤར་དུ་བསྒྲིགས་ལ་བཤགས་སོ།

བློ་བཟང་འཇམ་དཔལ་གྱིས་བོད་དའི་གཞིར་བྱས་ཏེ།

སྣར་ལེགས་སྤར་སྐད་དུ་བསྒྲིགས་པའོ།

༄༅། །རྒྱ་གར་སྐད་དུ། མ་དྷྱ་མ་ཀ་ཨ་ལཾ་ཀཱ་ར་ཥྲྀཏྟི།

བོད་སྐད་དུ། དབུ་མའི་རྒྱན་གྱི་འགྲེལ་བ།

འཇམ་དཔལ་གཞོན་ནུར་གྱུར་པ་ལ་ཕྱག་འཚལ་ལོ། །

གང་དག་སུ་རྣམས་དག་བདེན་བློ་མངའ་ས་ལ་བཤགས།

ཚེས་ཆུལ་ཟབ་མོ་རྒྱ་མཚོ་ལྷ་བུའི་པ་རོལ་གཟིགས།

ལྷག་པར་མོས་པ་ཡིངས་བསྐྱེམས་ཕྱགས་མངའ་ཆེ་རྣམས་ཀྱི།

བླ་བཤགས་དེ་དག་རྣམས་ལ་དག་ཏུ་ཕྱག་འཚལ་ལོ།། །།

བདག་དང་གཞན་གྱི་དོན་ཕུན་སུམ་ཚོགས་པ་བསྒྲུབ་པར་ཅི་ལ་ཡང་མ་རག་པར་རྣམ་པ། དངོས་པོའི་རྣམ་པ་མ་བཏགས་གཅིག་པུ་ན་དག་བ་མ་ལུས་པ་གཟུགས་བཞན་ལ་སོགས་པ་ལྷ་བྱར། ཡང་དག་པར་རང་བཞིན་མེད་པར་རྟོགས་ན་ཉིན་མོངས་པ་དང་། ཤེས་བྱའི་སྒྲིབ་པ་མཐའ་དག་སྤོང་བར་འགྱུར་ཏེ།

དེ་བས་ན་རིགས་པ་དང་ལུང་གིས། ཚེས་ཐམས་ཅད་རང་བཞིན་མེད་པར་བོད་དུ་ཆུད་པར་བྱ་བའི་ཕྱིར་རབ་ཏུ་འབད་དོ། །དེ་ལ་ལུང་དངོས་པོའི་སྟོབས་ཀྱིས་ཞུགས་པའི་རྗེས་སུ་དཔག་པ་ལ་དང་བྲལ་བ་ནི་དད་པས་རྗེས་སུ་འབྲང་བ་རྣམས་ཀྱང་ཤིན་ཏུ་ཡོངས་སུ་ཚོམ་པར་མི་འགྱུར་བས་རིགས་པ་རྗེ་བརྗོད་པར་བྱའོ། །

བདག་དང་གཞན་སྨྲ་དངོས་འདི་དག །ཡང་དག་ཏུ་ན་གཅིག་པ་དང་།

དུ་མའི་རོ་བོས་ཐལ་བའི་ཕྱིར། །རང་བཞིན་མེད་དེ་གཟུགས་བརྙན་བཞིན།། ༡ །།

རང་བཞིན་ཡོད་པར་འགྱུར་ན་ནི། གཅིག་པ་དམ་གཅིག་ཤོས་ལས་མི་འདའ་བོ། །དེ་དག་ནི་ཕན་ཚུན་སྤངས་ཏེ། གནས་པའི་མཚན་ཉིད་ཡིན་པས་ལུང་པོ་གཞན་སེལ་བར་བྱེད་དོ། །རང་གི་ངེ་བ་དང་། ཕྱི་རོལ་ལ་དག་གིས

སྐྱེས་པའི་ཕྱིར་པོ་དང་། །གཙོ་བོ་ལ་སོགས་པ་དེ་དག་ཡང་དག་པར་ན་མེད་དེ། རང་བཞིན་མེད་པར་གསལ་
བར་ཞེས་སོ། །གང་ཏུ་ཚོགས་འདི་མ་གྲུབ་པོ་སྐྱེ་མ་ུ་མ་སེམས་ཞིག །

འབྲས་བུ་རིམ་ཅན་ཉེར་སྟོར་བས། །རྟག་རྣམས་གཅིག་པུའི་བདག་ཉིད་མིན།

འབྲས་བུ་རེ་རེ་ཐ་དད་ན། །དེ་དག་རྟག་ལས་ཉམས་པར་འགྱུར།། ༡ །།

རང་གི་སྟེ་པ་དང་། གཞན་གྱིས་ཁས་བླངས་པའི་དངོས་པོ་དེ་དག་ནི་རྟག་པའམ་གཅིག་ཤོས་དང་། ཕུང་པོ་
གཉིས་སུ་རྣམ་པར་གནས་གྱུར་ན། དེ་ལ་དང་པོ་ནི་འབྲས་བུ་རིམ་ཅན་དགའ་བ་དང་། གདུང་བ་ལ་སོགས་པ་
སྐྱེད་པས་རིམ་ཅན་མ་ཡིན་པ་དང་། གཅིག་པུའི་བདག་ཉིད་ུ་མི་རིགས་ཏེ། དེ་དག་གི་འབྲས་བུ་རྣམས་གྱུང་
ཅིག་ཅར་ཏུ་འབྱུང་བར་འགྱུར་བའི་ཕྱིར་རོ། །

འབྲས་བུ་རྣམས་ནི་རྒྱུ་མ་ཚང་ན་ཤོལ་གྱི། གང་གི་ཚེ་རྒྱུའི་ནུས་པ་ཕོགས་པ་མེད་པར་གྱུར་པ་དེའི་ཚེ། དེ་དག་
ལ་ཕོལ་བ་སྐྱེད་པར་ག་ལ་འགྱུར། ཤོལ་ན་ནི་དེ་ལ་ཡོད་པའི་རྗེས་སུ་འགྲོ་བ་དང་། སྟོག་པའི་རྗེས་སུ་མི་བྱེད་
པའི་ཕྱིར། འདི་དག་དེའི་འབྲས་བུར་ག་ལ་འགྱུར། ྩེ་བྲག་ཏུ་བསྒྱུར་ུ་མི་རུང་བ་རྣམས་ནི་ལྷན་ཅིག་བྱེད་པའི་
རྒྱུ་ལ་སྟོས་པར་མི་འཐད་པར་ཞིག་གསལས་ལོ། །

གཞན་ཡང་འབྲས་བུ་བྱེད་པའི་ནུས་ན་ལྷན་ཅིག་བྱེད་པའི་རྒྱེན་དང་འདག་པའི་དངོས་པོ་གང་ཡིན་པ་དེ་ཉིད་ལྷན་
ཅིག་བྱེད་པའི་རྒྱུ་དང་ཕྲལ་བའི་ནུས་ན་ཡང་འདོད་ན་ནི་དེའི་རྗེས་སུ་འདྲུག་བ་ཉིད་ཀྱི་ཕྱིར་དེའི་ཚེ་ལྷན་ཅིག་བྱེད་
པའི་རྒྱེན་རྣམས་གྱུང་མགུལ་ནས་བཏགས་པ་བཞིན་ུ་སྟོབས་ཀྱིས་དྲངས་ནས་གནས་ཏེ། འབྲས་བུ་རྒྱུན་མི་
འཆད་པ་བརྟོག་པ་མེད་པ་ཉིད་ུ་འགྱུར་རོ། །

འདིས་ནི་གང་དག་ལྷན་ཅིག་བྱེད་པའི་རྒྱུའི་ཉིད་ནུས་པའི་སྐྱར་བརྗོད་དེ། དེའི་རིམ་གྱིས་འབྲས་བུའི་རིམ་བྱུར་
སོ་ཞེས་སྨྲ་བ་དེ་དག་ལ་ལན་བཏབ་པར་གྱུར་ཏེ། །རྗེ་སྟེ་ཉེས་པ་འདིར་འགྱུར་ུ་འོང་ཞེས་ཏེ། འབྲས་བུ་རིམ་
ཅན་རྣམས་ལ་དེ་དག་གི་རང་བཞིན་གཞན་དང་གཞན་ུ་རིམ་ཅན་ཉིད་དོ་ཞེ་ནི། དེ་དག་ལ་རྟག་པར་འདོད་
པ་དོར་བར་བུ་སྟེ། འབྲས་བུ་སོ་སོ་བས་སྐྱ་མ་དང་ཕྱི་མའི་རང་བཞིན་འཇིག་པ་དང་འབྱུང་བའི་ཕྱིར་རོ། །

རང་གི་སྟེ་པ་གང་དག་བསྒོམས་པའི་སྟོབས་ཚད་ཀྱིས་བྱུང་བའི་ཞེས་པའི་དམིགས་པ་ལ་འདུས་བྱས་ཀྱི་འདུག་པ་
ཐམས་ཅད་དང་མི་མཐུན་པ་རང་ལ་དམིགས་པའི་ཡིད་ཚམ་ཡང་དགོས་པ་མེད་པའི་འདུས་མ་བྱས་ནི་དེ་ཁོ་ན་

ཤེས་པའི་ཡུལ་ཡིན་པའི་ཕྱིར་རྟེན་དམ་པར་ཡོད་དོ་ཞེས་སྐྱ་བ་དེ་དག་གི་ལུགས་ལྟར་ན་རང་བཞིན་གཅིག་པུ་ཉིད་
དུ་འགལ་བ་མེད་དོ་ཞེན། འགལ་ཏེ་འདི་ལྟར།

བསྐྱེམས་ལས་བྱུང་བའི་ཤེས་པ་ཡིས། །ཤེས་བྱ་འདུས་མ་བྱས་སྐྱ་བའི།

ལུགས་ལའང་གཅིག་མིན་དེ་དག་ནི། །རིམ་ཅན་ཤེས་དང་འབྲེལ་ཕྱིར་རོ། ༣ །།

ཡུལ་དང་ཡུལ་ཅན་ཡིན་པའི་ཕྱིར་རྣམ་པར་ཤེས་པ་རིམ་ཅན་དང་འབྲེལ་པ་ཅན་དག་ཀྱང་ཅི་གཅིག་པུའི་རང་
བཞིན་དུ་མི་འགྱུར་རམ་ཞེ་ན་མི་འགྱུར་ཏེ། འདི་ལྟར།

རྣམ་ཤེས་སྐུ་མས་ཤེས་བྱ་བའི། །རང་བཞིན་རྟེས་སུ་འབྲངས་ན་ནི།

ཤེས་པ་སྐུ་མའང་ཕྱི་མར་འགྱུར། །དེ་བཞིན་ཕྱི་མའང་སྐུ་མར་འགྱུར།། ༤ །།

དེ་སྐུ་མ་ཡིན་ན་རྣམ་པར་ཤེས་པ་སྐུ་མས་ཤེས་པར་བུ་བ་འདུས་མ་བུས་ཀྱི་རང་བཞིན་ནི་ཕྱི་མའི་དུས་ན་འང་ཡོད་
ལ། རྣམ་པར་ཤེས་པ་སྐུ་མ་ནི་མེད་པ་དང་། དེ་བཞིན་དུ་ཤེས་པ་ཕྱི་མས་ཤེས་པར་བུ་བ་ནི་སྐུ་ན་ཡོད་ལ།
ཤེས་པ་ཕྱི་མ་ནི་མེད་དོ་ཞེས་བུ་བ་ཉམས་པར་འགྱུར་རོ། །ཅི་སྟེ་ཤེས་པ་ཕྱི་མ་དང་སྐུ་མས་ཤེས་པར་བུ་བ་དེའི་ངོ་
བོ་སྟོན་དང་ཕྱི་མའི་གནས་དག་ན་མེད་ན། གལ་ཏེ་དེ་ལྟ་ན་ནི།

སྟོན་དང་ཕྱི་མའི་གནས་རྣམས་སུ། །དེ་ཡི་ངོ་བོ་མི་འབྱུང་ན།

འདུས་མ་བུས་དེ་ཤེས་པ་བཞིན། །སྐྱེད་ཅིག་འབྱུང་བར་ཤེས་པར་བུ།། ༥ །།

བསམ་གཏན་གྱི་ཕྱུར་མས་བློ་གྲོས་ཀྱི་མིག་ཕྱེ་བ་རྣམས་ཀྱིས་རྣམ་པར་ཤེས་པ་བྱུང་མ་ཐག་ཏུ་འཇིག་པ་ཅན་དུ་
འབབ་པ། ཡུལ་དེ་ལ་འཇུག་པ་གནན་གྱི་དུས་ན་མེད་པའི་རང་བཞིན་ལྟར་དེ་ཡང་སྐྱད་ཅིག་དེ་རེ་ལ་འཇིག་པ་
ལས་མི་འདའ་བར་འགྱུར་རོ། །དེ་ལྟར་ན། དེའི་མིང་དོན་དང་མཐུན་པ་ཡང་རིགས་པ་མ་ཡིན་པ་ཉིད་དུ་བསྟན་
པ།

སྐུ་མ་སྐུ་མའི་སྐྱེད་ཅིག་གི། །མཐུ་ཡིས་འབྱུང་བར་འགྱུར་བ་ན།

འདུས་མ་བུས་སུ་འདི་མི་འགྱུར། །སེམས་དང་སེམས་ལས་བྱུང་བ་བཞིན།། ༦ །།

ཅི་སྟེ་སྐྱད་ཅིག་ཕྱི་མ་ཕྱི་མ་རྣམས་རང་དབང་དུ་འབྱུང་རོ་ཞེན། དེ་ལྟར་འགྱུར་བར་ནི་མི་ནུས་ཏེ།

སྐྱེད་ཅིག་མ་རྣམས་འདི་དག་ཏུ། །རང་དབང་འབྱུང་བར་འདོད་ན་ནི།

གཞན་ལ་བློས་པ་མེད་པའི་ཕྱིར། །རྟག་ཏུ་ཡོད་པའམ་མེད་པར་འགྱུར།། ༧ །།

རེས་འགའན་འབྱུང་བའི་ཕྱིར་དེ་དག་ཀུན་ སེམས་དང་སེམས་ལས་བྱུང་བ་དེ་བཞིན་དུ་རྟེན་ཅིང་འབྲེལ་པར་འབྱུང་
བ་ཉིད་དུ་གསལ་བར་ཤེས་པར་བྱའོ། །འདི་དག་ཐམས་ཅད་ནི་བདག་གིས་རྟོམས་ཏེ་སྐྱེས་སུ་ཟད་དུ་གྱི་ དོན་དུ་
བར་ནུས་པ་རྣམ་པར་བཏག་པའི་ཡུལ་ཡིན་པའི་ཕྱིར་རོ། །གཞན་དུ་ན།

 དོན་བྱེད་ནུས་པ་མ་ཡིན་ལ། །དེ་འདོད་བདགགས་ལས་ཅི་ཞིག་བྱ།

མ་ཉིད་གཟུགས་བཟང་མི་བཟང་ཞེས། །འདོད་ལྡན་རྣམས་ཀྱིས་བདགགས་ཅི་ཕན། ༢ །།

དེ་བས་ན་ མཁས་པ་རྣམས་ཀྱིས་ནི་དོན་བྱེད་ནུས་པ་ལ་དངོས་པོའི་མཚན་ཉིད་ཅེས་སྐྱའོ། །དངོས་པོ་རྣམས་པ་དེ་ལྟ་
བུ་ལ། གང་ཟག་དང་ཆོས་ལ་བདག་མེད་པ་ལ་སོགས་པ་སྟོང་ཅིད་དེ་ལས་བཟློག་པ་ལ་སྟོ་བཏགས་པའི་དོ་བོ་ནི་
དགག་པར་བྱེད་དེ། སྐྱེ་བུའི་དོན་ཅེས་བརྗོད་པ་འབན་བུ་འབྱུང་བ་ནི་འདི་ཉིད་ལ་རག་ལས་པའི་ཕྱིར་རོ། །
གཞན་ནི་སྐྱབ་པ་ཡང་མེད་དགག་པ་ཡང་མེད་དེ། དེ་ནི་བདང་སྟོམས་སུ་བྱ་བ་ཉིད་དུ་གནས་པའི་ཕྱིར་རོ། །དེ་
ལྟར་ན་དངོས་པོ་ཡུལ་ཐམས་ཅད་བདག་མེད་པ་ལ་སོགས་པར་མ་བསྟན་ཏེ་སྐྱམ་དུ་མ་སེམས་ཤིག །ཐམས་ཅད་
ཅེས་བུ་བའི་སྐྱ་ནི་བརྗོད་པར་འདོད་པའི་དོན་མ་ལུས་པ་ལ་བརྗོད་པའི་ཕྱིར་ཏེ། བརྗོད་པར་འདོད་པ་ནི་དངོས་
པོ་ཐམས་ཅད་དོ། །དེ་ལྟ་བས་ན་དོན་བྱེད་ནུས་པ་ནི་སྐྱད་ཅིག་པ་ཉིད་དུ་རིགས་སོ། །

གཞན་ནི་རིམ་དང་ཅིག་ཤོས་ཀྱི་དོན་བྱེད་པར་མི་འཐད་པའི་ཕྱིར་རོ། །གང་ཟག་སྐྱད་ཅིག་པ་འདམ། སྐྱད་ཅིག་པ་ལ་
མ་ཡིན་པར་བརྗོད་དུ་མེད་པའི་རང་བཞིན་མེད་པ་ཉིད་དེ། ནམ་མཁའི་མེ་ཏོག་ལ་སོགས་པ་ལྟར་བསྐྱིམ་མི་
དགོས་པར་གྱུབ་བོ། །གཞན་ཡང་།

སྐྱད་ཅིག་སྐྱད་ཅིག་མ་ཡིན་པར། །གང་ཟག་བསྟན་དུ་མི་རུང་བས།

གཅིག་དང་དུ་མའི་རང་བཞིན་དང་། །ཁྱབ་པར་གསལ་བར་རབ་དུ་ཤེས།། ༠ །།

ཕ་རོལ་གྱིས་བས་བླངས་པའི་གང་ཟང་ཆོས་ཅན་ལ། གདན་ཚིགས་ཀྱི་རྒྱ་བ་གཅིག་དང་དུ་མའི་རང་བཞིན་དང་
ཁྱབ་བ་ཉིད་ཚིགས་མེད་པ་ཉིད་དུ་འགྱུབ་བོ། །སྐྱད་ཅིག་པར་གྱུབ་ན་ནི་དུ་མའི་རང་བཞིན་དུ་འགྱུབ་ཏེ། སྐྱད་
ཅིག་རེ་རེ་ལ་ཡང་རང་བཞིན་གཞན་དང་གཞན་འབྱུང་བའི་ཕྱིར་རོ། །སྐྱད་ཅིག་མ་ཡིན་ན་ནི་བརྟན་པ་གཅིག་
པུའི་དོ་བོ་ཡིན་པའི་ཕྱིར་གཅིག་པུའི་རང་བཞིན་དུ་འགྱུར་རོ། །གཉི་ག་ལྟར་ཡང་བརྗོད་དུ་མེད་ན་ནི་ཚོགས་མེད་
པར་གཅིག་དང་དུ་མའི་རང་བཞིན་གྱིས་སྟོང་པ་ཉིད་དུ་གྱུབ་བོ། །

106

གཞན་ཡང་གཞན་དག་གིས་གཞན་དུ་དངོས་པོ་རྣམས་ལ་ཁྱབ་པ་དང་མ་ཁྱབ་པའི་ཕྱིར་པོ་གཉིས་སུ་ཁས་བླངས་
ཏེ། དེ་ལ་ཁྱབ་པ་ནི་ནམ་མཁའ་ལ་སོགས་པའོ། །མ་ཁྱབ་པ་ནི་རྒགས་པ་དང་རྡུལ་ཕྲ་རབ་རྣམས་སོ། །དེ་དག་
ཐམས་ཅད་ཀྱང་གཅིག་པུའི་རང་བཞིན་དང་འགལ་བར་བསྟན་པ།

ཐ་དད་ཕྱོགས་ཅན་དང་འཛིན་ཕྱིར། །ཁྱབ་རྣམས་གཅིག་པུར་ག་ལ་གྱུར།

བསྐྱེབས་དང་མ་བསྐྱེབས་དངོས་སོགས་ཕྱིར། །རྒགས་པ་རྣམས་ཀྱང་གཅིག་པུ་མིན།། ༡༠ །།
ནམ་མཁའ་ལ་སོགས་པ་ཕྱོགས་ཐ་དད་པའི་ཤིང་ལ་སོགས་པ་དང་འབྲེལ་བ་དེ་དག་གི་གཅིག་དང་འབྲེལ་པའི་
རང་བཞིན་གང་ཡིན་པ་དེ་ཉིད་གཞན་དང་འབྲེལ་པ་ཅན་ཡང་ཡིན་ན་ནི་ངེས་ན་དེ་དང་འབྲེལ་པའི་ཕྱིར་དེ་གཅིག་
པུའི་བདག་ཉིད་ཡིན་པ་བཞིན་དུ་གཞན་ཡང་དེ་དང་ཐ་དད་པ་མ་ཡིན་པར་འགྱུར་རོ། །འོན་ཏེ་དེ་ཕྱོགས་ཐ་དང་
ན་ནི་རང་བཞིན་དེ་ཉིད་གཞན་དང་འབྲེལ་པ་ཅན་མ་ཡིན་པར་འགྱུར་རོ། །

རྒགས་པར་འདོད་པ་ལུས་ལ་སོགས་པ་ཡང་བསྐྱེབས་པ་དང་། མ་བསྐྱེབས་པ་དང་། གཡོ་བ་དང་། མི་གཡོ་
བ་དང་། ཆོན་གྱིས་བསྐྱུར་བ་དང་། མ་བསྐྱུར་བ་དང་། ཆེག་པ་དང་མ་ཆེག་པ་ལ་སོགས་པ་མི་མཐུན་པའི་
ཕྱོགས་གཞན་པའི་རང་བཞིན་འཛིན་ན་གཅིག་པུའི་རང་བཞིན་དུ་ཇི་ལྟར་རིགས་པར་འགྱུར།

གལ་ཏེ་བསྐྱེབས་པ་ལ་སོགས་པ་དག་ཡན་ལག་རྣམས་ཀྱི་ཡིན་གྱི་ཡན་ལག་ཅན་གྱི་མ་ཡིན་ཞེ་ན། ཅི་ཡན་ལག་
ཅན་འདི་དག་དེ་དག་དང་འདུ་བ་མ་ཡིན་ནམ། འདི་དག་མ་ཡིན་ནོ། གལ་ཏེ་དེ་བདེན་དུ་གཏུན་ན་ནོ་ན་
བསྐྱེབས་པ་དང་། མ་བསྐྱེབས་པ་ཞེས་བྱ་བ་ལ་སོགས་པ་ཕན་ཆུན་མི་མཐུན་པ་ཀུང་པ་དང་ལུས་ལ་སོགས་པའི་
དངོས་པོའི་གཉིས་སུ་ཅིའི་ཕྱིར་མིག་གི་སྟོང་ཡུལ་དུ་མི་འགྱུར།

གལ་ཏེ་དེ་དག་ཀུང་དེའི་ཡིན་ནོ་ཞེ་ན། ཅི་ཡན་ལག་གཞན་དང་ལྷན་པ་ཉིད་དམ་དེ་ཉིད་དོ། །གཞན་དུ་ན་
རྒགས་པ་གཅིག་པུར་མི་འགྱུར་རོ། །འདི་ནི་དེ་བས་ཆེས་རྒགས་ཏེ། ཡན་ལག་ལྷག་མ་རྣམས་དང་ལྷན་ན་ནི།
དེ་ལྷ་བུའི་ཆོས་ཁོ་ནར་དམིགས་པར་འགྱུར་རོ། །འོན་ཀུང་གང་ཕྱོག་མར་དེ་ཚོམ་པའམ། རྒས་པ་གདགས་
པའི་རྒྱུ་ཧྱལ་ལྷུ་རབ་དོན་དམ་པ་གཅིག་པུའི་རང་བཞིན་དུ་འགྱུར་རོ། །

དེ་ཡང་དེ་ལྟར་འགྱུར་བར་མི་རིགས་ཏེ། དེ་ཡང་འཛུར་བར་འགྱུར་ན་ནི་ཇི་ལྟར་གནེགས་ཟན་པ་དག་ན་རེ།
ཕྱུད་དེ་ཚོགས་ན་དགོས་པ་ཀུམ་མོ་ཞེས་ཟེར་བ་ལྟ་བུའབམ། ཡང་ན་ཕན་ཆུན་མཐུས་འཛིན་གྱིས་མ་འགྱུར་བའི་
རང་བཞིན་པར་ཡོད་ཅིང་བསྒྱིར་བ་སྟེ། ཇི་ལྟར་ཁ་ཅིག་ན་རེ།

ཐ་དད་ཕྱོགས་ནས་མང་པོ་དག །འགའ་ཞ་ལ་ཀུན་ནས་བསྐོར་ཚམ་དུ། །

བརྟོད་པར་ཟན་གྱི་རྡུལ་དེ་ནི། །ཆ་ཤས་བཅས་པའི་བདག་ཉིད་མིན། །

ཞེས་ཟེར་བ་ལྟ་བུ་འམ། ཡང་ན་མང་པོ་དག་པར་མེད་དེ། དེ་ལྟར་རྡུལ་ཕྲ་རབ་རྣམས་མི་རེག་ཀུང་པར་མེད་
པས་རེག་པར་འདུ་ཞེས་སོ་ཞེས་བྱ་བ་ལྟ་བུ་ཡང་མི་རུང་སྟེ། རྣམ་པར་གཞག་པ་འདི་དག་ཐམས་ཅད་ནི་བཏགས་
པ་ཙམ་ཁོ་འི་སྐྱེ་པོ་རན་དོ། །

བདག་ཉིད་ཐམས་ཅད་ཀྱིས་འབྱུར་ན་ནི་རྫས་རྣམས་འདྲེས་པར་འགྱུར་ཏེ། རྡུལ་གྱི་རང་བཞིན་གཅིག་པུ་གང་
གིས་ཀུན་འབྱུར་བ་དེ་ཉིད་གཞན་དང་ཡང་འབྱུར་བའི་ཕྱིར་རོ། ཕྱོགས་གཅིག་གིས་འབྱུར་ན་ནི་ཆ་ཤས་ཡོད་
པར་འབྱུར་ཏེ། རང་བཞིན་གཞན་དང་གཞན་དག་གིས་རྡུག་གཞན་དང་འབྱུར་བའི་ཕྱིར་རོ། །

བར་ཡོད་པ་ཡང་བར་དག་ཏུ་སྤྲུང་བ་དང་སྤུན་པའི་རྡུལ་ཕྲ་རབ་རྣམས་ཀྱི་གོ་སྐབས་ཡོད་པར་འགྱུར་ཏེ། སྤུག་ནི་
སྤུན་པ་དང་སྤུང་བའི་བདག་ཉིད་ཡིན་པའི་ཕྱིར་དེ་དག་དང་འབྱུར་བར་འགྱུར་རོ། །བར་མེད་པའི་ཕྱོགས་ཀྱུང་
འབྱུར་བའི་ཕྱོགས་ཐ་དད་མེད་པ་ཉིད་དེ། བར་མེད་པ་ནི་ཕྱག་མེད་པའོ། སྤུན་པ་དང་འབྱུར་བ་ཞེས་བྱ་བ་ནི་
དོན་ཐ་དད་པ་མ་ཡིན་ཏེ། ཤིན་ཏུ་ཆེན་པོ་རྣམས་ཀྱིས་ལམ་པོ་ཆེ་བཏོད་ཟིན་ཏོ། །དེ་ལྟ་ཡིན་ཡང་མངོན་བསུས་
དེ་རྣམ་པར་བཏག་པར་བྱའོ། །

འབྱུར་བ་དང་ནི་བསྐོར་བ་འམ། །བར་མེད་རྣམ་པར་གནས་ཀུན་དུ། །

དབུས་གནས་རྡུལ་ཕྲན་རྡུལ་གཅིག་ལ། །བསྐས་པའི་རང་བཞིན་གང་ཡིན་པ།། *11* ॥

ཡང་དག་འབྱུར་དང་བསྐོར་བ་འམ། །བར་མེད་རྣམ་པར་གནས་ཀུན་དུ།

དབུས་གནས་རྡུལ་ཕྲན་རྡུལ་གཅིག་ལ། །བསྐས་པའི་རང་བཞིན་གང་ཡིན་པ། ། དེ་ཁོ་ཉིད་བསྡུས་པ་ལ་   ཚིགས་བཅད་ *1150*

རྡུལ་ཕྲན་གཞན་ལ་ལྟ་བ་ཡང་། །དེ་ཉིད་གལ་ཏེ་ཡིན་བརྟོད་ན། །

དེ་ལྟ་ཡིན་ནས་ཅུ་སོགས། །རི་ལྟར་རྒྱས་འགྱུར་བ་ཡིན་ནམ།། *12* ॥

རྡུལ་ཕྲན་གཞན་ལ་ལྟ་བ་ཡང་། །དེ་ཉིད་གལ་ཏེ་ཡིན་ཚོག་ན།
དེ་ལྟ་ཡིན་ནས་འཛིན་སོགས། །རྒྱས་པར་འགྱུར་བ་རི་རགས་ས་ཡིན། ། དེ་ཁོ་ན་ *1150*

ཕྱོགས་གསུམ་ཆར་ཡང་ཕྱོགས་བཅུ་འི་རྣམ་པར་གནས་པའི་རྡུལ་ཕྲ་མོ་རྣམས་ཀྱི་དབུས་ན་གནས་པའི་རྡུལ་ཕྲ་
རབ་གང་ཡིན་པ་དེ་ཤར་ཕྱོགས་ན་གནས་པའི་རྡུལ་ཕྲ་རབ་ལ་བལྟས་པའི་རང་བཞིན་གང་ཡིན་པ་དེ་ཉིད་གལ་ཏེ་
ཕྱོགས་ལྷག་མ་ན་རྣམ་པར་གནས་པའི་རྡུལ་ཕྲ་རབ་རྣམས་ལ་བལྟས་པ་ཡང་ཡིན་ན་ནི་དེ་འི་ཚོ་འི་རང་བཞིན་ལ་

བསྐལ་པ་ཉིད་ཀྱི་ཕྱིར་དེར་ཕྱོགས་ན་གནས་པར་འདོད་པའི་རྡུལ་ཕྲ་མོ་ལྟ་བུའམ། །དེར་ཕྱོགས་ཀྱི་ཁད་པ་ལ་

ཁད་པ་གཅིག་བསྐལ་པ་ལ་ལྟ་བུར་ཕྱོགས་ལྔག་མ་གནན་ན་གནས་པ་རྣམས་དོན་ཏེ་ལྟ་བ་ཞིན་མི་འགྱུར་རོ། །དེ་

ལྟ་བས་ན་དེར་དང་ནུབ་ལ་སོགས་པའི་ཆ་ཅན་མི་གནས་པས་སའི་དཀྱིལ་འཁོར་ལ་སོགས་པ་གནས་པར་མི་

འགྱུར་རོ། །ཅི་སྟེ་ཉེས་པ་འདིར་འགྱུར་དུ་འོང་ཞེས་ཏེ།

རྡུལ་ཕྲན་གནན་ལ་ལྟ་བའི་དོས། །གལ་ཏེ་གནན་དུ་འདོད་ན་ནི།

གལ་ཏེ་དེ་ལྟ་ཡིན་ན།

རབ་ཏུ་ཕྲ་རྡུལ་ཇི་ལྟ་བུར། །གཅིག་པུ་ཆ་ཤས་མེད་པར་འགྱུར།། ༡༣ །།
རྡུལ་ཕྲན་གནན་ལ་ལྟ་བའི་དོས། །གལ་ཏེ་གནན་དུ་འདོད་ན་ནི།
རྡུལ་ཕྲན་གཅིག་པུ་ཆ་ཤས་ནི། །མེད་པ་དུ་ནི་ཇི་ལྟར་འགྱུར། ། དེ་བོ་ན་ ༡༦༦༡

ཕྱོགས་བཅུ་ན་གནས་པའི་རྡུལ་རབ་ཏུ་གྱུར་པའི་གྲངས་ཀྱི་རང་བཞིན་དང་ལྡན་པའི་ཕྱིར། འདི་ལྟར་གཅིག་པུ་

རྣམ་པར་གནལག་པ་སྙོས་ཤིག །རང་བཞིན་ཐ་དད་པའི་མཚན་ཉིད་ཡིན་པས་དོས་པོ་ཐ་དད་དེ། རྡུལ་ཕྲ་རབ་

དེ་དག་ཀུང་དེ་སྟེད་དུ་འགྱུར་རོ། །ཁད་གི་ཕྱིར་དེ་ལྟར།

རྡུལ་ཕྲན་རང་བཞིན་མེད་གྱུབ་པ། །དེའི་ཕྱིར་མིག་དང་རྫས་ལ་སོགས།

བདག་དང་གནན་སྐྱེས་མང་པོ་དག །རང་བཞིན་མེད་པར་མཛོན་པ་ཡིན།། ༡༤ །།

རྡུལ་ཕྲ་རབ་རྣམས་མེད་པ་ཉིད་དུ་ཞེས་ན་རང་གི་སྟེ་པ་དག་མིག་དང་གཟུགས་དང་དེའི་རྣམ་པར་ཤེས་པ་ལ་

སོགས་པ་དེ་ཁོན་ཉིད་དུ་འདོད་པ་དང་། གཟིག་ཞན་པ་ལ་སོགས་པས་སྙམ་པའི་རྫས་དང་ཡོན་ཏན་ལ་སོགས་

པ་བསྒྲིམ་མི་དགོས་པར་རང་བཞིན་གྱིས་སྟོང་པར་ཞེས་སོ། །ཅི་འདི་རྒྱལ་པོའི་བཀའ་ཡིན་ནམ་ཞེན། མ་ཡིན་

ཏེ།

དེ་ཡི་རང་བཞིན་དེས་བཀྲམས་དང་། །དེ་ཡི་ཡོན་ཏན་དེ་ལས་བདག །

དེ་ཡི་སྐྱེ་དང་ཁྱད་པར་ཡང་། དེ་དག་དེ་དང་འདུ་བ་ཅན།། ༡༥ །།

རང་གི་སྟེ་པ་དག་ནི་གཟུགས་ཅན་གྱི་ཁམས་བཅུ་པོ་དེ་དག་རྡུལ་ཕྲ་རབ་ལ་སོགས་པ་ཡིན་པར་བཟོད་དེ། དེ་

དག་མེད་ན་མི་རུང་ངོ་། །འདི་ལྟར་མིག་དང་གཟུགས་རྣམས་ལ་བརྟེན་ནས་མིག་གི་རྣམ་པར་ཤེས་པ་འབྱུང་

ཞེས་བྱ་བ་ལ་སོགས་པ་དེ་ལ་བརྟེན་པ་དང་དམིགས་པ་རྣམ་པར་ཤེས་པའི་ཁམས་ལྟ་ཡང་དེ་མེད་ན་ཅི་ལ་བརྟེན

དེ་སྐྱེ་བར་འགྱུར། རྣམ་པར་ཤེས་པའི་ཁམས་སུ་མེད་ན་དེ་མ་ཐག་པའི་རྐྱེན་དེས་མངོན་པར་བསྐྱེབས་པའི་ཡིད་
ཀྱི་རྣམ་པར་ཤེས་པ་ཡང་མི་འབྱད་པའི་རང་བཞིན་ཉིད་དོ། །

དེ་ལྟར་རྣམ་པར་ཤེས་པ་དྲུག་གི་ཚོགས་མ་གྲུབ་ན། རྣམ་པར་ཤེས་པ་དེ་འདས་མ་ཐག་པའི་ཡིད་ཀྱང་ཡང་དག་
པར་རྣམ་པར་བཞག་པ་མི་རིགས་སོ། །དེ་ལྟར་སེམས་རང་བཞིན་མེད་པར་འགྱུར་ན་དེ་དང་གྲུབ་པ་དང་བདེ་བ་
གཅིག་པ་དང་ཚོར་བ་དང་འདུ་ཤེས་དང་སེམས་པ་ལ་སོགས་པ་སེམས་ལས་བྱུང་བ་རྣམས་ཀྱང་རང་བཞིན་མེད་
པར་བདེ་བླག་ཏུ་ཤེས་སོ། །

ལྡན་པ་མ་ཡིན་པའི་འདུ་བྱེད་རྣམས་ཀྱང་རྣམ་པར་རྟོག་པ་ལ་ལ་དཔའ་བ་མཁས་པ་རྣམས་ཀྱིས་ལན་བཅུར་དུ་མ་བུ་
ཧུལ་བུར་བཞིག་ཞིན་པས་ཤེ་ཞིན་པ་དེ་དག་ལ་བརྟན་མི་དགོས་སོ། །ཡང་ན་གཟུགས་ལ་སོགས་པ་དེ་དག་དང་
དངོས་སུ་འམ་བརྒྱུད་ནས་འབྲེལ་པ་ཅན་དེ་དག་ཀྱང་དེ་མེད་པས་གཏིང་མ་ནས་མ་སྐྱེས་པ་ཉིད་དོ། །

རྣམ་པར་རིག་བྱེད་མ་ཡིན་པ་འབྱུང་བ་ཆེན་པོ་རྣམས་རྒྱུ་བྱས་པས་གྲུབ་པར་བརྗོད་པ་དེ་ཡང་དེ་དག་མེད་ན་
མེད་པ་ཉིད་དོ། །ནམ་མཁའ་ལ་སོགས་པ་འདུས་མ་བྱས་མཐའ་དག་ཀྱང་སྤྱར་བསྟན་ཞིན་ཏེ། ཁམས་བཙོ
བཀྱུད་པོ་དེ་དག་ནི་རང་བཞིན་མེད་པ་ཉིད་དུ་གསལ་ལོ། །ཧུལ་གཉིས་པ་ལ་སོགས་པའི་ཡན་ལག་ཅན། ཧུལ་
ཕ་རབ་དེ་དག་གིས་དངོས་དང་གཅིག་ནས་གཅིག་ཏུ་བཀྱུད་དེ་བརྣམས་པར་འདོད་པ་དེ་དག་ཀྱང་དེ་མེད་ན་མེད་
དོ། །གཟུགས་དང་རོ་དང་དྲི་ལ་སོགས་པ་ཡོན་ཏན་རྣམས་ཀྱི་ཕལ་ཆེ་འཕུས་བུ་དང་བཙས་པ་དེ་དག་གི་ཉིད་
ཀྱི་ཡིན་ནོ། །འདེགས་པ་ལ་སོགས་པ་ལས་ཀྱི་དངོས་པོ་རྣམས་ཀྱང་དེའི་ལས་ཀྱི་དོ་ཉིད་ལོ་ནའོ། །སྐྱི་དང་
སྐྱིའི་ཁྱད་པར་དང་ཁྱད་པར་ཡང་ཡོན་པ་དང་། ས་ལ་སོགས་པ་ཕལ་ཆེར་བརྟེན་པ་དང་ཉེ་བར་བརྟེན་པ་ལ་
སོགས་པ་དང་བཙས་པ་དེ་དག་ཉིད་ཀྱི་ཡིན་ཏེ། དེ་དག་ཀྱང་དེ་དང་འབྲེལ་བ་ཅན་དུ་འདོད་དོ། །དེ་བས་ན་
འབྲེལ་པ་ཅན་མེད་པའི་འབྲེལ་བ་ཡང་རང་བཞིན་མེད་པའོ་ནོ། །

ཧུག་པའི་དངོས་པོ་ནམ་མཁའ་དང་། དུས་དང་། ཕྱོགས་དང་། བདག་དང་། ཕྲ་རབ་དག་ཀྱང་བསལ་
ཏེ། །རང་བཞིན་མེད་པ་སྟེར་བསྟན་ཞིན་ཏོ། །གཟུགས་ཀྱི་ཕུང་པོ་དཔྱད་པའི་ཞར་ལ་རྣམ་པར་ཤེས་པའི་ཕུང་
པོ་མཚུངས་པར་ཕྱན་པ་དང་བཙས་པ་ཡང་རང་བཞིན་མེད་པར་བསྟན་ཏོ། །

དེ་ནི་རང་གི་ངོ་བོ་དང་གཞན་གྱིས་གཉིས་དང་གཉིས་མ་ཡིན་པའི་ཚུལ་དུ་བརྟེན་པ་དངོས་སུ་བསྟན་པར་
བྱའོ། །དེ་གཉིས་ཀྱི་ཚུལ་ནི་གང་དག་གཟུང་བ་དང་འཛིན་པ་གཉིས་ཡང་དག་པར་ཡོད་པར་འདོད་ལ། རྣམ་
པར་ཤེས་པ་ནི་ཤེལ་སྒོང་དག་པ་ལྟ་བུ་ཡུལ་གྱི་རྣམ་པ་ནི་འཛིན་པར་བརྟོན་པ་སྟེ། དེ་དག་གི་དཔྱད་པར་བྱའོ། །

རྣམ་ཤེས་ཐེམ་པོའི་རང་བཞིན་ལས། །བརྫོག་པ་རབ་ཏུ་སྐྱེ་བ་སྟེ།
ཤེམ་མིན་རང་བཞིན་གང་ཡིན་པ། །དེ་འདི་བདག་ཉིད་ཤེས་པ་ཡིན།། ༡༦ ||
<small>རྣམ་ཤེས་ཐེམ་པོའི་རང་བཞིན་ལས། །བརྫོག་པ་རབ་ཏུ་སྐྱེ་བ་སྟེ།
ཤེམ་མིན་རང་བཞིན་གང་ཡིན་པ། །དེ་འདི་བདག་ཉིད་ཤེས་པ་ཡིན། ། དེ་བོན་ ༡༠༠༠</small>

དེ་ལ་རེ་ཞིག་གཉིས་ཀྱི་ཚུལ་རྣམ་པ་མེད་པའི་རྣམ་པར་ཤེས་པའི་ཕྱོགས་ནི། རྣམ་པར་ཤེས་པ་ཡུལ་གྱི་སྣང་བ་
དང་མ་ཕྱད་པ། བདག་ཚམ་རིག་པ་ཚམ་ལ་གཟིལ་བ་ལོ་ནར་ཟད་ལས། བདག་དང་ཐ་དད་པའི་དོན་མྱོང་བའི་
བདག་ཉིད་དུ་མི་རུང་ངོ། །

འདི་རང་རིག་པའི་རང་བཞིན་དུ་རྣམ་པར་གནས་པ་ནི་རང་བཞིན་གྱིས་གསལ་བའི་བདག་ཉིད་ཡིན་པའི་ཕྱིར་ཏེ།
ཤིང་ཏུ་ལ་སོགས་པ་ལ་རིག་པ་མེད་པའི་རང་བཞིན་ལས་བཟློག་པའི་ཕྱིར་རོ། །དེ་ནི་རང་གི་ངོ་བོ་རིག་པར་བྱ་
བའི་ཕྱིར་སྟོན་པོ་ལ་སོགས་པ་བཞིན་དུ་རིག་པར་བྱེད་པ་གཞན་ལ་མི་ལྟོས་པས་ཏེ། རིག་པ་མེད་པ་མ་ཡིན་ཞེས་
བྱ་བའི་དོན་འདི་ནི་རང་རིག་པ་ཞེས་བརྫོད་དོ། །

གཅིག་པ་ལ་ཚ་མེད་རང་བཞིན་ལ། །གསུམ་གྱི་རང་བཞིན་མི་འཐད་ཕྱིར།
དེ་ཡི་རང་གིས་རིག་པ་ནི། །བྱ་དང་བྱེད་པའི་དངོས་པོ་མིན།། ༡༧ ||
<small>གཅིག་པ་ལ་ཚ་མེད་རང་བཞིན་ལས། །གསུམ་གྱི་རང་བཞིན་མི་འཐད་ཕྱིར།
འདི་ཡི་རང་གིས་རིག་པ་ནི། །བྱ་དང་བྱེད་པའི་ཌོ་བོ་མིན། ། དེ་བོན་ ༡༠༠༠</small>

ཇི་སྐྱེད་དུ་ཡུལ་རང་གི་རྣམ་པ་འཛོག་ནུས་པ་ནི་རྒྱུ་ཉིད་དེ་རིག་པར་བྱ་བ་ཉིད་ཡིན་པ་དང་། རྣམ་པར་ཤེས་པ་
ཡུལ་གྱི་ཌོ་བོར་བཞག་པ་ནི་བསྐྱེད་པར་བྱ་བ་ཉིད་དེ་རིག་པ་པོ་ཉིད་དོ་ཞེས་རྣམ་པ་དང་བཅས་པའི་ཤེས་པའི་ཚུལ་
ལ་བརྟོན་པ་ལྟ་བུར་རང་རིག་པ་ལ་ནི་དེ་ལྟར་རྣམ་པར་གཞག་པར་མི་འཐད་དེ། རྣམ་པར་ཤེས་པ་ཚ་མེད་པའི་
བདག་ཉིད་ལས་བསྐྱེད་པར་བྱ་བ་དང་། སྐྱེད་པ་པོ་དང་། བསྐྱེད་པའི་བྱ་བའི་ཚུལ་དུ་འམ། རིག་པར་བྱ་བ་དང་།
རིག་པ་པོ་དང་། རིག་པའི་བྱེ་བྲག་གིས་གསུམ་གྱི་ཚུལ་དུ་མི་དམིགས་པའི་ཕྱིར་ཏེ། འདི་ལྟར་སྐྱེ་བའི་ལྟ་ལོགས
ན་ནི་མེད་ལས་ནུས་པ་མེད་ལ། ནུས་པའི་དུས་ན་ནི་སྐྱེད་པོར་འདོད་པའི་ཌོ་བོ་བཞིན་དུ་དེ་དག་ཐ་མི་དད་པ

བསྐྱེད་པར་བྱ་བར་འདོད་པའི་རོ་བོ་ཡང་ཡོངས་སུ་གྲུབ་སྟེ། བདག་ཉིད་ལ་ཕྱིན་པ་ནི་འགལ་ལོ། དེ་ལྟ་བས་
ན་གསལ་བར་བྱེད་པ་གཞན་ལ་མི་ལྟོས་པར་རང་གསལ་བའི་བདག་ཉིད་ནི་རྣམ་པར་ཤེས་པའི་རང་རིག་པ་
ཞེས་བྱའོ། །

དེའི་ཕྱིར་འདི་ནི་ཤེས་པ་ཡི། །རང་བཞིན་ཡིན་པས་བདག་ཤེས་སྡུང་།
རོན་གྱི་རང་བཞིན་གཞན་དག་ལ། །དེ་ཡིས་ཇི་ལྟར་ཤེས་པར་འགྱུར།། ༡༧ ||

དེ་ཕྱིར་འདི་ནི་ཤེས་པ་ཡི། །རང་བཞིན་ཡིན་པས་བདག་ཤེས་སྡུང་།
རོན་གྱི་རོ་བོ་གཞན་པའི། །དེ་ཡིས་ཇི་ལྟར་ཤེས་པར་འགྱུར། ། དེ་ལྟོན་ ༡༠༠༡

དཔེར་ན་བདག་ཉིད་གསལ་བའི་རོ་བོ་ཡིན་པས་རང་གི་རོ་བོ་གསལ་བར་བྱེད་པ་ལ་གསལ་བར་འདོད་པ་དེ་
བཞིན་དུ་རྣམ་པར་ཤེས་པ་ཡང་སྐྱོང་བའི་བདག་ཉིད་ཡིན་པའི་ཕྱིར་རང་རིག་པར་འདོད་དོ། །ཅི་སྟེ་རྣམ་པར་
ཤེས་པ་ནི་ཡུལ་སོ་སོར་རྣམ་པར་རིག་པའི་མཚན་ཉིད་ཡིན་པས་དེ་ནི་རོན་ཡོངས་སུ་དཔྱོད་པའི་རོ་བོ་ཉིད་གུང་
ཡིན་ཏེ། དེའི་ཕྱིར་རང་གི་རོ་བོ་བཞིན་དུ་རོན་གུང་སྐྱོང་བར་འདོད་དོ་ཞེན། དེ་ནི་མི་རུང་སྟེ།

དེ་ཡི་རང་བཞིན་གཞན་ལ་མེད། །གང་གིས་དེ་ཤེས་གཞན་ཡང་ཤེས།
ཤེས་དང་ཤེས་པར་བྱ་བའི་དོན། །ཁྱད་པར་བར་ནི་འདོད་ཕྱིར་རོ།། ༡༨ ||

དེ་ཡི་རང་བཞིན་གཞན་ལ་མེད། །གང་གིས་དེ་ཤེས་གཞན་ཡང་ཤེས།
དངོས་པོ་རྣམས་ནི་དོན་དམ་པར། །ཁྱད་པར་བའི་འདོན་གནས་ཕྱིར་རོ། ། དེ་ལྟོན་ ༡༠༠༡

ཡོངས་སུ་གཅོད་ཅེས་བྱ་བའི་རོ་བོ་དེ་ནི་ཤེས་པའི་ཐུན་མོང་མ་ཡིན་པ་སྟེ། བདེ་བ་ལ་སོགས་པའི་བདེ་བ་ཉིད་ལ་
སོགས་པ་ལྟ་བུ་ཡིན། དེ་འདུ་བ་དེ་གཞན་ལ་ཇི་ལྟར་ཡོད། འཁྲུལ་པ་གང་གིས་ན། འདིའི་འདི་ཞེས་བསྣན་
པ་སྐྱོང་བར་འགྱུར། དེ་ལས་བྱུང་བ་དེ་ཙམ་གྱིས་ནི་དོན་སྐྱོང་བར་མི་འགྱུབ་སྟེ། མིག་ལ་སོགས་པ་ལ་ཡང་ཐལ་
བར་འགྱུར་བའི་ཕྱིར་རོ། །གལ་ཏེ་དོན་གུང་ཡོངས་སུ་གཅོད་པའི་བདག་ཉིད་དུ་འགྱུར་ལ། རྣམ་པར་ཤེས་པ་
ཡང་དེའི་བདག་ཉིད་ཡིན་ན་ནི། དེ་ལྟ་བས་ན་དེའི་ཚེ་ཤེས་པའི་དོན་ཡོངས་སུ་གཅོད་པའི་རོ་བོ་ཡིན་པས་སྐྱོང་
བའི་རོ་བོར་ཐ་མི་དད་པའི་ཕྱིར། ཤེས་པ་རིག་པས་དོན་རིག་པར་ཡང་འགྱུར་བ་ཞིག་ན། ཕྱི་རོལ་དོན་ལ་མངོན་
པར་ཞེན་པའི་དུག་གིས་མ་རུངས་པར་བྱས་པའི་བསམ་པ་ཅན་གྱི་ལུགས་ལ་ནི་དེ་མི་སྲིད་དོ། དོན་དང་ཤེས་པ
གཉིས་ཐ་དད་པའི་ཕྱིར་རོ། །

གང་རྣམ་པ་བཞིན་དུ་ཤེས་པ་ཡང་རིག་པ་མེད་པར་འདོད་པ་དེའི་ལྷན་ན་གཉིག་ལ་རིག་པ་མེད་དེ་དོན་དང་ཤེས་པ་ཞེས་བྱ་བར་འགྱུབ་པར་བསྐྱེད་དུ་མེད་དོ། །ཤེས་པ་ནི་གསལ་བ་ཡིན་ན་གསལ་བ་ནི་གསལ་བར་མ་གྱུར་ཏེ། གསལ་བ་གསལ་བ་མ་ཡིན་པའི་ཕྱིར་མི་གནན་གྱི་མཚན་སུམ་དུ་འདོད་པ་དོན་བཞིན་དུ་འདོད་པ་དོན་ཀུན་མཚན་སུམ་དུ་མི་འགྱུར་ལ་རབ་ཏུ་འབྲེལ་པའི་རྒྱ་ཡང་མེད་པའི་ཕྱིར་རོ།

གཞན་ཡང་ཤེས་པ་རྣམ་པ་མེད་པའི་ཕྱོགས་འདི་ནི་ཤེས་པ་རྣམ་པ་དང་བཅས་པའི་ཕྱོགས་ཤིན་དུ་འབྲེལ་པ་མེད་པས་ཀུང་ཚེས་དམན་པར་བསྟན་པ།

ཤེས་པ་རྣམ་བཅས་ཕྱོགས་ལ་ནི། །དངོས་སུ་དེ་གཉིས་ཐ་དད་ཀྱང་།
དེ་དང་གཟུགས་བརྐྱན་འདུ་བས་ན། །བདག་ས་པ་ཙམ་གྱིས་ཆོར་བར་རུང་།། ༣༠ །།
ཤེས་པ་རྣམ་བཅས་ཕྱོགས་ལ་ནི། །དངོས་སུ་དེ་ཉིད་ཐ་དད་ཀྱང་།
དེ་དང་གཟུགས་བཅུན་འདུ་བས་ན། །གདགས་པ་ཙམ་གྱིས་ཆོར་བར་རུང་། །དེ་ཁོ་ན་ ༡༠༠༩

དེས་གལ་བཞིག་པ་ཤེས་པའི་བདག་ཉིད་དུ་གྱུར་པའི་གཟུགས་བརྐྱན་རིག་པ་གང་ཡིན་པ་དེ་ཉིད་དོན་ཤེས་པ་པོ། །དེའི་ཕྱིར་ན་དོན་གྱི་འབྲས་བུ་གཟུགས་བརྐྱན་སྤྱོང་བ་ལ་དོན་ཀུང་སྤྱོང་དོ་ཞེས་གདགས་སོ། །

དོན་གྱི་རྣམ་པས་བསླྱུར་སྤྱང་པའི། །རྣམ་ཤེས་སུ་ཞིག་མི་འདོད་པ།
དེ་ལ་ཕྱི་རོལ་རིག་པ་ཡི། །རྣམ་པ་འདི་ཡང་ཡོད་མ་ཡིན།། ༣༡ །།
དོན་གྱི་རྣམ་པས་བསླྱུར་སྤྱང་པའི། །རྣམ་ཤེས་སུ་ཞིག་མི་འདོད་པ།
དེ་ལ་ཕྱི་རོལ་རིག་པ་ཡི། །རྣམ་པ་འདི་ཡང་ཡོད་མ་ཡིན། ། ༡༠༠༥ དབུ་མ་རྒྱན་འདི་བསྐྱན་པ་སྩ་དང་དུ་ཡེ་ཤེས་སྙི་ལ་སྩོགས་པས་བསྐྱན། དེ་ཁོ་ན་ཉིད་བསྟན་པའི་ནི་བསྐྱན་པ་ཕྱི་དང་དུ་དུ་རྒྱུ་རྒྱན་དོན་གྱི་ཀྱུང་ཞིག་དོན་ཀྱིས་བསྐྱན་པ། གཉུང་ཆེན་ཚོ་བ་བཞིན་ཡོན་པས། སྩ་འགྱུན་ཉིང་ཞི་དོན་ཀྱིས་གནང་འདི་ནས་སྒྲུབས་པར་མཛད་དོ། །

རིག་པ་མེད་པའི་རང་བཞིན་ཡིན་པས་རིག་པའི་དོན་གྱི་དངོས་པོ་ནི་དོན་ལས་རིང་དུ་གྱུར་པ་ཉིད་དོ། །འབྲེལ་པའི་རྒྱ་གཟུགས་བཅུན་ཡང་ཁམས་མི་ཡིན་པས་གདགས་པ་ཡང་མི་སྱིད་དོ། །གལ་ཏེ་དེ་ལྟན་ཤེས་པ་རྣམ་པ་དང་བཅས་པ་ཉིད་དུ་མི་རུང་དོ། །དེ་ཡང་དེ་ལྟ་མ་ཡིན་ཏེ།

འདི་ལ་ཡང་།

ཤེས་གཅིག་ཐ་དད་མ་ཡིན་པས། །རྣམ་པ་མང་པོར་མི་འགྱུར་ཏེ།
དེའི་ཕྱིར་དེ་ཡི་མཐུ་ཡིས་ནི། །དོན་ཤེས་འགྱུར་བར་གཞག་པ་མེད།། ༣༣ །།
དེས་ན་དེ་ཡི་སྐྱོབས་ཀྱིས་ནི། །དོན་རིག་གཞས་པ་ཡོད་མ་ཡིན། དེ་ཁོ་ན་ ༡༠༥༠

113

རེ་མོ་རྒྱང་པ་ལ་སོགས་པ་ལ་ལ་དམིགས་པའི་རྣམ་པར་ཤེས་པ་ནི་སྟོན་པོ་དང་། སེར་པོ་ལ་སོགས་པ་སྟུག་ཡུལ་གྱི་ཉེ་བྲག་ཏེ་སྟེང་པ་དེ་སྟེང་གི་གྲངས་ཀྱི་ཉེ་བྲག་གི་རྣམ་པ་གཏན་མི་ཟ་བར་འབྱུང་ངོ་། །དེ་ལྟ་མ་ཡིན་ན་ཤེས་པ་དེ་དང་མཐུན་པར་མི་འགྱུར་རོ། །

རྣམ་པ་དེ་དག་གི་སྐུ་ཚོགས་པ་འདི་ནི་རིགས་པ་ལ་མ་ཡིན་ཏེ། རྣམ་པར་ཤེས་པ་གཅིག་དང་ཐ་དད་པ་ལ་མ་ཡིན་པའི་ཕྱིར་ཤེས་པ་དེའི་རང་གི་དོ་བོ་བཞིན་ནོ། །དེའི་ཕྱིར་རྣམ་པ་ལ་སྐུ་ཚོགས་ཀྱི་རྒྱས་དེ་ལ་འདི་ནི་སྟོན་པོའི། །འདི་ནི་སེར་པོའི་ཞེས་བྱ་བ་ལ་སོགས་པ་དོན་སྐུ་ཚོགས་རིག་པའི་རྒྱུ་རྣམ་པ་སྐུ་ཚོགས་སུ་རྣམ་པར་གནོག་པ་མེད་པར་འགྱུར་རོ། །

ཅི་སྟེ་ཡང་གསལ་བར་མཛོན་རྣམ་དུ་བྱལ་པ་རྣམ་པ་སྐུ་ཚོགས་ཡོད་པར་ཤེས་པར་བས་བྲུད་དུ་རེས་སོ་ཞེ་ན། དེ་ལྟ་ཡང་།

རྣམ་པ་རྣམས་དང་མ་བྲལ་བས། །རྣམ་ཤེས་གཅིག་ཕྱུར་མི་འགྱུར་རོ།
དེ་ལྟ་མིན་ན་འདི་གཉིས་ལས། །གཅིག་ཉེས་དེ་སྐྱད་བཏོང་པར་བྱ།། ༢༢ །།
རྣམ་པ་དང་ཐ་མི་དད་ཕྱིར། །ཤེས་པའང་གཅིག་ཉིད་དུ་མི་འགྱུར།
གནན་དུ་འདི་ལ་གཅིག་ཉིད་དུ། །ཇི་ལྟར་ཡོངས་སུ་བཏག་པར་འགྱུར། ། དེ་བོ་ན ༡༠༡༢

རྣམ་པར་ཤེས་པ་དེ་རྣམ་པ་དུ་མ་དང་ཐ་དད་པ་མ་ཡིན་པའི་ལུས་ཡིན་ན་ནི། རྣམ་པ་དེ་དག་གི་བྱེ་བྲག་བཞིན་དུ་དུ་མར་འགྱུར་རོ། །གལ་ཏེ་རྣམ་པར་ཤེས་པ་ནི་གཅིག་ཁྱོ་བོ་ནའི་རང་བཞིན་ཡིན་ལ། རྣམ་པ་ནི་དུ་མ་ཡིན་ན་དེའི་ཚོ་འགལ་བའི་ཚོས་སུ་གནས་པས་རྣམ་པ་དང་རྣམ་པར་ཤེས་པ་ཉིད་ཐ་དད་པ་མ་ཡིན་པར་ནི་འགལ་ལོ། །འདི་ལྟར་འདོད་དེ།

དགར་པོ་དག་ལ་སོགས་པ་ལ། །ཤེས་པ་དེ་ནི་རིམ་འབྱུང་སྟེ།
མགྱོགས་པར་འབྱུང་ཕྱིར་བླུན་པོ་དག །ཅིག་ཅར་སྐྱམ་དུ་ཤེས་པའི།། ༢༠ །།
རྣམ་ཊོག་རིམ་གྱིས་སྐྱེ་ཉིད། །ཡིན་ཡང་མགགས་མི་འཁོར་ལོ་བཞིན།
མྱུར་པར་འདུག་ལ་ཅིག་ཅར་བར། །མཚོན་པ་སེམས་པ་ཡིན་ཞེས། ། དོ་བོ་ཉིད་ཅིགཆས་བཅད ༡༡༠༦

མེ་ཊོག་ཨུཏྤལའི་འདབ་མ་བརྒྱ་འབིགས་པ་བཞིན་དུ། ཤིན་ཏུ་མྱུར་བའི་རིམ་གྱིས་དངོས་པོ་ལ་ཡང་ཅིག་ཆའི་སྐྱམ་དུ་ཤེས་སོ་ཤེས་འཛོར་ཏེ། དཔེར་ན་མགལ་མེ་འཁོར་ལོ་མཐོང་བ་བཞིན་ཏེ། མཐོང་བ་དེ་ནི་མྱུར་དུ་བསྐོར་བའི་ཕྱིར་པོ་ཞེས་ཟེར་རོ། །གལ་ཏེ་དེ་ལྟ་ན།

ཕྱུག་མའི་སྐྲ་ལ་སོགས་པའི་བློ། །རབ་ཏུ་མགྱོགས་པར་འབྱུང་ཡིན་ན།
དེའི་ཕྱིར་ཅིག་ཅར་འབྱུང་བ་ཡིན། །འདིར་ཡང་ཅིའི་ཕྱིར་འབྱུར་མི་འགྱུར།། ༢༥ །།

འདིར་ཕྱུག་མའི་སྐྲ་ཞེས་བསྒྲར་བ་ལ་གཤུན་གི་གྷོ་བ་བརྒྱལ་པར་མི་ལམ་རེན་པོ་ཆེས། སྨྲ་ཡང་ལེགས་སུ་ཆེག །ལ་ཏུ་ཞེས་པ་ཕྱུགས་མའི་མིད་དང་། ཏུ་ལ་ཞེས་པ་ཞིང་ཏུ་འདིའི་མིད་ཞེས་གསུངས་པའི་གཤུན་གི་དགོས་ས་ཏྲོགས་པ་ལ་ས་པ་ཆེན་པོ་བསྒྲར་པར་མཛད་དོ། །

ཕྱུག་མའི་སྐྲ་ལ་སོགས་རྣམས་ཀྱིས། །གྷོ་ནི་ཧེན་ཏུ་སྐྱུར་འབྱུང་བ།
སྔན་ཅིག་ཡོད་པའི་རྒྱལ་ཏེ། །འདིར་ཡང་ཅིའི་ཕྱིར་འབྱུར་མི་འགྱུར། །དེ་གོ་རིན་༡༩༥༠ པར་པོ་ཅིང་པར་མར་ཆིག་ཀྲུང་གཤིག་འཚད་པ་ལེགས་སུ་བསྒྲར་ནས་པ་བཀྲལ་པ་སྟེ་དགེ་སྔར་པར་སོགས་པར་ཞིབ་གཏུགས་བྱ་དགོས་སོ།

ཕྱུག་མ་(སྟེ) ལ་ཏུ)དང་། ཏུ་ལ་དང་། (ས་རྃ)མཚོ་དང་། (ར་ས)ཕོ་བྷོ་བ་དང་ཞེས་བུ་བ་ལ་སོགས་པ་ཡི་གིའི་འབུའི་ཡུལ་རྣམས་ཀྱི་བློ་དག་ཀུང་རབ་ཏུ་མགྱོགས་པར་འབྱུང་དུ་འདུ་སྟེ། དེ་བས་ན་མགྱོགས་པར་འབྱུང་བའི་ཕྱིར་རེ་མོ་བཀྱང་ལ་སོགས་པ་བཞིན་དུ་ཅིག་ཅར་དུ་ཅིའི་ཕྱིར་མི་ཞེས། རྒྱུ་འདུ་བའི་འབྲས་བུ་ནི་ཐ་དད་པར་མི་རིགས་ཏེ། རྒྱུ་མ་ཡིན་པར་འབྱུར་བའི་ཕྱིར་རོ། །

ཡིད་ཀྱི་རྟོག་པ་འབའ་ཞིག་ལའང་། །རིམ་ཏུ་ཤེས་པར་མི་འགྱུར་རོ།
རིང་དུ་གནས་པ་མ་ཡིན་པས། །བློ་རྣམས་ཀུན་ཀྱང་མགྱོགས་འབྱུང་འདུ།། ༢༦ །།

ཡིད་ཀྱི་རྟོག་པ་འབའ་ཞིག་ལའང་། །རིམ་ཏུ་རིས་པ་བས་བྱེད་མིན།
བློ་རྣམས་ཀུན་ཀྱང་སྐྱུར་འབྱུར་ཞིང་། །རིམ་ཏུ་གནས་པ་བ་པར་མཆུངས། །
དེ་གོ་རིན་༡༩༥༧ འདིར་ཡང་དཔེ་གནན་དང་གཏུགས་དགོས་སོ།

སེམས་པ་ལ་དང་དཔྱོད་པ་ལ་སོགས་པའི་དུན་ན་འབྱུང་བ་ཅན་རིགས་མི་འདུ་བ་མིག་ལ་སོགས་པའི་ཤེས་པ་ལ་དང་མ་འདྲེ་པ་བར་མ་ཆད་མེད་པ་ལ་འབྱུང་བ་ཡང་གསལ་བར་མགྱོགས་པར་འབྱུང་ན་ཅིའི་ཕྱིར་ཅིག་ཅར་དུ་མི་ཞེས། གཅིག་ཏུ་ན་འདིའི་ཕྱིར་སྐྱུར་དུ་འབྱུང་བའི་ཕྱིར་རོ་ཞེས་བུ་བ་འདི་ནི་ལན་དུ་མི་རུང་སྟེ། ཕ་རོལ་གྱི་ལུགས་ལས། ཀུང་རབ་ཏུ་སྐྱུར་དུ་འཇིག་པ་ལ་དང་ལྡན་པའི་བློ་རྣམས་ནི་གང་ཡང་ཡུན་རིང་དུ་གནས་པ་མེད་དོ་ཞེས་འབྱུང་སྟེ།

དེའི་ཕྱིར་ཡུལ་རྣམས་ཐམས་ཅད་ལ། །རིམ་གྱིས་འཛིན་པར་མི་འགྱུར་གྱི།
རྣམ་པ་དགའ་ནི་ཐ་དད་ལྟར། །ཅིག་ཅར་འཛིན་པར་སྟུང་བར་འགྱུར།། ༢༧ །།

དེའི་ཕྱིར་ཡུལ་རྣམས་ཐམས་ཅད་ལ། །རིམ་གྱིས་འཛིན་པར་མི་འགྱུར་གྱི།
སྐྲ་ལ་སོགས་པའི་བློ་ཞིན་དུ། །ཅིག་ཅར་འཛིན་པར་སྟུང་བར་འགྱུར། །དེ་གོ་རིན་༡༩༥༢

དེའི་ཕྱིར་མགྱོགས་པར་ཏེ་བྲག་མེད་པའི་ཕྱིར། དོན་ཐམས་ཅད་འཛིན་པ་ལ་རྣམ་པའི་ཏེ་བྲག་བཞིན་དུ་རིམ་པ་མ་ཡིན་པར་འགྱུར་བ་བརྗོག་པར་དགའོ། །རྒྱུ་རྣམ་པ་ཐམས་ཅད་དུ་འདུ་བའི་འབྲས་བུ་མི་འདུ་བ་ནི་མི་རིགས

115

ཏེ། རྒྱུ་མ་ཡིན་པར་འགྱུར་བར་སྟེར་བཞེད་ཅིན་ཏོ། །མགལ་མེའི་འཁོར་ལོ་མཐོང་བའི་དཔེ་ཡང་རྡུང་བ་མ་ཡིན་
ཏེ། འདི་ལྟར།

མགལ་མེ་ལ་ཡང་ཅིག་ཅར་དུ། །འཁོར་ལོར་སྟེར་བའི་འཁྱུལ་བ་འགྱུར། །
གསལ་བར་རབ་ཏུ་སྟེང་བའི་ཕྱིར། །མཐོང་བའི་མཚམས་སྟོར་མ་ཡིན་ནོ།། ༢༥ །།

མགལ་མེ་ལ་ཡང་འཁྱུལ་བ་ཡིས།
ཅིག་ཅར་འཁོར་ལོར་སྟེང་བར་འགྱུང་།
གསལ་བར་སོ་སོར་སྟེང་བའི་ཕྱིར།
མཐོང་བས་མཚམས་སྟོར་མ་ཡིན་ནོ། ། དེ་ལྟོན་ ༡༢༥༧

ཅི་གསལ་བར་སྟེང་བ་དང་དང་མཚམས་སྟོར་བ་ལ་འགལ་ལམ། འགལ་ཏེ།

འདི་ལྟར་མཚམས་རྣམས་སྟོར་བ་ནི། །དུན་བས་བྱེད་པ་ཉིད་ཡིན་གྱི། །
མཐོང་བས་མ་ཡིན་འདས་པ་ཡི། །ཡུལ་ལ་འཛིན་པ་མེད་ཕྱིར་རོ།། ༢༩ །།

འདི་ལྟར་མཚམས་རྣམས་སྟོར་བ་ནི། །དུན་བར་བྱེད་བས་སྟོར་ཡིན་གྱི།
མཐོང་བས་མིན་ཏེ་འདས་པ་ཡི། །ཡུལ་དང་འཛིན་པ་མེད་ཕྱིར་རོ། ། དེ་ལྟོན་ ༡༢༥༧

དུན་པ་ནི་ཡུལ་དུ་བྱས་པ་ཉིད་མཚམས་སྟོར་ཏེ། མ་ཟིན་པ་ལ་ནི་མཚམས་སྟོར་བ་མི་ནུས་པའི་ཕྱིར་རོ། །དེས་
ཅིར་འགྱུར་སྙམས་པ།

དེ་ཡི་ཡུལ་དུ་གང་གྱུར་པ། །དེ་ནི་ཞིག་བས་གསལ་མ་ཡིན། །
དེའི་ཕྱིར་འཁོར་ལོར་སྟེང་བ་འདེ། །གསལ་བ་མ་ཡིན་འགྱུར་བའི་རིགས།། ༣༠ །།

དེ་ཡི་ཡུལ་དུ་གང་གྱུར་པ། །དེ་ནི་ཞིག་བས་གསལ་མ་ཡིན།
དེའི་ཕྱིར་འཁོར་ལོར་སྟེང་བ་འདེ། །གསལ་བ་མིན་པར་འགྱུར་བའི་ཕྱིར། ། དེ་ལྟོན་ ༡༢༥༥

དུན་པ་ནི་མཐུན་ན་འདུག་པའི་དངོས་པོ་ལ་ཡང་ཤིན་ཏུ་གསལ་བར་ཐོགས་པ་མ་ཡིན་ནོ། །དེའི་བདག་ཉིད་དུ་
གྱུར་པ་མགལ་མེའི་འཁོར་ལོ་མཐོང་བ་ཡང་དེ་བཞིན་དུ་འགྱུར་བའི་རིགས་ན། མགལ་མེ་ལ་ནི་འཁོར་ལོར་
གསལ་བར་སྟེང་བ་འདི་ཡང་སྟོང་རོ། །ཡུངྷུལའི་འདབ་མ་བརྒྱ་ཅིག་ཅར་ཕིགས་པར་ཤེས་གང་ཉིན་པ་དེ་
ཡང་གསལ་བར་སྟེང་བ་མ་ཡིན་ནོ། །ཅིག་ཅར་ཕིགས་སོ། །སྐྲ་མ་ལ་ནི་ཚོ་ཚ་མའི་གཤོད་པ་ཡང་ཡོད་པའི་
ཕྱིར་དེ་ལ་ཅིག་ཅར་ཡང་མ་ཡིན་པར་གསས་པར་རིགས་ཏེ། ཞིབ་པ་ཇེ་གའུའི་པ་ཤེས་རབ་ཀྱི་མིག་དང་ལྡན་པ་
དགའ་ནི་དེ་ལ་རིམ་དུ་དེས་པར་བྱེད་ཏོ། །མང་པོ་དག་བྱེད་པ་གཅིག་པ་གཅིག་གིས་འབིགས་པ་གང་ཡིན་པ་དེ་
ནི་རིམ་གྱིས་འགྱུར་ཏེ། དཔེར་ན་ཟངས་ཀྱི་སྣྱིགས་མ་ལ་སོགས་པ་ལྟ་བུ་སྟེ། །ཡུངྷུལའི་འདབ་མ་མང་པོ་

འབིགས་པ་འདི་ཡང་མིའི་བྱེད་པ་གཅིག་གིས་བྱས་པས་རྟེས་སུ་དཔོག་གོ །གང་དག་རིགས་མ་ཐུན་པའི་ཤེས་པ་
རྣམས་ཀྱང་རྣམ་པའི་གྱངས་བཞིན་དུ་རེ་མོའི་གནི་ལ་སོགས་པ་ལ་ལྟར་ཅིག་ཏུ་མང་དུ་འབྱུང་སྟེ། གསུམས་དང་
སྐྱ་དང་ལ་སོགས་པའི་ཤེས་པ་རིགས་མི་མཐུན་པ་བཞིན་ནོ་སྣམ་དུ་སེམས་པ་དེ་དག་གི་ལུགས་བསྟུན་པར་
བྱའོ །

དེ་མོ་གཞི་རྣམས་མཐོང་བའི་ཚེ། །དེ་ལ་དེ་བཞིན་སེམས་མང་པོ།

དི་སྟེ་གཅིགགའི་རྒྱལ་གྱིས་སུ། །འབྱུང་བར་འགྱུར་བ་འདོད་ན་གོ། ༣༢ །།
གལ་ཏེ་དེ་ལྟ་ན།

དེ་ལྟ་ཡིན་ན་དགར་ལ་སོགས། །རྣམ་པ་སྣ་གཅིག་ཤེས་པ་ཡང་།

ཐོག་མ་དབུས་མཐའ་བ་དང་བས། །དམིགས་པ་སྣ་ཚོགས་ཉིད་དུ་འགྱུར།། ༣༣ །།
དི་ལྟར་སྟོན་པོ་དང་། དགར་པོ་ལ་སོགས་པ་རྣམས་པ་མང་པོ་དེ་བཞིན་དུ་གཅིག་ཕྱར་འདོད་པ་དགར་པོ་ལ་
སོགས་པ་ལ་ཡང་ཆུ་རོལ་དང་། ཕ་རོལ་དང་དབུས་ཀྱི་ཆའི་པོའི་རྣམ་པ་མང་པོ་ཉིད་དེ། དེ་ལ་ཡང་དེའི་
བདག་ཉིད་ཀྱི་ཤེས་པ་ཉིད་དུ་མ་ཉིད་དུ་འགྱུར་རོ །

དུ་མར་འདོད་དོ་ཞེ་ན། དོ་ན་གཅིག་ཕྱར་གྱུར་པ་གང་ཡིན། གང་ཡན་ལག་མེད་པའི་རྡུལ་གྱི་ཡུལ་འཛིན་པ་སྟེ།
ཡུལ་དེའི་ཡན་ལག་རྣམ་པར་དབྱེ་བར་ཟེས་པར་བྱེད་པ་ནི། ཤིན་དུ་ཞིབ་པའི་ཤེས་རབ་ཅན་རྣམས་ཀྱིས་ཀྱང་མི་
ནུས་སོ། །ལྟ་བ་དེ་ཡང་སྐྱོང་བ་མ་ཡིན་པར་བརྟོད་པ།

དུལ་ཕྲན་བདག་ཉིད་དགར་ལ་སོགས། །གཅིག་ཕུའི་བདག་ཉིད་ཆ་མེད་པ།

ཤེས་པ་གང་ལའང་སྣང་གྱུར་པར། །བདག་གིས་རབ་ཏུ་ཚོར་བ་མེད།། ༣༣ །།
བདག་གི་སེམས་རབ་ཏུ་བཏུད་ཀྱང་། ཚ་ཤས་ཐམས་ཅད་ཀྱིས་སྟོང་པའི་དུལ་མ་མཐོང་སྟེ། མ་མཐོང་བཞིན་དུ་
དེ་ཁས་བླངས་ཤིན་བདག་ལ་དི་ལྟར་བརྒྱ། ཏོག་པ་དང་ལྟན་པ་རྣམས་ཀྱིས་ཡོད་པར་ཁས་ལེན་པའི་རྒྱུ་ནི་
དམིགས་པ་ཡིན་ན། དེ་ནི་མེད་པས་རྡུ་བ་མ་ཡིན་ནོ །

གཞན་ཡང་བཅོས་མ་དང་བཅོས་མ་མ་ཡིན་པའི་ཕྱེ་མ་ལེབ་ཁྲ་བོ་ལ་སོགས་པ་ལ་ཇེ་ལྟར་གཅིག་ཕུའི་བདག་ཉིད་མ་
ཡིན་པ་དེ་བཞིན་དུ་རྣམ་པ་སྣ་ཚོགས་པའི་རྣམ་པར་ཤེས་པ་ཡང་གཅིག་ཕུའི་རང་བཞིན་དུ་གདགས་པར་མ་ཡིན་
པར་འཐད་པ་མེད་དོ །

དོན་སྨྲ་ཚོགས་མ་ཡིན་པའི་རྣམ་པར་ཤེས་པ་གང་ཡིན་པ་དེ་གཅིག་པུའི་རང་བཞིན་དུ་འགྱུར་རོ། །དེ་ཡང་དེ་ལྟར་མི་རུང་སྟེ། ཐམས་ཅད་ཀྱི་ལྟ་བ་རྣམས་ལ་ཡང་། དེ་ལ་སྨྲ་ཚོགས་སྣང་བས་ཡུལ་དུ་མ་ཡོད་དེ་འདི་ལྟར་རེ་ཞིག་རང་གི་སྟེ་པའི་ལུགས་ལས།

རྣམ་ཤེས་ཕྱི་ཡི་ཁམས་རྣམས་ནི། །བསགས་ལ་དམིགས་པའི་རྣམ་པ་ཡིན།

སེམས་དང་སེམས་བྱུང་དམིགས་པ་ནི། །དུག་པར་བཤད་པ་བྱེད་པ་ཡིན།། ༣༥ ॥

དབང་པོ་གཟུགས་ཅན་ལ་བརྟེན་པ་རྣམ་པར་ཤེས་པའི་ཁམས་ལྔའི་ཡུལ་ནི་རྡུལ་ཕྲ་རབ་དུ་མ་འདུས་པ་ཡིན་ལས། རྣམ་པ་དེ་སྟེད་ཀྱི་རྫས་སུ་འབྲེལ་པའི་སྨྲ་ཚོགས་ཉིད་ལས་མི་འདའ་དོ། །ཡིན་ཀྱི་རྣམ་པར་ཤེས་པ་ཡང་དེ་དང་དོན་མཐུན་ཏེ། དེ་དང་གྱུབ་པ་དང་བའི་བ་གཅིག་པའོ། །

ཚོས་ཀྱི་ཁམས་རྣམ་པར་རིག་བྱེད་མ་ཡིན་པ་དང་། འདུས་མ་བྱས་ཀུན་གྱི་མི་རིགས་པའི་ཕྱིར་ཚོར་བ་ལ་སོགས་པ་ལྔང་པོ་གསུམ་ཀྱི་བདག་ཉིད་དེ། དེ་ལ་དམིགས་པའི་ཡིད་ཀྱི་རྣམ་པར་ཤེས་པ་ཡང་སེམས་ལས་བྱུང་བ་འབའ་ཞིག་ལ་མི་འཇིན་གྱི། སེམས་དང་སེམས་ལས་བྱུང་བའི་ཚོགས་ལ་དམིགས་ཏེ། དེའི་གནས་སྟེད་ཀྱི་རྣམ་པ་དང་ལྟན་པའི་ཕྱིར་སྨྲ་ཚོགས་པ་ལས་མི་འདའ་དོ། །

གང་དག་བདེ་བར་བཤེགས་པའི་གསུང་རབ་ལེགས་པར་གསུངས་པ་འདི་ལས་ཕྱིར་རོལ་དུ་གནས་པ་གཟིགས་ཐན་དང་སེར་སྐྱ་ལ་སོགས་པའི་ལུགས་ལ་འཆལ་བ། འཁྲུལ་པའི་རྩ་ལ་སོགས་པ་དོན་གཅིག་གི་ཡུལ་ཤེས་པར་སྨྲ་བ་དེ་དག་གི་ལུགས་སྤྱར་ན། དོན་གཅིག་པུ་དེའི་རྣམ་པར་ཤེས་པའི་བདག་ཉིད་དུ་འཁྱལ་བ་མེད་དོ་ཞེ་ན། མི་རུང་སྟེ་འདི་ལྟར།

ཕྱི་གཞུང་རྣམས་ལ་འདང་རྣམ་ཤེས་ནི། །གཅིག་ཏུ་སྣང་བར་མི་འགྱུར་ཏེ།

ཡོན་ཏན་ལ་སོགས་ལྔར་པ་ཡི། །རྫས་ལ་སོགས་པར་དམིགས་ཕྱིར་རོ།། ༣༦ ॥

དེ་དག་ནི་གཞུགས་ལ་སོགས་པ་ཡོན་ཏན་རྣམས་དང་། བསྐྱེད་པ་ལ་སོགས་པ་ལས་རྣམས་དང་། ལག་པ་ལ་སོགས་རང་གི་ཡན་ལག་རྣམས་དང་། སྤྱི་ལ་སོགས་པ་དང་ལྔན་པའི་ལུས་ལ་སོགས་པའི་རྫས་ལ་དམིགས་སོ་ཞེས་སྨྲ་སྟེ། ཡོན་ཏན་ལ་སོགས་པ་ཡང་རྫས་ལ་སོགས་པ་དང་ལྟན་ནོ་ཞིའོ། །དེ་དག་གི་ལུགས་ལྟར་ན་ཡང་རྣམ་པར་ཤེས་པ་ལ་དོན་དུ་མ་སྣང་བ་ཉིད་དོ། །རྒྱལ་བ་པ་དང་། རྒྱལ་དཔོག་བ་རྣམས་ཀྱི་ལྟར་ན་ཡང་།

ཚོར་བུ་གཉི་ཡི་བདག་ཉིད་ལྟར། །དངོས་པོ་ཀུན་ཅེས་ལྟ་བ་ལ།

དེ་ལ་འཛིན་པའི་སེམས་ཀྱང་ནི། །གཅིག་བུའི་དོ་བོར་སྟང་མི་རིགས།། ༣༦ །།
དེ་དག་སྐྱབ་ནི།

དུ་མའི་དོ་བོའི་དངོས་པོ་ལ། །བརྟེན་པར་འདོད་པ་དོ་བོར་འདོད།
ཅིག་ཅའམ་རིམ་གྱིས་རྒྱལ་གཉིས་ལས། །ཚིག་གི་ཕྱ་བ་གཞན་མེད་དོ། །
དཔེར་ན་ཁྱུའི་ཁ་དོག་ལས། །ཇི་ལྟར་འདོད་བཞིན་ཁ་དོག་འཛིན།
དེ་བཞིན་དངོས་ལ་སྣ་ཚོགས་ཕྱིར། །ཐ་དད་ཐ་དད་མིན་པར་རྟོག །
ཅེས་ཟེར་རོ། །

ཡུལ་སྣ་ཚོགས་ལ་རྣམ་པར་ཤེས་པ་སྣ་ཚོགས་མ་ཡིན་པ་སྟང་བ་ནི་མི་རིགས་ཏེ། དེ་དག་དང་མཐུན་པར་མི་
འཇུག་པས་མི་འཛིན་པར་འགྱུར་བའི་ཕྱིར་རོ། སྤྱིའི་བླ་མའི་ལྟ་བའི་རྗེས་སུ་འབྲང་བ་ལ་སྨྲས་པ།

ས་ལ་སོགས་པ་འདུས་པ་ལ། །ཁྱུ་དང་དབང་པོ་ཀུན་འཛོག་པ།
སུ་འདོད་དེ་ཡི་ལྟགས་ལ་ཡང་། །དངོས་པོ་གཅིག་དང་མཐུན་འཛག་མེད།། ༣༡ །།
འདུས་པ་རྣམ་པར་གཞག་པའི་རྒྱུའི་འདུས་པ་ཅན་དུ་མ་ཡིན་པས་འདུས་པ་ལ་འཛིན་པའི་ཤེས་པ་ནི་གཅིག་དང་
མཐུན་པར་འཛག་པར་མི་རིགས་སོ། །

སེར་སྐྱའི་དབང་དུ་བྱས་ནས་སྨྲ་བ།

སྤྱིང་སྟོབས་ལ་སོགས་བདག་སྣ་སོགས། །ཕྱོགས་ལ་འང་དོན་གཅིག་སྟང་བ་ཅན།
ཤེས་པ་རིགས་པ་མ་ཡིན་ཏེ། །གསུམ་གྱི་བདག་ཉིད་ཡུལ་སྟང་ཕྱིར།། ༣༢ །།
ཅི་སྟེ་གསུམ་གྱི་བདག་ཉིད་ཁོ་ནར་ཡུལ་སྟང་བ་མ་ཡིན་གྱི། སྤྱིང་སྟོབས་ལ་སོགས་པ་གང་གི་ཤས་ཆེ་བ་དེ་
དམིགས་ཏེ་གཞན་ནི་མ་ཡིན་ནོ་ཞེ་ན། དེ་ཡང་དེ་ལྟར་མི་རུང་སྟེ། རིགས་དང་བསྐོམས་པའི་བྱེ་དྲག་གིས་སྣ་ལ་
སོགས་པ་གཅིག་ཁོ་ན་ལ་མང་པོ་དག་གི་གདུང་བ་དང་ཞུ་བ་ལ་དང་དགའ་བ་ལ་སོགས་པ་ལ་སྟོང་དོ། །
ཡོན་ཅན་གཉིས་ཀྱི་ཤས་ཆུན་ན་སྟོང་བ་འདི་ཇི་ལྟར་མངོན་སུམ་དུ་རབ་དུ་འགྱུབ། མི་སྟང་བ་ལ་སོགས་པའི་
དབང་གིས་ལྡག་མའི་དོ་བོ་མི་མཐོང་བར་འདོད་དོ་ཞེན། འདི་ཡང་ཉིན་ཏུ་མི་རིགས་པར་བརྗོད་པ།

དངོས་པོའི་དོ་བོ་རྣམ་གསུམ་ལ། །དེ་ནི་གལ་ཏེ་རྣམ་གཅིག་སྟེ།
དེ་དང་མི་མཐུན་སྟང་ན་གོ །དེ་ནི་དེར་འཛིན་ཇི་ལྟར་འདོད།། ༣༠ །།
དངོས་པོའི་དོ་བོ་རྣམ་གསུམ་པ། །དེ་ཡི་རིགས་པ་རྣམ་གཅིག་ཅན།

དེ་དང་མི་མཐུན་དེ་དག་ནི། །དེ་ལས་ཡང་དག་རེ་ལྷུར་རིགས། སོ་ དེ་ལྟོ་ནེ་ཉིད་ ༣༠ འདང་གནས་འདུའོ།

ཡུལ་རྗེ་ལྟར་གནས་པའི་རང་བཞིན་དང་མཐུན་པར་འདྲུག་ན་རྣམ་པར་ཤེས་པ་དམིགས་པ་འརྫོན་པར་འགྱུར་གྱི།
གནན་དུ་ན་དོན་གནན་བཞིན་དུ་ཡུལ་དུ་འརྫོད་པ་ཡང་ཡུལ་དུ་མི་འགྱུར་ཏེ། སྐྱུ་ལ་སོགས་པ་ནི་གསུམ་གྱི་རང་
བཞིན་ཡིན་ལ་རྣམ་པར་ཤེས་པ་ནི་གཅིག་གི་ངོ་བོ་དང་མཐུན་པར་འདྲུག་སྟེ་དེ་དང་མཐུན་པར་མི་འདྲུག་པའི་
ཕྱིར་རོ། །

གསན་པ་ལ་གདད་དག །

ཕྱི་རོལ་ཡུལ་རྣམས་མེད་པར་ཡང་། །སྐུ་ཚོགས་སྣང་ལ་དགག་པ་སྟེ།
ཅིག་ཅའམ་རྗེ་སྟེ་རིམ་འབྱུང་བའི། །རྣམ་ཤེས་རྡུང་བར་ཤིན་ཏུ་དགགས། ༣༠ །

རྗེ་སྐྱད་བརྫོད་པ་དེ་དག་གི་ཕྱོགས་ལ་ཡང་སྐུ་ཚོགས་སུ་སྣུ་བ་ཉིད་དེ། འདི་ལྟར་སྟོན་ཕོ་དང་སེར་སྐྱའི་རྣམ་པ་དུ
མ་ཅིག་ཅར་སྣང་བའི་རྣམ་པར་ཤེས་པ་ནི་རྣམ་པ་དུ་མ་དག་དང་ཐ་དང་མ་ཡིན་པའི་ཕྱིར་རྣམ་པ་དེའི་རང་གི་ངོ་བོ
བཞིན་དུ་དུ་མར་འགྱུར་རོ། །རིམ་པ་ལ་ཡང་གསུབས་དང་སྐུ་ལ་སོགས་པར་སྣང་བ་ནི་གཅན་ཚོགས་དང་དའི
གཉིས་པོ་འདི་དག་ཉིད་ཀྱིས་དུ་མར་འགྱུར་བ་ལས་མི་འདའ་བ་ཉིད་དོ། །གནན་དུ་ན་འདི་གཉིས་གཅིག་ཏུ་རྗེ་
ལྷར་བརྫོད་དེ་ཉེས་པ་ལྱ་སྨ་བཞིན་ནོ། །རིམ་གྱི་ཕྱོགས་ལ་ཉེས་པ་གནན་འདི་ཡང་ཡོད་དེ། རྣམ་པ་གཅིག་རིག་
པར་འརྫོད་པ་ན་དེ་དག་རྣམ་པར་ཤེས་པ་ཐ་མི་དད་པའི་ཕྱིར་རྣམ་པར་ཤེས་པ་དེའི་རང་གི་ངོ་བོ་ལྟ་བུའམ།
འརྫོད་པའི་རྣམ་པར་ལྷ་བྱར་སྨ་དང་ཕྱི་མའི་རྣམ་པ་ཡང་རིག་པར་འགྱུར་ཏེ། དེ་གཉིས་ཀྱང་འདག་པའི་ཕྱིར་
རོ། །

ནམ་མཁའ་དང་སོ་སོར་བརྟགས་པས་འགོག་པ་ལ་སོགས་པ་གང་དག་ཀུན་རྫོབ་ཏུ་ཡོད་པར་བརྫོད་པ་དེ་དག
འརྫོན་པའི་ཤེས་པ་ནི་སྐུ་ཚོགས་སུ་སྣང་བ་མ་ཡིན་པར་འགྱུར་རོ་ཞིན། དེ་ལྟར་ཡང་མ་ཡིན་པར་བརྫོད་པ།
ནམ་མཁའ་ལ་སོགས་ཤེས་པ་རྣམས། །མིང་ཙམ་དུ་ནི་སྣང་བ་དག
ཡི་གེ་དུ་མ་སྣང་བའི་ཕྱིར། །སྐུ་ཚོགས་གསལ་བར་སྣང་བ་ཡིན།། ༣༡ །

རྣམ་ཤེས་སྐུ་ཚོགས་མི་སྣང་བ། །འདབའ་ཞིག་ཡོད་པར་བཤགས་ན་ཡང་།
ཚོན་ཀྱང་ཡང་དག་གཤམ་མི་རུང་། །མཚན་ཉིད་བཅས་ལ་གནོད་མཐོང་ཕྱིར།། ༣༢ །

མཚན་ཉིད་དང་ལྷན་པ་ལ་ནི་གནོད་པ་དམིགས་ཏེ། དེའི་མཚན་ཉིད་སྱུང་ཕྱུང་བའི་ཕྱིར་ཐམས་ཅད་དུ་དབགས་
མི་ཕྱིན་ཏེ། །དེ་ལྟར་ཐམས་ཅད་ཀྱི་ཕྱོགས་རྣམས་ལ་ཡང་།

དེའི་ཕྱིར་སྐྱེ་ཚོགས་སྐྱེང་བ་ཡི། །རྣམ་ཤེས་རྣམ་པ་ཀུན་ཏུ་གནས། །

དེ་ནི་རྣམ་པ་ཐ་དད་ལྷུར། །གཅིག་ཕུའི་བདག་ཉིད་མི་རིགས་སོ།། ༩༣ །།

སྐབས་ཀྱི་མཇུག་སྡུད་དོ། །འདིར་གཞུངས་པ།

སོར་མོ་ཚོགས་རྣམས་ལས་གཞན་མིན། །གཞན་མ་ཡིན་པ་ཡོང་མ་ཡིན། །

དེ་ལྟར་མ་གྲུབ་ཚོགས་སོགས་མེད། །དེ་ཕྱིར་ཚོགས་པ་ཙམ་ཡང་མེད། །

ཚོགས་པ་དང་ནི་བཅས་པ་ཡི། །སོར་མོ་ལ་སོགས་རྣམས་ཀྱིས་ནི། །

དངོས་པོ་ཐམས་ཅད་མེད་པར་བསྒྲུན། །ཚོགས་མ་གཏོགས་པའི་དངོས་ཕྱུ་མེད། །

དེ་ལྟར་དོན་གཅིག་ཤེས་བྱེད་པ། །བློའི་གང་དུ་བཏག་པར་བྱ། །

སེམས་བྱུང་ཚོགས་དང་བཅས་སེམས་ཀྱི། །དམིགས་པ་གཅིག་འདིར་ཇི་ལྟར་འགྱུར། །

རང་གི་སྟེ་བ་སེམས་ཙམ་གྱི་རྒྱལ་ལ་བརྟེན་པ་བློ་གྲོས་དཀར་བ་གང་དག་རྣམ་པར་ཤེས་པ་ནི་མཐུན་པའི་བག་ ཚགས་ཡོངས་སུ་སྨིན་པ་ལ་རག་ལས་ནས་འབྱུང་སྟེ། བྱུང་མ་ཐག་ཏུ་འཇིགས་པ་དང་དོན་དུ་ཚོར་བར་བྱ་བ་དང་ ཚོར་བ་པོའི་རྣམ་པ་མེད་དོ་ཞེས་སྨྲ་བ་དེ་དག་གི་ལུགས་ལ་དགོས་པ་བསུ་སྟེ།

ཇི་སྟེ་ཐོག་མ་མེད་རྒྱུད་ཀྱི། །བག་ཆགས་སྨིན་པས་སྐུལ་བ་ཡི། །

རྣམ་པ་དག་ནི་སྡུང་བ་ཡང་། །འོར་བས་སྐྱ་མའི་རང་བཞིན་འདུ།། ༩༩ །།

གཟུགས་ལ་སོགས་པའི་སྐྱེད་མཆེད་ཀྱི་དུལ་ཕྲ་རབ་རྣམས་དང་རྡུལ་དང་ཡོན་ཏན་ལ་སོགས་པ་མཚིག་དང་ མཆོག་མ་ཡིན་པའི་ལྟ་བའི་རྟེ་སུ་འབྱུང་བ་རྣམས་ཀྱིས་བརྟོད་པ་དག་མི་རིགས་པ་དང་ཚོར་བར་བྱ་བ་དང་ཚོར་ བ་པོའི་མཆན་ཉིད་དང་ཡང་ཐབ་ལ་བའི་ཕྱིར་དུ་ཟེའི་གྲོང་ཁྱེར་དང་། མགལ་མེ་འཁོར་ལོ་དང་། སྒྱུལ་བ་དང་། སྨི་ལམ་དང་། སྒྱུ་མ་དང་། ཆུ་ཟླ་ལྤ་བུ་ལོ་ན་སྟེ། དམིགས་པ་བདེན་པར་འདོད་པའི་ཤེས་པ་ལ་སྣང་བའི་རྣམ་ པ་འདི་དག་ཀུན་ཐོག་མ་མེད་པའི་སྲིད་པར་འབྱུང་བ་ཅན་དངོས་པོ་ལ་མཚོན་པར་ཞེན་པའི་བག་ཆགས་ཡོངས་སུ་ སྨིན་པའི་མཐུས་སྐུ་དོ། །

དེ་དག་འོན་ཀྱང་དེ་དག་གི །དངོས་དེ་ཡང་དག་ཉིད་དམ་ཅེ། །

འོན་ཏེ་མ་བརྟགས་གཅིག་པུ་ན། །དགའ་བར་བས་ལེན་འདི་བསམ་མོ།། ༩༥ །།

ལྱགས་འདི་ནི་ཚད་མ་དང་ལུང་ཉིད་ཀྱི་གཞལ་བས་ཤེས་པར་བྱ་བ་དང་། དངོགས་པ་ཅན་མཐའ་ཡས་པ་དག་

གི་མདོན་པར་ཞེན་པ་འདར་པའི་གཞེན་པོ་ཡང་ཡིན་པས་ཤེན་ཏུ་དགར་བ་སྟེ་འདི་ལྟར་རྟུལ་ཕྱུ་རབ་ལ་སོགས་པ་

ཡོད་པ་དག་དགག་པར་བྱེད་པ་ཆོར་བར་བྱ་བ་དང་ཆོར་བ་པོའི་མཆན་ཉིད་དང་འཁལ་བ་ཡང་སྟོན་པ་སྟར་

བཞད་པའི་ཚད་མ་ནི་ཆུལ་འདི་རབ་ཏུ་གཞལ་བར་བྱེད་པའོ། །ཆུལ་འདི་ནི་ཡུད་དང་ཕྱེན་པ་ཡང་ཡིན་ཏེ། ཡང་

གར་གཞིགས་པའི་མདོ་ལས།

ཐོག་མ་མེད་པའི་སྐྱོ་བསྐྱེད་པས། །སེམས་ནི་གཟུགས་བརྙན་ལྟ་བུ་སྟེ།

དོན་གྱི་རྣམ་པར་སྣང་ཡང་ནི། །ཡང་དག་ཏེ་བཞིན་དོན་མཐོང་མེད། །

གང་ཟག་སྐྱུད་དང་ཡུད་པོ་དང་། །རྒྱུན་དང་དེ་བཞིན་དུ་རྣམས་དང་།

གཙོ་བོ་དབང་ཕྱུག་བྱེད་པ་དག། སེམས་ཙམ་པོ་ལས་རྣམ་པར་བརྟགས། །

ལེའུ་གཞིས་པ། ཚིགས་བཅད་༡༢༡།

དོན་ཡོད་མ་ཡིན་སེམས་ཉིད་དེ། །ཕྱི་རོལ་དོན་མཐོང་ལོག་པ་ཡིན།

རིགས་པས་རྣམ་པར་བསྟན་ནས་ནི། །གཟུང་དང་འཛིན་པ་འགག་པར་འགྱུར། །

ལེའུ་བདུན་པ། ཚིགས་བཅད་༡༤༡། ༤༤

མ་གཞན་པ་དག་ཆུལ་འདི་ལ་བརྟེན་ནས་བདག་དང་བདག་གི་དང་གཟུང་བ་དང་འཛིན་པ་རབ་ཏུ་དཔྱེ་བ་བཅས་པ་

རྣམས་ལ་ཕྱིན་ཅི་ལོག་ཏུ་གྱུར་པ་རྣམས་སེལ་ཏོ། །འོན་ཀྱང་འདི་ལ་དཔྱད་པར་བྱ་བ་ཅུང་ཟད་འདི་ཡོད་དེ། ཅི་

རྣམ་པ་དེ་དག་དེ་ཁོ་ན་ཉིད་ཡིན་ནམ་འོན་ཏེ་གཟུགས་བརྟན་ལ་སོགས་པ་ལྟར་མ་བདགས་པ་གཅིག་པུན་ཉམས་

དགའ་བ་ཞིག་ཡིན།

གལ་ཏེ་ཡང་དག་རྣམ་པར་ཤེས། །དུ་མར་འགྱུར་རོ་ཡང་ན་ནི།

དེ་དག་གཅིག་འགྱུར་འགལ་ལྱན་པས། །གཉིན་མི་ཟ་བར་སོ་སོར་འགྱུར།། ༤༤ །།

ཡང་དག་པའི་རྣམ་པ་དང་ཐ་དད་པ་མ་ཡིན་པས་རྣམ་པའི་རང་གི་ངོ་བོ་བཞིན་དུ་རྣམ་པར་ཤེས་པ་དུ་མར་འགྱུར་

བའམ་ཡང་ན་རྣམ་པར་ཤེས་པ་གཅིག་པུ་དང་ཐ་མི་དད་པས་རྣམ་པ་རྣམས་ཀྱང་རྣམ་པར་ཤེས་པའི་རང་གི་ངོ་བོ་

བཞིན་དུ་གཅིག་པུ་ཉིད་དུ་འགྱུར་བ་བཟློག་པར་དགའོ། །འགལ་བའི་ཚོས་གནས་པ་ཉིད་པས་དོང་དག་པར་ན་

རྣམ་པ་དང་རྣམ་པར་ཤེས་པ་ཉིད་ཐ་དད་ཉིད་དུ་འགྱུར་རོ། །

ཉེས་པ་གཞན་ཡང་བརྗོད་པ།

རྣམ་པ་ཐ་དད་མ་ཡིན་ན། །གཡོ་དང་མི་གཡོ་ལ་སོགས་པ། །

གཅིག་གིས་ཁྱབས་ཅད་གཡོ་ལ་སོགས། །ཐལ་བར་འགྱུར་ཏེ་ཡིན་གད་དག །ༀ༔ །།

ཐ་དད་པ་མ་ཡིན་ཞེས་བྱ་ནི་དེ་ཉིད་ཡིན་ནོ་ཞེས་བསྟན་པར་འགྱུར་རོ། །དེ་བས་ན་གལ་ཏེ་རྣམ་པ་གཅིག་གཡོ་བ་ལ་སོགས་པའི་བྱེད་པ་ཟིན་ཏམ། སེར་པོ་ལ་སོགས་པའི་བདག་ཉིད་དུ་གྱུར་ན་ལྷག་མ་རྣམས་ཀྱང་རྣམ་པ་དེ་ལྟ་བུར་འགྱུར་རོ། །ཐལ་བ་འདི་ནི་ཕྱི་རོལ་གྱི་དོན་གྱི་ཕྱོགས་ཡང་རྣམ་པ་དང་མཚན་པའི་ཞེས་པ་ལས་ཞེན་ན་མཆོངས་པ་རབ་ཏུ་སྟོན་ཏེ།

ཕྱི་རོལ་དོན་གྱི་ཆུལ་ལ་ཡང༌། །དེ་ལྟར་རྣམ་པ་མ་གྲུབ་ན།

གཅིག་གི་ཚོས་སུ་ཐམས་ཅད་ཀྱང༌། །འདུག་པར་འགྱུར་བ་བཟློག་པ་མེད།། ༠༩ །།

མི་མཐུན་པའི་ཚོས་སུ་གནས་ན་ནི་དེ་ཉིད་ངེས་པར་ཐ་དད་པར་འགྱུར་རོ། །གང་དག་བདེ་བ་ལ་སོགས་པ་ལྷར་སྟོན་པོ་ལ་སོགས་པའི་རྣམ་པ་རྣམས་ཀྱང་སྟོང་པའི་བདག་ཉིད་ཁོ་ན་སྟེ་ཞེས་པ་དེ་དག་ནི་མེད་ལ་དེ་དག་ཀུན་རིགས་མཐུན་པ་ལ་དུ་སྒྲུ་སྟེ། རིགས་མི་མཐུན་པའི་ཞེས་པ་བཞིན་དུ་འབྱུང་དོ་ཞེས་སྐྱ་བ་དེ་དག་གི་ནི་གང་ཟག་ཕྱི་མེད་པར་སེམས་གཉིས་འབྱུང་བ་འདི་ནི་གནས་མ་ཡིན་ཏེ་གོ་སྐབས་མེད་དོ་ཞེས་བྱ་བ་དང༌། དེ་བཞིན་དུ་སེམས་ཅན་ཐམས་ཅད་ནི་རྣམ་པར་ཞེས་པ་རྒྱུད་གཅིག་པའི་ཞེས་བྱ་བའི་ཡུང་དང་འགལ་བ་བཟློག་པར་དགའོ། །རྣམ་པར་སྨིན་པའི་རྣམ་པར་ཞེས་པའི་དབང་དུ་མཛད་དེ། །དེ་སྐད་གསུངས་པར་མཛད་དོ་ཞེན། གལ་ཏེ་དེ་ལྟར་ན་འདི་ནི་སྟོང་གི་སྟོབ་དཔོན་གྱི་ཆུལ།

དེ་རྣམས་རིགས་མཐུན་པ་ཉིད་ལས། །ཞེས་པ་ངེས་པར་གྱུར་པ་ཡིན། །

འདི་ལྟར་རྣམ་པར་རྟོག་པ་རྣམས། །རིམ་གྱིས་འབྱུང་བར་ཡང་དག་རྟོགས། །

ཞེས་བྱ་བ་དང་འགལ་ལོ། །དེའི་ཚེ་མི་མཐུན་པའི་ཕྱོགས་དང་གཉེན་པོའི་སེམས་ཀྱི་དབང་དུ་མཛད་ནས་སེམས་གཉིས་སྐྱེན་ཆིག་འབྱུང་བ་བཀག་པ་སྟེ། རིགས་པས་ཞིན་ཏུ་གསལ་བར་ཁོ་བོ་དེ་སྐྱེ་དུ་སྐྱེའོ། །གཅིག་ཅེས་བྱ་བའི་སྐྲ་ནི་འབའ་ཞིག་ཅེས་བྱ་བའི་རྣམ་གྲངས་སུ་གཏོགས་པ་ཡིན་གྱི་དེ་གྲག་གི་ཚིག་ནི་མ་ཡིན་ཏེ། དེ་དག་ལ་བདག་དང་བདག་གི་དང་གཟུང་བ་དང་འཛིན་པ་ལ་སོགས་པ་དང་ཐལ་བའི་སེམས་ཉིད་ཡོད་ཀྱི་གཞན་ནི་ཙ་ཡང་མེད་དོ་ཞེས་བསྟན་པར་འགྱུར་རོ། །

དེ་བས་ན་རྣམ་པར་སྐྱེན་པའི་རྣམ་པར་ཤེས་པ་ཁྱད་དང་ལྡོང་ས་སྟོང་དང་གནས་སུ་སྲུང་བའི་རྣམ་པ་ཐ་དད་དང་པས་
ཐ་དད་པར་ཐལ་བར་འགྱུར་གྱི་གནོད་པ་ནི་ཅི་ཡང་མི་སྐྱེད་དོ། །

ཅི་ལྱགས་འདི་སྐྲ་མེད་པ་ཡིན་ནམ། མ་ཡིན་པར་བརྗོད་པ།

ཇི་སྟེ་རྣམ་པའི་གྲངས་བཞིན་དུ། །རྣམ་པར་ཤེས་པ་ཁས་ལེན་ན།

དེའི་ཚེ་དུལ་ཕྲན་འདུར་འགྱུར་བ། དཔྱོད་པ་འདི་ལ་བརྟིག་པར་དགའ།། ༩༢ །།

གལ་ཏེ་བར་མེད་པར་གནས་པའི་དུལ་ཕྲ་རབ་ཀྱི་རོ་བོ་རྣམས་སྣར་རིགས་མཐུན་པའི་རྣམ་པ་ར་ཤེས་པ་མང་པོ་
འདི་དག་ཀྱིང་འབྱུང་ན། དེའི་ཚེ་དུལ་ཕྲ་རབ་ལ་དཔྱད་ཅི་འབྱུང་བ་སྣར་ཐུས་པ་དེ་འདུ་བ་ཉིད་རྣམ་པར་ཤེས་པ་
རྣམས་ལ་བརྗོག་པར་དགའ་བར་འགྱུར་ཏེ། འདི་ལྟར་དགས་སུ་འདོད་པའི་རྣམ་པར་ཤེས་པ་དུལ་ཀྱིས་བསྐོར་
བ་ལྟ་བུར་འདོད་པ་གང་ཡིན་པ་དེའི་རང་བཞིན་གང་གིས་གཅིག་ལ་མདོན་པར་ཕྱོགས་པ་དེ་ཉིད་ཀྱི་ཅི་གཞན་
ལ་ཡང་ཕྱོགས་སམ་འོན་ཏེ་གཞན་གྱི་ཕྱོགས་ཤེས་རྣམ་པར་དོག་པའི་ཉེས་པ་དེ་ཉིད་དོ། །

བར་མེད་པར་རིགས་གཅིག་པའི་དུལ་དུ་མ་འཛིན་པ་ན་རགས་པ་གོང་བུ་གཅིག་ཏུ་འབྱུལ་པ་དང་བར་མེད་པར་
དུ་མ་སྐྱིང་བའི་བདག་ཉིད་སྟོན་པོ་ལ་སོགས་པ་རིག་པ་ལ་གཅིག་ཏུ་ཤེས་བྱ་བ་འདི་ལ་ཇེ་བྲག་ཅི་ཡོད་དེ། སྟོན་
པོ་ལ་སོགས་པ་ལ་བར་མེད་པར་སྣང་བ་དེ་ཉིད་ཁ་ཅིག་དུལ་ཕྲ་རབ་ཀྱི་བདག་ཉིད་དུ་ཁས་ལེན། གཞན་ཉི་རིག་
པའི་རོ་བོ་ཞེས་ཟེར་བ་སྐྱེན་མཆུངས་པ་ཉིད་ལས་མི་འདའ། །

གང་དུ་ནོར་བུ་གཇི་ཟ་བཞིན་དུ་རྣམ་པར་ཤེས་པ་གཅིག་བོ་ནས་སྣ་ཚོགས་ཀྱི་རོ་བོར་སྣང་སོ་ཞེས་བྱ་བ་དེ་དག་གི་
ལྱགས་ལ་དགོས་པ་བརྗོད་པ།

གལ་ཏེ་སྣ་ཚོགས་དེ་གཅིག་ན། །རམ་མཁའི་གོས་ཅན་ལྱགས་སམ་ཅི།
འདི་ནི་རམ་མཁའི་གོས་འཆད་པའི་ལྟ་བ། །དུ་མའི་རོ་བོ་དངས་པོ་ལ། བརྟེད་པར་འདོད་པས་རོ་བོར་
འདོད། །གཅིག་ཅམ་རིམ་གྱིས་ཆུལ་གཉིས་ལས། ཚོག་གི་བྱ་བ་གཞན་མེད་དོ། །ཞེས་བྱ་བ་ལ་དེ་ལ་བརྟེན་
ཏམ། དེ་ལྟའི་ཞེ་ན། དེ་ཡང་རིགས་པ་མ་ཡིན་ཏེ།

སྣ་ཚོགས་གཅིག་པའི་རང་བཞིན་མིན། །རིན་ཆེན་སྣ་ཚོགས་ལ་སོགས་འདུ།། ༥༠ །།

སྣ་ཚོགས་གང་ཡང་དེ་གཅིག་མིན།
སྣ་ཚོགས་རིགས་ཀྱི་རིན་ཆེན་བཞིན། །དེ་པོན་ ༡༧༢༢

སྐུ་ཚོགས་ཞེས་བྱ་བ་ནི་རྣམ་པ་ཐ་དད་པ་ལ་བྱ་སྟེ། དེ་ནི་ཡང་དག་པར་ན་གཅིག་གི་རང་བཞིན་དང་འགལ་
ལོ། །རྣམ་པ་དེ་དག་ཏེ་སྟེང་པར་རང་བཞིན་དེ་སྟེད་དེ། རང་བཞིན་ཐ་དད་པའི་མཚན་ཉིད་ནི་དངོས་པོ་ཐ་དད་
པའོ། །

སྐུ་ཚོགས་གཅིག་པའི་རང་བཞིན་ན། །སྐུ་ཚོགས་དོ་བོར་སྐྱང་བ་དང་།

བསྐྲིབས་དང་མ་བསྐྲིབས་ལ་སོགས་པ། །ཐ་དད་དེ་ནི་ཇི་ལྟར་འགྱུར།། ༥༡ །།
རིན་པོ་གཟི་ལ་སོགས་པ་ལ་སྐུ་ཚོགས་ཀྱི་དོ་བོ་གཅིག་པའི་བདག་ཉིད་དུ་གྱུར་ན་རྣམ་པ་ཐ་དད་པའི་རྣམ་པ་སྐྱང་
བ་དང་འགལ་ལོ། །དེ་ནི། རྣམ་པ་ཐ་དད་པའི་བདག་ཉིད་དུ་འཁྱུལ་པ་མེད་དེ། རིན་པོ་ཆེའི་རྣམ་པ་དང་
མཚུངས་སོ། །ཐ་དད་པ་མེད་པའི་ཕྱིར་གཅིག་བསྐྲིབས་པས་ཐམས་ཅད་བསྐྲིབས་པར་ཡང་འགྱུར་རོ། །དེ་
བཞིན་དུ་གཅིག་རྟོགས་པས་ཐམས་ཅད་རྟོགས་པ་ལ་སོགས་པར་འགྱུར་རོ། །

ཇི་སྟེ་དོ་བོ་ཉིད་དུ་དེའི། །རྣམ་པ་འདི་དག་མེད་པ་སྟེ།

ཡང་དག་ཏུ་ན་རྣམ་མེད་པའི། །རྣམ་པར་ཤེས་པས་ནོར་བས་སྐུང་།། ༥༢ །།
རྣམ་པར་ཤེས་པ་དེ་ནི་དོན་དམ་པར་ན་ཤེས་ལ་སྐྱོང་དག་པ་ལྟ་བུ་སྟེ། སྟོན་པོ་ལ་སོགས་པའི་རྣམ་པ་ཇི་ཉག་ཏུ་
གྱུར་པ་མ་ཡིན་ན། དེ་ལྟ་བུ་དེ་ལ་ཡང་ཕོག་མ་མེད་པའི་དུས་ཀྱི་ཕྱིན་ཅི་ལོག་གི་བག་ཆགས་སྨིན་པའི་མཐུས་རྣམ་
པ་རྣམས་སྐྱང་སྟེ་སྐྱགས་ལ་སོགས་པས་དགུགས་པའི་མིག་ཅན་རྣམས་ལ་འཛིམ་པའི་དུ་བུ་ལ་སོགས་པ་ར་དང་
གུང་པོ་ཆེ་ལ་སོགས་པར་སྐྱང་བ་བཞིན་ནོ་ཞེའོ། །

གལ་ཏེ་མེད་ན་ཇི་ལྟ་བུར། །དི་དག་འདི་ལྟར་གསལ་བར་ཚོར།
དེ་ཡི་དངོས་ལས་ཐ་དད་པའི། །ཤེས་པ་དེ་འདྲ་མ་ཡིན་ནོ།། ༥༣ །།
དེ་པོན་ཉིད་དུ་དེ་དག་མེད་གྱང་ཞིན་ཏུ་གསལ་བར་ཤེས་པར་མི་འཐད་པ་ཅི་ཡོད་ཅེ་ན། སྨྲས་པ།
འདི་ལྟར་གང་ལ་དངོས་གང་མེད། །དེ་ལ་དེ་ཤེས་ཡོད་མ་ཡིན།
བདེ་བ་མིན་ལ་བདེ་སོགས་དང་། །དཀར་བ་རྣམས་ལ་འདང་མི་དཀར་བཞིན།། ༥༤ །།
འདི་ལས་བསྐྱབ་པར་བྱ་བའི་ཚོར་ལས་བརྟོག་པ་ལ་དང་སྐྱབ་པའི་ཚོར་འགལ་བ་ཅི་ཞིག་ཡོད་ན། འདི་ལྟར་མི་
མཐུན་པའི་ཕྱོགས་ལས་ལྡོག་པ་ལ་སོ་སོའི་སྐྱབས་མེད་པར་འགྱུར་རོ་ཞེན། སྨྲས་པ།
རྣམ་པ་འདི་ལ་ཤེས་པའི་དོན། །དངོས་སུ་འབད་པ་མ་ཡིན་ཏེ།

ཤེས་པའི་བདག་དང་བྲལ་བའི་ཕྱིར། །ནམ་མཁའི་མེ་ཏོག་ལ་སོགས་བཞིན།། ༥༥ །།

རྣམ་པར་ཤེས་པ་ཞེས་པའི་དོ་བོ་མ་ཡིན་པའི་རང་བཞིན་དུ་གནས་པ་གང་ཡིན་དེ་བདགས་པ་མ་ཡིན་པར་
རིག་པའི་ཚིག་གི་དོན་ཡིན་ན། ནམ་མཁའི་མེ་ཏོག་ལྟ་བུ་སྟོན་པོ་ལ་སོགས་པའི་རྣམ་པ་དེ་ལྟ་བུ་ནི་རྣམ་པར་ཤེས་
པའི་དོ་བོ་དང་བྲལ་བའི་ཕྱིར་མི་སྲིད་དོ། །

མེད་པ་ཉམས་པ་མེད་པས་ན། །གཏགས་པ་འང་མི་རུང་དུ་དུ་བཞིན།
མེད་པ་བདག་སྐྱེ་ཤེས་སྐྱེད་པར། །ནུས་པ་རྩུང་བ་མ་ཡིན་ནོ།། ༥༦ །།

རང་སྟུང་བའི་རྣམ་པར་ཤེས་པ་བསྐྱེད་པའི་མཐུ་མེད་པའི་རྣམ་པ་ལ་ནི་གདགས་པ་ཙམ་དུ་ཡང་རིག་པའི་དོན་མི་
སྲིད་པ་ཉིད་དོ། །ཧྲ་རུ་མེད་པ་ནི་རང་སྟུང་བའི་རྣམ་པར་ཤེས་པ་བསྐྱེད་པར་མི་འགྱུར་ཏེ་རིག་ལ་གདགས་པའི་
ཀྱར་མི་འགྱུར་རོ། །འདི་གཞན་དུ་ཡང་འདིར་དགྱུད་པར་བྱ་སྟེ་རྣམ་པ་དེ།

གང་ཕྱིར་དེ་ཡོད་རེས་ཚོར་བར། །ཤེས་དང་འབྲེལ་པ་ཅི་ཞིག་ཡོད།
བདག་མེད་དེ་ཡི་བདག་ཉིད་དང་། །དེ་ལས་འབྱུང་བ་མ་ཡིན་ནོ།། ༥༧ །།

དེ་ནི་ཤེས་པའི་བདག་ཉིད་མ་ཡིན་ཏེ། ཤེས་པ་བཞིན་དུ་ཡོད་པའི་སྐྱོན་དུ་འགྱུར་བའམ་རྣམ་པ་བཞིན་དུ་རྣམ་
པར་ཤེས་པ་ཡང་མེད་པའི་སྐྱོན་དུ་འགྱུར་བའི་ཕྱིར་རོ། །མེད་པའི་དོ་བོ་དེ་ཤེས་པ་ལས་འབྱུང་བ་ཡང་མ་ཡིན་ཏེ།
བསྐྱེད་པར་བྱ་བའི་དོ་བོ་ཉིད་མེད་པའི་ཕྱིར་རོ། །དེ་ལས་བྱུང་ན་ཡང་ལྟ་ཕྱི་ཡོད་ལས་ཅིག་ཙར་དུ་རིག་པ་མེད་
པའི་སྐྱོན་དུ་ཡང་འགྱུར་ཏེ། འདི་ནི་རེ་ཞིག་བཤད་སྟོམས་སུ་བོར་རོ། །ཤེས་པ་དང་དུས་མཉམ་དུ་དམིགས་པའི་
རྣམ་པ། །

རྒྱུ་མེད་ན་ནི་གང་ཞིག་གིས། །རེས་འགའ་འཆུང་བ་འདི་རུ་འགྱུར།
རྒྱུ་དང་ལྷུན་ན་གང་ཞིག་གིས། །གཞན་གྱི་དབང་ལས་བརྫོག་པར་འགྱུར།། ༥༩ །།

རྣམ་པ་ནི་མེད་པ་ཉིད་ཀྱི་ཕྱིར། རྒྱུ་མེད་པ་ཉིད་དོ། །རྒྱུ་མེད་ན་རེས་འགའ་འཆུང་བར་མི་སྲིད་དེ། སྟོས་པ་མེད་
པ་ཉིད་ཀྱི་ཕྱིར་རོ། །ཅི་སྟེ་ཤེས་པ་འདི་འཆུང་དུ་འོང་ཞེས་པ་རྒྱུ་དང་ལྷུན་པར་ཁས་ལེན་ན་གལ་ཏེ་དེ་ལྟ་ཡོན་པར་
ཁས་བླངས་མ་ཐག་པ་མེད་ན་མི་འབྱུང་བའི་གཞན་གྱི་དབང་ཉིད་དུ་དེ་འགྱུར་བ་ལ་ཇེ་ལྟར་ལན་གདབ་པར་ནུས།
རྟེན་ཅིང་འབྲེལ་པར་འབྱུང་བ་ལས་གཞན་གྱི་དབང་དུ་ནི་གུད་ན་མེད་དོ། །རྒྱུན་ལས་འབྱུང་བའི་རང་བཞིན་
ལས་ཀྱང་ཡོད་པ་གཞན་མ་ཡིན་ནོ། །རྣམ་པ་མེད་པར་ཁས་ལེན་ན་ཤེས་པ་གཞན་ཡང་སྐྱུས་པ།

དེ་མེད་ན་ནི་ཤེས་དེ་ཡང་། །རྣམ་པ་མེད་པ་ཉིད་ཀྱིས་འགྱུར། །
ཤེས་སྟོང་དག་པ་འདུ་བ་ཡིན། །ཤེས་པ་རབ་ཏུ་ཚོར་བ་མེད།། ༥༩ ༎

མིག་ལ་སོགས་པའི་རྣམ་པར་ཤེས་པའི་རང་བཞིན་སྟོན་པོ་ལ་སོགས་པའི་རྣམ་པ་དང་བྲལ་བ་ནི་བར་བཞག་པས་
ཁ་སྐྱར་བ་མེད་པའི་ཤེས་སྟོང་ལྟ་བུའི་མི་དམིགས་སོ། །ནང་དང་ཕྱི་རོལ་དུ་གྱུར་པའི་རྣམ་པ་མེད་ན་སྟོབས་ཀྱིས་
འདི་འབའ་ཞིག་དམིགས་པར་འགྱུར་རོ། །སྲིག་རྒྱ་ལ་སོགས་པས་ཡེས་པ་མི་ཡིན་པར་ཡང་མི་འགྱུར་ཏེ།
བཀག་ཞིང་བཏག་པ་མཐུན་པའི་ཕྱིར་རོ། །

འདི་ནི་འཁྲུལ་པས་ཤེས་ཤེ་ན། །དེ་ཅི་འཁྲུལ་ལ་རག་ལས་སམ། །
དེ་ཡིས་མཐུ་ཡིས་བྱུང་ན་ནི། །དེ་ཡང་གཞན་གྱི་དབང་ཉིད་དོ།། ༦༠ ༎

དཔེར་ན་མིག་སེར་གྱི་ནད་ཀྱིས་བདག་པའི་མིག་ཅན་གྱིས་མེད་བཞིན་དུ་དུང་ལ་གསེར་གྱི་རྣམ་པ་ལྟ་བུ་རིག་པ་
བཞིན་དུ་འཁྲུལ་པའི་བག་ཆགས་ཀྱིས་དབང་གིས་མེད་ཀྱང་སེར་པོ་ལ་སོགས་པའི་རྣམ་པ་བདེན་པར་མཛིན་པར་
འདོད་ཅེའོ། །འདིར་ཡང་འདི་འཁྲུལ་པའི་བག་ཆགས་ལ་རག་ལས་པ་ཡིན་ནོ། །ཅི་ཞེས་བསམས་པར་བྱའོ། །
དེ་ལས་བྱུང་བའི་མཚན་ཉིད་ཀྱི་འབྲེལ་པ་ཡིན་ན་ནི། །དེ་ཉིད་རྟེན་ཅིང་འབྲེལ་པར་འབྱུང་བའི་ཕྱིར། གཞན་གྱི་
དབང་དུ་འགྱུར་རོ། །བག་ཆགས་ཀྱི་འབྲས་བུའི་བདག་ཉིད་འཁྲུལ་པ་ལ་འདེ་བདག་ཉིད་ཀྱི་མཚན་ཉིད་ཀྱིས་
འབྲེལ་པ་ཡིན་ན་ནི་འཁྲུལ་པ་བཞིན་དུ་གཞན་གྱི་དབང་ཉིད་དུ་འགྱུར་བ་བཟློག་པར་དཀའ་བར་འགྱུར་
རོ། །འདིས་ནི།

དཔེར་ན་ཐག་རིང་རྒྱུ་དང་ན། །རྐྱང་དུ་ཆེན་པོར་སྣང་བ་བཞིན།
ཞེས་བྱ་བ་ལ་སོགས་པས་ཕྱི་རོལ་གྱི་དོན་ལ་མངོན་པར་ཞེན་པས་དབང་མེད་པར་གྱུར་པའི་བློ་ཅན་ལ་རྣམ་པ་
མེད་ཀྱང་སྣང་རོ་ཞེས་སྨྲས་པའི་ལན་ཀྱང་བཏབ་ཟིན་ཏོ། །

དེ་བས་ན་དངོས་དང་གཅིག་ཤོས་ཀྱིས་རིག་པའི་དོན་མ་གྲུབ་པ་དང་འཁྲུལ་པའི་བག་ཆགས་ལ་སྟོབ་པོ་ལ་སོགས་
པའི་རྣམ་པ་མེད་པས་འབྲེལ་པ་མ་གྲུབ་པས (བརྩན་བ་དགེ་སྦྱང་)ཁ་ཅིག་ན་རེ།

རྣམ་ཤེས་རིག་པ་ཚམ་ཉིད་དེ། །བག་ཆགས་ཉེས་པས་དཀྲུགས་པས་ན།
སྟོན་པོ་ལ་སོགས་ཚོར་བ་ཡི། །རྣམ་པ་འབའ་ཞིག་སྐྱེ་བར་འགྱུར། །
དེ་ནི་སྐྱེ་སོགས་རྟོགས་པ་སྟེ། །སྐྱེ་ལ་སོགས་པའི་མཚན་ཉིད་མིན།

དེ་ནི་འཁྲུག་པ་སྐྱོངས་པའི་བདག །ཕྱི་རོལ་སྟེ་ལ་སོགས་པའི་སེམས། །

ཞེས་སྐྱ་བ་དེ་དག་གི་ལན་ཡང་བཏབ་ཟིན་ཏོ། །དེ་བས་ན་སྟོན་པོ་ལ་སོགས་པ་སོགས་པའི་རྣམ་པ་ནི་འབྲུལ་བ་

དང་དེའི་བག་ཆགས་དང་འདུལ་བར་མ་གྱུར་པས། དེ་ལོག་སྟེ་ཉིད་དུ་རྣམ་པར་དག་པའི་དུས་ན་ཡང་རྣམ་པ་

ཐམས་ཅད་སྤྱོག་པར་མི་རིགས་ཏེ།

འབྲེལ་པ་མེད་ན་གཅིག་ལོག་པས་གཞན་ཡང་སྤྱོག་པར་ངེས་པ་མེད་དེ། བ་ལང་དང་རྟ་ལ་སོགས་པ་བཞིན་

ནོ། །དཔེར་ན།

དངོས་པོ་གང་དང་གང་དབྱད་པ། །དེ་དང་དེ་ལ་གཅིག་ཉིད་མེད།

གང་ལ་གཅིག་ཉིད་ཡོད་མིན་པ། །དེ་ལ་དུ་མ་ཉིད་ཀྱང་མེད།། ༦༡ ॥

དེ་ལྟར་སྤྱོགས་རྣམས་ཐམས་ཅད་ལ། །བདག་ཉིད་གཅིག་པུ་ནི་མི་རིགས།
གཅིག་ནི་མ་གྲུབ་པ་ཡི་ཕྱིར། །དུ་མའི་རང་བཞིན་ཡང་མི་སྲིད། །   དེ་ལོན་ ༡༥༥

ཕ་རོལ་དང་བདག་གི་ལྟ་བའི་རྟེས་སུ་འབྲང་བ་དག་གིས་ཁས་བླངས་པ་ཏྟག་པ་དང་། མི་རྟག་པ་དང་། ཅིག་

ཤོས་དང་། རྡུལ་དང་། རགས་པ་དང་། ཤེས་བྱ་དང་། ཤེས་པ་ལ་སོགས་པ་སོ་སོར་ཕ་དང་པའི་དངོས་པོ་

གང་ལ་གཅིག་པུར་བདག་ན་དེ་ལེ་འི་ལྟར་བདག་གས་པ་དེའི་ཚོ། བདག་པའི་དུར་སྤྱི་བ་བརྟོ་པ་ལྟ་རབ་ཚམ་ཡང་

མེད་དོ། །གང་གཅིག་པའི་རང་བཞིན་མི་འཕད་དེ་དུ་མའི་བདག་ཉིད་དུ་ཁས་བླངས་པ་ནི་རིགས་པ་མ་ཡིན་

པ་ཉིད་དེ། འདི་ལྟར་དུ་མ་ནི་གཅིག་བསགས་པའི་མཚན་ཉིད་དོ། །གཅིག་མེད་ན་དེ་ཡང་མེད་དེ། ཤེར་ལ་

སོགས་པ་ལ་མེད་ན་ནགས་ཚལ་ལ་སོགས་པ་མེད་པ་བཞིན་ནོ། །དེའི་ཕྱིར།

དངོས་པོ་གང་དང་གང་བཏགས་པ། །དེ་དང་དེ་ལ་གཅིག་པ་མེད།
གང་ལ་གཅིག་པ་ཡོད་མིན་པ། །དེ་ལ་དུ་མའང་མེད་པ་ཡིན། །

ཞེས་གསུངས་སོ། །མདོ་དེ་ཉིད་ལས།

བློ་ཡིས་རྣམ་པར་གཞིགས་ནས་ནི། །ངོ་བོ་ཉིད་ནི་གཟུང་དུ་མེད།
དེ་ཕྱིར་དེ་དག་བརྗོད་མེད་དང་། །ངོ་བོ་ཉིད་ཀྱང་མེད་པར་བཤད། །   ཡང་གཤེགས ༡ ༡༡༦
བློ་ཡིས་རྣམ་པར་གཞིགས་ནས་ནི། །གཞན་དང་དང་མེད་ཅིང་བཏགས་པ་མེད།
གྲུབ་པའི་དངོས་པོ་ཡོད་མེད་ན། །བློ་ཡིས་དེ་ལྟར་རྣམ་པར་བཏགས། །   ཡང་གཤེགས ༡ ༡༡༦
རང་བཞིན་མེད་ཅིང་རྣམ་རིག་མེད། །དངོས་པོ་མེད་ཅིང་ཀུན་གཞི་མེད། །

རོ་མ་ཆུངས་ཀྱིས་པ་ཆོག་གི་པ། །འན་པ་རྣམས་ཀྱིས་འདི་དག་བརྟགས། ། ལུང་གཤེགས་ ༩ ༥༢

མཆན་མ་དངོས་པོ་རྣམ་རིག་དང་། །ཡིད་ཀྱི་གཡོ་བ་གང་ཡིན་ལས།

ང་ཡི་སྙས་རྣམས་རབ་འདས་ནས། །དེ་དག་རྣམ་པར་མི་རྟོག་སྟོང་། ། ལུང་གཤེགས་ ༩ ༥༣

ཅེས་གསུངས་སོ། །དེ་བས་ན་བློ་གྲོས་དཀར་པོ་རྣམས་ཀྱིས་དོན་འདི་ནི་དང་དེར་སློར་ཏེ།

གང་གིས་དངོས་རྣམས་རེ་བདག་ནས། །ཡང་དག་ཏུན་དངོས་དེ་མེད།

འདི་སླར་དེ་དག་གཅིག་པུ་དང་། །དུ་མའི་རང་བཞིན་ཡོད་མ་ཡིན།། རྣམ་འབྱེལ་མཚོན་ཤུམ་ལེའུ ༡༦༠

སྐུ་ཚོགས་དངོས་པོ་དོན་རྣམས་ལ། །གལ་ཏེ་གཅིག་ཉིད་མི་རིགས་ན།

དེ་བློ་སྐུ་ཚོགས་སྤྱང་བ་ཡང་། །ཇི་སླར་ཁྱར་ན་གཅིག་པུར་འགྱུར།། རྣམ་འབྱེལ་མཚོན་ཤུམ་ལེའུ ༡༠༢

མ་གཏས་པ་རྣམས་ཀྱིས་གང་གསུངས་པ། །དེ་ནི་གསལ་བར་འོས་པ་ཡིན།

ཇི་ལྟ་ཇི་ལྟར་དོན་བསམས་པ། །དེ་ལྟར་དེ་ལྟར་རྣམ་པར་འབྲལ།། རྣམ་འབྱེལ་མཚོན་ཤུམ་ལེའུ ༡༠༦

གནུང་དང་འཛིན་པའི་རྣམ་པ་ཡི། །ཕྱི་རོལ་མཆན་ཉིད་ཡོད་མ་ཡིན། ཚིག་རྐང་འདིའི་གཉིས་འདི་མེད

དེ་བས་མཆན་ཉིད་སྟོང་པའི་ཕྱིར། །རང་བཞིན་མེད་པ་བདུ་བཞུད།། རྣམ་འབྱེལ་མཚོན་ཤུམ་ལེའུ ༡༠༥

ཞེ་ནོ། །དེ་སླར་རིགས་པ་དང་ལུང་དང་ལུན་པའི་ཤེས་རབ་ཀྱིས་བརྟགས་ན། དངོས་པོ་མ་ལུས་པ་བཅུ་ཆལ་དུ་གཞིགས་ཏེ་གཅིག་པ་དང་དུ་མའི་རང་བཞིན་དང་བྲལ་བའི་གཏན་ཚིགས་གྲུབ་བོ། །

གཏན་ཚིགས་གྲུབ་ཏུ་ཟིན་ཀྱང་ཚེས་གཉིས་ཀ་དང་ལུན་པའི་པའི་མ་གྲུབ་པ་མ་ཡིན་ནམ། ཇི་སླར་ཞེ་ན། མེ་ལོང་གི་དོས་ལ་མིག་གི་འོད་རེར་ཕོག་ནས་སྣར་ཕོག་པས་རང་གི་བཞིན་ལ་སོགས་པ་དེ་སླར་དངོས་པའི་ཕྱིར་རོ། །ཡང་ན་མེ་ལོང་ལ་སོགས་པའི་ནང་དུ་ཤིན་ཏུ་དང་བའི་གཟུགས་གཞན་ཞིག་འབྱུང་བའི་ཕྱིར་རོ། །ཡང་ན་དངོས་པོའི་ནུས་པ་བསམ་ཀྱིས་མི་ཁྱབ་པའི་མཐུས་དེ་སླར་སྣང་བའི་རྣམ་པར་ཤེས་པ་ཚམ་འབྱུང་བའི་ཕྱིར་རོ། །གལ་ཏེ་དེ་སླར་ན་ཡང་དེ་མ་ལུས་པ་དཔུད་ཉིན་བས་ཡང་དབུང་བ་མི་རིགས་སོ། །

གཞན་ཡང་གལ་ཏེ་མེ་ལོང་གི་དོས་ལ་སོགས་པ་ལ་མིག་གི་འོད་རེར་ཕོག་ནས་སྣུར་ལོག་པ་ལ་རང་གི་བཞིན་ལ་སོགས་པ་དང་འབྲལ་བ་ལ་དེ་འཛིན་པའི་རྒྱུ་འགྱུར་ན། དེ་སླར་ན་མེ་ལོང་གི་དོས་བུད་ཕྱོགས་སུ་བ་བླུན་ན་གཟུགས་བཅན་ལྡོ་ཕྱོགས་སུ་བཞས་པ་མཐོང་བ་དང་། མེ་ལོང་གི་དོས་ཆུང་དུ་ལ་རང་གི་བཞིན་ཆེན་པའི་གཟུགས་བཅན་ཆུང་ངུར་སྣུང་བ་ཡང་མི་རིགས་པ་དང་། མེ་ལོང་གི་དོས་ཀྱི་ནང་དུ་ལོང་བར་སྣུང་བ་ཡང་མི་རིགས་པ་དང་། ཆུ་ཤུངས་པའི་མཚོ་དེའི་འགྲམ་ན་འདུག་པའི་རི་དང་ཤིང་གི་རྗེ་མོ་དང་ཡལ་ག་ཀྱིན་དུ་བཞུས་པ

མང་པོའི་གཟུགས་བརྐྱན་ཡལ་ག་དང་རྩེ་མོ་ཕྲ་དུ་བཤས་པར་དམིགས་པར་ཡང་མི་འགྱུར་ཏེ། དེ་བས་ན
གཟུགས་བརྐྱན་ཞེས་པ་དེ་དང་མི་འདྲ་བར་སྟང་བའི་ཕྱིར་རང་གི་བཞིན་ལ་སོགས་པ་འཛིན་པ་མ་ཡིན་ཏེ། སྐྱ་ལ
སོགས་པའི་ཤེས་པ་བཞིན་དུ་རྟེས་སུ་དཔག་པར་ནུས་སོ། །

གཟུགས་གཞན་འབྱུང་བ་ཡང་རིགས་པ་མ་ཡིན་པ་ཉིད་དེ། གཟུགས་རྣམས་ལྷན་ཅིག་མི་གནས་པའི་ཕྱིར་ཏེ
གཟུགས་བརྐྱན་རྣམས་ནི་མེ་ལོང་གི་དོས་ཀྱི་ཕྱོགས་དེ་ཉིད་ན་དམིགས་ལ། ལུས་ཅན་གྱི་དངོས་པོ་རྣམས་ནི
ཕྱོགས་མཚུངས་པར་ནམ་ཡང་མི་འགྱུར་ཏེ། དེ་དག་གཅིག་པུའི་བདག་ཉིད་དུ་འགྱུར་བའི་ཕྱིར་རོ། །དེར་སྣང
བའི་ཤེས་པ་ཚལ་ཡང་འབྱུང་བར་ཞད་དེ། དེ་ཕྱག་མེད་ན་དེ་སྣག་མ་རྣམས་ཀྱི་ཅིའི་ཕྱིར་མི་འདོད། འདི་ལྟར
དུལ་ཕྲ་རབ་རྣམས་དང་ཡས་ལགས་ཅན་རྣམས་མི་རིགས་པ་དང་། གཟུང་བའི་མཚན་ཉིད་དང་འགལ་བར་ཐལ་བས
ཅད་ཏེ་བར་སྡུར་བས་ཁྱབ་པ་གྲུབ་པའི་ཕྱིར་རོ། །

འདིས་སྐྱ་མ་དང་། སྐྲ་ལམ་དང་། སྨིག་རྒྱུ་དང་། དྲི་ཟའི་གྲོང་ཁྱེར་དང་། མགལ་མེའི་འཁོར་ལོ་ལ་སོགས
པའི་དཔེ་ཡང་བཤད་དོ། །དེ་ལ་འཛིན་པའི་དུས་བུ་ལ་སོགས་པ་ཡོད་དུ་ཟིན་ཀྱང་། དེ་སྐྱ་མ་ལ་སོགས་པར་མི
བཟོད་དེ། གང་གཟུང་པོ་ཆེ་ལ་སོགས་པའི་དེ་ལྟར་དམིགས་པ་དེ་ཉིད་དཔེ་ཕྱེ་ཀྱི། འཛིམ་པའི་དུས་བུ་ལ་སོགས
པ་ནི་དེ་ལྟར་དམིགས་པ་མ་ཡིན་ནོ། །ཞེས་བ་རྣམ་པ་དང་བཅས་པ་དང་། རྣམ་པ་མེད་པའི་ཕྱོགས་གཉི་ག་ལ
ཡང་གང་གི་དོ་བོར་སྣང་བ་དང་། རིག་པ་དེ་ཉིད་དམིགས་པ་ཡིན་གྱི་རྒྱུ་ཚན་ནི་མ་ཡིན་ཏེ། སྨིག་ལ་སོགས་པ
ལ་ཡང་ཐལ་བར་འགྱུར་བའི་ཕྱིར་རོ། །དེ་བས་ན།

སྐྱེ་བ་འདི་དང་གཞན་དང་ནི། །དུས་དེ་དང་ནི་དུས་གཞན་ན།
ཐམས་ཅད་དུ་ནི་ཕྱི་རོལ་དམིགས། །ཁྱལ་དང་དུས་གཞན་བདག་ཉིད་དོ། །
སྐྲ་ལམ་ཤེས་པའི་སྐྱོད་ཁྱལ་ནི། །ཁྱལ་དེ་དང་ནི་ཁྱལ་གཞན་ནོ།
མགལ་མེའི་འཁོར་ལོ་འཁལ་བ་ནི། །སྒྱུར་དུ་བསྒྱུར་བར་བྱུལ་པ་ཡིན། །
དྲི་ཟའི་གྲོང་ཁྱེར་སྐྱེན་རྣམས་དང་། །སོན་ཤེས་ཁྲིམ་ལ་སོགས་པ་ཡིན
སྐྱིག་རྒྱུ་ཡི་རྣམ་ཤེས་ལ། །དགོན་དུ་འོང་ཟེར་གདུངས་དེ་བཞིན། །

ཞེས་བུ་བ་ནི་གནས་མེད་དོ། །དེ་དག་རྒྱུ་ཉིད་ཡོང་ཀྱང་དམིགས་པ་ཉིད་དུ་མི་རིགས་ཏེ། རྒྱུའི་དོན་ཀྱང་གནས
ལ་དམིགས་པའི་དོན་ཀྱང་གནས་ཏེ། བཏད་མ་ཐག་ལས་རྒྱུ་ཆེར་མི་དགོས་སོ། །འདི་ཕྱོགས་དང་མཐུན་པའི

ཕྱོགས་ལ་ཡོད་པར་གྱུར་དུ་ཟིན་ཀྱང་མི་མཐུན་པའི་ཕྱོགས་ལས་ལྡོག་པར་རྗེ་ལྟར་རེས་ཏེ། གང་གིས་ན་ལྡོག་པ་
ལ་ཐེ་ཚོམ་གྱི་སྐྱོན་དུ་མི་འགྱུར་སྣམས་པའི་རེ་བ་འདི་ནི་བརྟན་པའོ། །དེ་བས་འདི་བརྗོད་དེ།

གཉིག་དང་དུ་མ་གཏོགས་པར། །རྣམ་པ་གཞན་དང་ལྡན་པ་ཡི།

དངོས་པོ་མི་རུང་འདི་གཉིས་ནི། །ཕན་ཚུན་སྤྱངས་ཏེ་གནས་ཕྱིར་རོ།། ⽷ ⽷

གཉིས་ཕུའི་བདག་ཉིད་དང་། དུ་མའི་བདག་ཉིད་ནི་ཕན་ཚུན་སྤྱངས་ཏེ་གནས་པའི་མཚན་ཉིད་ཡིན་པས་ཕུང་པོ་
གཞན་སེལ་ཏེ། དེ་བས་ན་རྣམ་པ་གཞན་དུ་གཤག་པའི་དངོས་པོ་མེད་པའི་ཕྱིར་འདི་ལ་ལྷོག་པ་མི་ལྷོག་པ་མེད་
དོ། །གཏན་ཚིགས་འདི་ལ་ནི་དམ་བཅའ་བའི་དོན་གྱི་ཕྱོགས་ཀྱི་གཉིག་ལ་ཡང་མེད་དེ། གྲུབ་པའི་ཡུལ་གྱིས་
ཡུལ་ཅན་ཤེས་པ་དང་། སྐྱ་དང་བ་སྐྱ་རྣམས་གྲུབ་པའི་ཕྱིར་ཏེ། དཔེར་ན་འདི་ནི་བ་གྱུང་སྟེ་ལྷོག་ཤལ་ལ་
སོགས་པ་འདུས་པའི་བདག་ཉིད་ཀྱི་ཕྱི་རོ་ཞེས་བྱ་བ་དང་འདར་རྗེ་སྐྱད་སྐྱམས་པའི་འཆང་ན་རྣམས་ཀྱིས།
གཉིག་དང་དུ་མའི་རང་བཞིན་དང་ཕྲལ་བར་བསྟན་དུ་ཟིན་ཀྱང་། གང་དག་ཕྱོག་མ་མེད་པའི་འཆོར་བ་ནས་ཕྱིར་
ཅི་ལྷོག་གཉིག་ནས་གཉིག་ཏུ་བརྒྱུད་དེ། དངོས་པོ་ལ་མངོན་པར་ཞེན་པས་ཡོངས་སུ་འཕེལ་བ་སྟང་བར་དགང་
བ་དང་། ཆུལ་བཞིན་ཡིད་ལ་བྱེད་པས་གོམས་པར་བྱེད་པའི་ཕྱིར་སྐྱང་དགང་བས་ཡང་དག་པར་ན་དངོས་པོ་
མཐའ་དག་ལ་ཁྱབ་པའི་རང་བཞིན་མེད་པ་དེས་པར་མི་སེམས་མི་བརྟོད་ཅིང་། གཞན་དག་ལ་ཡང་རེས་པར་
བསྐྲེ་པར་འདོད་པས་ཐ་སྐྱད་འདོགས་པར་མི་བྱེད་པ་འདི་དེ་ལྟར་ཤེས་པ་དང་སྐྱ་དང་བ་སྐྱ་ཀྱི་ཡུལ་ཉིད་དུ་
བསྐྱབ་སྟེ། དམིགས་སུ་ཡོད་པའི་མཚན་ཉིད་དུ་གྱུར་པ་ལས་མི་དམིགས་པས་མེད་ཅེས་བྱ་བ་ལྟ་བུའོ། །
འདི་ཐམས་ཅད་ནི་བཙོམ་ལྡན་འདས་ཉིད་ཀྱིས་ཀྱང་གསུངས་ཏེ། ཡབ་དང་སྲས་མཇལ་བའི་མདོ་ལས་ཀྱང་།
འདི་སྐད་དུ།

མེ་ལོང་ཤིན་ཏུ་ཡོངས་དག་ལ། །ཇི་ལྟར་རང་བཞིན་མེད་པ་ཡི།

གཟུགས་བརྙན་སྣང་བ་དེ་བཞིན་དུ། །སྟོན་པ་ཚོམས་འདི་ཤེས་པར་གྱིས། །

ང་ཡིས་རང་བཞིན་སྟོང་པ་ཞེས། །གང་བཤད་སྟོང་པར་བཤ་བར་གྱིས།

བྱིས་པ་ལོག་པའི་བློ་ཅན་རྣམས། །རང་བཞིན་སྟོང་པ་མི་ཤེས་པ། །

དེ་དག་རྣམས་ལ་བསྟན་པའི་ཕྱིར། །རང་བཞིན་སྟོང་ཞེས་བདེ་གཤེགས་སྟོན།

ཀུན་ཏུ་རྟོག་ལས་རྟོག་པ་བསྐྱེད། །ཡང་དག་མ་ཡིན་རྟོག་ལས་བཅིངས། །

131

ཞེས་གསུངས་པ་ལྟ་བུའོ། །ལྡང་ཀྲུར་གཤེགས་པའི་མདོ་ལས་ཀྱང་།

གཅིག་དང་གཉེན་ཉིད་སྤངས་པ་ཡིས། །ཁྲུགས་ནི་རི་རྩེ་སྨེ་ལོང་ལ།

སྣང་ཡང་དེ་ན་ཡོད་མ་ཡིན། །དེ་བཞིན་དངོས་པོའི་རོ་བོ་ཉིད། ། ༡༠ ༣༠༩

ཅེས་བསྟན་ཏོ། །གང་གི་ཕྱིར་དེ་དེ་ལྟར་གྱུར་པ།

དེའི་ཕྱིར་དངོས་པོ་འདི་དག་ནི། །ཀུན་རྫོབ་ལོ་འདི་མཚན་ཉིད་འཛིན།

གལ་ཏེ་འདི་བདག་རོན་འདོད་ན། །དེ་ལ་བདག་གིས་ཅི་ཞིག་བྱ། ༦༣ ༎

ཇི་སྐྱེད་བཤད་རིགས་པ་དག་གིས། དངོས་པོ་ཐམས་ཅད་ནི་བདག་མི་བརྟོག་པའི་ཕྱིར་མ་བརྟགས་ན་ཉམས་དགའ་བ་ལོའའི་བདག་ཉིད་དུ་འཛིན་ཏེ། སྐྱུ་མའི་གྲུང་པོ་ཆེ་དང་དུ་དང་མི་ལ་སོགས་པ་བཞིན་ནོ། །གལ་ཏེ་རྣམ་པ་དེ་ལྟར་གཞན་གྱིས་མ་བཅོས་པའི་དངོས་པོ་ཐམས་ཅད་རོ་བོ་རེས་པར་འཛིན་པར་འདོད་ན་དེ་ལ་བོ་བོས་དགག་ཏུ་ཅི་ཡོད། དེ་དག་གིས་དངོས་པོའི་རོ་བོ་འདི་བདག་ཉིད་ཀྱིས་རང་གིར་བྱས་ཀྱི། འདི་ནི་སུ་དག་གིས་ཀྱང་ལྤགས་ཀྱུ་མེད་པའི་འདོད་པས་འདི་དག་ལ་གཤག་པ་མེད་དོ། །

ཇི་ལྟར་གསེན་པའི་དངོས་པོའི་དེ་ལོ་ན་ལ་མཁས་པའི་དེ་བཞིན་གཤེགས་པ་རྣམས་ཀྱིས་དེ་དང་དེ་དག་ཏུ་རབ་ཏུ་བཤད་དེ། ཚོས་ཐམས་ཅད་ཡང་དག་པར་སྣང་ལ་ལས་ཇི་སྐྱེད་དུ། བྱང་ཆུབ་སེམས་དཔའི་བཞིན་གཤེགས་པ་དག་བཅོས་པ་ཡང་དག་པར་རྟོགས་པའི་སངས་རྒྱས་རྣམས་ཀྱིས་ཆ་སྤྱད་དུ་སྟོན་པ་བཅུར་ཁོང་དུ་ཆུད་པར་བྱ་སྟེ། བཅུ་གང་ཞེ་ན། འདི་ལྟ་སྟེ་ཤུང་པོ་སྟོན་པ་དང་། ཁམས་སྟོན་པ་དང་། སྐྱེ་མཆེད་སྟོན་པ་དང་། སེམས་ཅན་སྟོན་པ་དང་། ལས་སྟོན་པ་དང་། སྐྱེ་བ་སྟོན་པ་དང་། རྒྱ་བ་སྟོན་པ་དང་། འཆི་བ་སྟོན་པ་དང་། འཆི་བའི་ཉིང་མཚམས་སྤོར་བ་སྟོན་པ་དང་། དེ་རབ་ཏུ་ཞི་བར་འགྱུར་པའི་སྲུ་ངན་ལས་འདས་པ་སྟོན་པ་ཞེས་གསུངས་པ་ལྟ་བུའོ།

དེ་བས་ན་དགོན་མཆོག་སྤྲིན་ལས་ཀྱང་། རིགས་ཀྱི་བུ་ཚོས་བཅུ་དང་ལྡན་ན། བྱང་ཆུབ་སེམས་དཔའ་ཀུན་རྫོབ་ལ་མཁས་པ་རྣམས་ཡིན་ནོ། །བཅུ་གང་ཞེ་ན། འདི་ལྟར་སྟེ། གཟུགས་སུ་ཡང་འདོགས་ལ། རོ་དང་པར་གཟུགས་སུ་ཡང་མི་དམིགས་ཤིང་མཐོང་པར་ཞེན་པ་མེད་དོ། །དེ་བཞིན་དུ་ཚོར་བ་དང་། འདུ་ཤེས་དང་། འདུ་བྱེད་རྣམས་དང་། རྣམ་པར་ཤེས་པ་ཞེས་རྒྱ་ཆེར་གསུངས་སོ། །དེ་བས་ན་འཕགས་པ་ལ་རྡོ་རྒྱལ་མི་ཟད་པ་བསྟན་པ་ལས་ཀྱང་། རྒྱལ་བཞིན་ཞེས་བྱ་བའི་ཚོས་ཐམས་ཅད་བདག་མེད་པ་སྟེ། དེ་བཞིན་དུ་ཚོས་ཐམས་ཅད

རིགས་པས་མཐོང་བའོ། །ཅི་ལྟར་སེམས་ཅན་བདག་མེད་པ་དེ་བཞིན་དུ་ཆོས་ཐམས་ཅད་རིགས་པས་མཐོང་
བའོ་ཞེས་བྱ་བ་གསུངས་སོ། །རྒྱལ་བ་བསྐྱེད་མ་ལས་ཀྱང་རྒྱལ་བས་རི་སྐྱེད་དུ་མཚན་ཉིད་སྟོང་པ་ཉིད་ཀྱི་ཕྱིར་
རྣམ་པར་ཤེས་པའི་བར་དུ་རྣམ་པར་ཤེས་པའི་རོ་བོ་ཉིད་ཀྱིས་སྟོང་དོ་ཞེས་གསུངས་པ་ལྟ་བུའོ། །

གལ་ཏེ་འདི་ནི་བརྟགས་པའི་རོ་བོ་ཉིད་ཀྱིས་སྟོང་པ་ཉིད་དོ་ཞེས་གསུངས་སོ་ཞེ་ན། དེ་བདེན་ཏེ་ཡང་དག་པར་
རང་བཞིན་དང་བཅས་པ་ལ་ཡང་ཡོད་དོ་ཞེས་བྱ་བ་དེ་ཡང་བརྟགས་པའི་རོ་བོ་ཉིད་ཁོ་ནའོ། །གཞན་གྱི་དབང་གི་རོ་
བོ་ཡང་དག་པར་ཡོད་པ་ཉིད་དུ་གྲུབ་ན་ནི་གཉིས་ལ་སོགས་པ་བརྟགས་པའི་ཞེས་བྱ་བ་དེ་གྲུབ་ན་སྟར་སྐྱེས་པའི་
ཆད་མའི་གནོད་པ་ཡོད་པས་དེ་ནི་མ་གྲུབ་བོ། །

སྐྱོང་པོ་ཆེའི་རྒྱལ་གྱི་མདོ་ལས་ཀྱང་། དུ་དྲེའི་བུ་འདི་ཇི་སྐྲ་དུ་སེམས། གང་ཆོས་རྣམས་ཀྱི་རོ་བོ་ཉིད་ཤེས་པ་
དེ་ཡོད་པ་ཡིན་ནམ། ཚོན་ཏེ་མེད་པ་ཡིན། གསོལ་པ། བཙོམ་ལྡན་འདས་གང་ཆོས་ཐམས་ཅད་ཀྱི་རོ་བོ་ཉིད་
འཆལ་བ་དེ་ནི་སྐྲ་མའི་རོ་བོ་ཉིད་འཆལ་བ་སྟེ། བཙོམ་ལྡན་འདས་དེ་ནི་མ་མཆིས་ཤིང་། མཆིས་པ་མ་ལགས་
སོ། དེ་ཅིའི་སྐྱད་དུ་ཞེ་ན། འདི་ལ་གང་ཡང་ཡང་དག་པར་ཆོས་གང་ཡང་མི་དམིགས་པའི་སྐྱད་དུའོ་ཞེས་བྱ་བ་
ལ་སོགས་པ་གསུངས་སོ། །

ལོ་ན་ཅི་སྟེ་ཀུན་རྟོབ་ཀྱི་རོ་བོ་འདི་གལ་ཏེ་ཅི་དངོས་པོ་མེད་པ་ཡིན་ནམ། འདི་དངོས་པོ་མེད་པ་ཡིན་ན་ནི་མཐོང་
བ་དང་འདོད་པའི་དོན་བྱེད་པ་འགལ་ལོ་ཞེ་ན། དེ་ནི་དེ་ལྷ་མ་ཡིན་པར་བསྟན་པ།

    མ་བརྟགས་གཅིག་པུ་ཉམས་དགའ་ཞིང་། །སྐྱེ་དང་འཇིག་པའི་ཆོས་ཅན་པ།
    དོན་བྱེད་པ་དག་ནུས་རྣམས་ཀྱི། །རང་བཞིན་ཀུན་རྟོབ་པ་ཡིན་ཏོགས། ༧༩ །།

ཀུན་རྟོབ་ནི་སྐྱེའི་ཐ་སྙད་ཙམ་གྱིས་བདག་ཉིད་མ་ཡིན་གྱི། མཐོང་བ་དང་འདོད་པའི་དངོས་པོ་རྟེན་ཅིང་འབྲེལ་
པར་འབྱུང་ང་རྣམས་ནི་བརྟག་མི་མཐོང་པས་ཡང་དག་པའི་ཀུན་རྟོབ་སྟེ། གདགས་པ་ཞེས་བྱ་བ་ལ་སོགས་པ་ཐ་
སྙད་དེ་ལྷ་བུར་ནུས་པའི་བདག་གིས་ཐ་སྙད་འདོགས་པར་བྱེད་པ་ན་དེའི་ཕྱིར་དོན་བྱེད་པ་དང་ཅིའི་ཕྱིར་འགལ་
ཏེ། འདི་སྐྲ་དུ།

    ཧེན་ཅིང་འབྲེལ་པར་གང་འབྱུང་བ། །དེ་ནི་སྟོང་པ་ཉིད་དུ་བཤད།
    དེ་ནི་རྒྱུར་བྱས་གདགས་པ་སྟེ། །དེ་ཉིད་དབུ་མའི་ལམ་ཡིན་ནོ། །

ཞེས་གསུངས་པ་ལྟ་བུའོ། །

འཕགས་པ་བློ་གྲོས་མི་ཟད་པས་བསྟན་པ་ལས། དེ་ལ་ཀུན་རྫོབ་ཀྱི་བདེན་པ་གང་ཞེན། འཇིག་རྟེན་གྱི་ཐ་སྙད་
རྗེ་སྐྱེད་པ་དང་། ཡི་གེ་དང་སྐད་དང་བརྗོད་བསྟན་པ་དགག་གོ །དོན་དམ་པའི་བདེན་པ་ནི་གང་ལ་སེམས་ཀྱི་རྒྱུ་བ་
ཡང་མེད་ན་ཡི་གེ་རྣམས་ལྟ་ཅི་སྨྲོས་ཞེས་གསུངས་པ་དེ་ལ་དོན་ནི་འདི་ཡིན་ཏེ། སེམས་ཅན་དང་སྐྱོང་གྱི་བདག་
ཉིད་ཀྱི་འཇིག་རྟེན་སྐྱོང་བར་བྱ་བ་དང་། སྐྱོང་བའི་དོ་བོའི་ཚུལ་འདིར་འཇིག་རྟེན་གྱི་ཐ་སྙད་དུ་དགོངས་པ་སྟེ།
བྱེད་པའི་སྐྱབ་པ་ཡོངས་སུ་བརྗོད་པའི་ཕྱིར་རོ། །བརྗོད་པའི་དོ་བོ་ནི་མ་ཡིན་ཏེ། དེ་ནི་ཡི་གེ་ལ་སོགས་པ་ལས་
བརྗོད་པའི་ཕྱིར་རོ། །རྗེ་སྐྱེད་པ་ཞེས་བྱ་བ་ནི་མ་ལུས་པའི་དོན་ཡིན་པར་བསྟན་ཏེ། དེའི་ཕྱིར་རྣམ་པར་མི་རྟོག་
པའི་ཤེས་པས་རྟོགས་པའི་བདག་ཉིད་གཟུགས་ལ་སོགས་པ་དང་། བདེ་བ་ལ་སོགས་པའི་ཀུན་རྫོབ་ཀྱི་བདེན་
པ་ཉིད་ལས་མི་འདའོ། དེའི་རྗེས་སུ་འབྲེལ་པའི་ཕྱིར་ཡི་གེ་ལ་སོགས་པ་ལ་ཡང་སྦྱར་རོ། །

དེའི་ཕྱིར་ལུང་ལས་བྱུང་བ་དང་། འཇིག་རྟེན་པ་ཡང་བསྟུ་སྟེ། དེ་ནི་ཡིད་ཀྱི་དང་དག་གི་ནོ། །དཔེར་ན་ཡིན་
གྱིས་བརྒྱ་བྱིན་ལ་ཚོས་མཆོ་པར་བཤད་པ་དང་། ཡིན་གྱི་ཚིགས་སུ་བཅད་པའི་ཡན་བཏབ་པར་དེ་དང་དེ་དག་
ནས་འབྱུང་བ་ལྟ་བུའོ། །དེ་བས་སྨྲོས་པའི་ཚོགས་ཐམས་ཅད་དང་ཁྱལ་བའི་དོན་དམ་པའི་བདེན་པ་ལ་ནི་སེམས་
ཀྱི་རྒྱུ་བ་ཡང་མེད་པར་བསྟན་ཏོ། །ཀུན་རྫོབ་འདི་ནི་རྒྱུ་མེད་པར་མི་རུང་སྟེ། ཤིང་རྟ་དང་སེམས་ལ་སོགས་པ་
བཏགས་པ་བཞིན་མ་ཡིན་ནམ། སྐྱོབ་པས་ཀྱང་།

   དཔེར་ན་ཡན་ལག་ཚོགས་རྣམས་ལ། །ཤིང་ད་ཞེས་ནི་བྱ་བར་འདོད།
   དེ་བཞིན་ཕུང་པོ་རྒྱུར་བྱས་ནས། །ཀུན་རྫོབ་ཏུའི་སེམས་ཅན་བརྗོད། །
ཅེས་གསུངས་སོ། །གལ་ཏེ་དེ་ལྟ་ན་ཡང་།

      བདག་པ་མ་བྱས་ཉམས་དགའ་བའང་། །བདག་རྒྱུ་སྟ་མ་སྟ་མ་ལ།
      བཟེན་ནས་ཕྱི་མ་ཕྱི་མ་ཡི། །འབྲས་བུ་དེ་འདུ་འབྱུང་བ་ཡིན།། ༦༥ །།
      དེའི་ཕྱིར་ཀུན་རྫོབ་རྒྱུ་མེད་ན། །རང་མིན་ཞེས་པབང་ལེགས་མ་ཡིན།
      གལ་ཏེ་འདི་ཡི་ཉེར་ལེན་ལ། །ཡང་དག་ཡིན་ན་དེ་སྨྲོས་ཤིག། ། ༦༦ །།
དེ་ནི་བཤད་ཟིན་ཏེ། བདག་མི་བཟོད་ལ་དོན་བྱེད་ནུས་པའི་དངོས་པོ་ཉིད་ནི་ཡང་དག་པའི་ཀུན་རྫོབ་ཅེས་བྱ་སྟེ།
གང་ཟག་ལ་སོགས་པ་ལྟར་སྒྱུ་ཚམ་ནི་མ་ཡིན་ནོ་ཞེས་བྱ་བའོ། །དེ་ལྟ་བུ་དེ་ལ་ཡང་བརྗོད་པའི་ཚུལ་གྱིས་བཏགས
པས་དཔྱད་མི་བཟོད་པའི་རང་གི་རྒྱུ་ལ་བརྟེན་ནས་འབྱུང་ན་རྒྱུ་མེད་པར་རྗེ་ལྟར་འགྱུར། ཞེས་རབ་དང་ཡི་ཞེས་

ཀྱིས་དཔྱད་ན་གང་གི་རྒྱུའི་རང་བཞིན་ཡོད་པ་དེ་བློ་གྲོས་དང་ལྡན་པས་སྐྱོབས་ཤིག །ཤིང་རྟ་ལ་སོགས་པ་ཡང་
ཚོས་ཉིད་འདི་ལས་མི་འདའ་ཉིད་དོ་ཞེས་ཐབས་ཅད་ཉེ་བར་སྒྲུབ་པར་བཤད་ཟིན་ཏོ། །འདིར་ཡང་གསུངས་པ།

ཡི་གེ་གཅིག་སྐྱགས་གང་ཡང་མེད། །ཡི་གེ་མང་པོ་གཞན་ཡང་མེད།
ཡི་གེ་འབགགས་པ་རྣམས་མིན་ལ། །བརྟེན་ནས་དེ་ནི་མེད་པ་ཡིན། །
དེ་བཞིན་རང་གི་ཡན་ལག་ལས། །སྤུན་ནི་གུད་ནས་མི་སྲང་ངོ༌། །
སྤུ་འི་གྲུང་པོ་སྲང་བ་དེ། །དེ་དག་ལས་མིན་གཞན་ཡང་མིན། །
ཉེན་ཅིང་འབྲེལ་པར་འབྱུང་བ་དེ། །ཡོད་དང་མེད་པར་སུ་ཞིག་འདོད། །
དེ་ལ་དམིགས་པར་བྱེད་པ་ཡི། །མིག་གི་རྣམ་ཤེས་བྱུང་བ་ལྟར། །
ལས་དང་ཉོན་མོངས་དབང་འབངས་པ། །ལེན་བཅས་སྲིད་ལས་འབྱུང་བ་དང༌། །
དེ་བཞིན་དུ་ནི་གཟུགས་འབྱུང་བ། །ཡོད་དམ་མེད་པར་སུ་ཞིག་འདོད། །
དེ་ལྟར་སྲིད་པའི་ཡན་ལག་ཀུན། །ཐ་སྙད་ཀྱིས་ནི་གདགས་པ་སྟེ། །
འདི་ལྟར་འགོག་ལ་སོགས་པ་ཡི། །ཚོས་ཀུན་དགོངས་ཏེ་གསུངས་པ་ཡིན། །
ཇི་ལྟར་སྒྲས་དེ་སྒྲས་མིན་དང༌། །ཇི་ལྟར་སྐྱེ་ཡང་སྐྱེ་མིན་ལ། །
དེ་ལྟར་བརྟེན་ནས་གསུངས་པ་དེ། །གཞིས་ཀ་འགྲུབ་པར་འགྱུར་མ་ཡིན། །

ཚོས་ཐམས་ཅད་རང་བཞིན་མེད་པ་ཡིན་དུ་ཟིན་ན། འཇིག་རྟེན་མཐའ་དག་ནས་མཁའི་མེ་ཏོག་བཞིན་དུ་འགྱུར་
ཏེ། དེའི་ཕྱིར་མཐོང་བ་དང༌། ཐོས་པ་དང༌། བྱེ་བྲག་འབྱེད་པ་དང༌། རྣམ་པར་ཤེས་པ་ལ་སོགས་པ་མེད་ལས་
འཕགས་པ་དང་འཕགས་པ་མ་ཡིན་པའི་ཐ་སྙད་ལ་སོགས་པ་རྣམ་པར་གཞག་པ་གྲུབ་པའི་མཐའ་དང་མི་འགལ་
བ་དེ་ལྟར་སྒྲུར་ཞེན། གྲུན་ཀ་འདི་ནི་སྙིང་པོ་ཡོང་པ་མ་ཡིན་ཏེ།

དངོས་པོ་ཀུན་གྱི་རང་བཞིན་ནི། །རིགས་པའི་ལམ་གྱི་རྗེས་འབྲང་བར། །
གཞན་དག་འདོད་པ་སེལ་བར་བྱེད། །དེའི་ཕྱིར་རྩོལ་འདས་གནས་མེད་དོ།། ༼༡༠ ༽ །
ཡོད་དང་མེད་དང་ཡོད་མེད་ཅེས། །ཁས་མི་ལེན་པ་གང་ཡིན་པ། །
དེ་ལ་ནན་ཏན་ལྡན་པས་ཀྱང༌། །ཅི་ཡང་ལ་ཀླན་ཀ་བྱ་མི་ནུས།། ༼༡༡ ༽

ཁྱིས་པའི་གནས་སྐབས་ནས་བརྗོད་སྟེ། ཐམས་ཅད་མཁྱེན་པའི་ཡེ་ཤེས་ཀྱི་བར་དུ་སྐྱོང་བ་གང་མ་བཏགས་
གཅིག་ཕུ་ན་ཡིན་དུ་འོང་བའི་རང་བཞིན་ལ་འོ་བོ་བཀག་པ་མེད་དེ། ཡང་དག་པར་ན་འཇུག་ཏུ་སྨྲ་ན་ཡོད་པ་
དང་། མེད་པ་དང་། གཉིས་ཀ་དང་། གཉིས་ཀ་མ་ཡིན་པར་སྐྱ་བ་སྐྱ་བ་ལ་སོགས་པ་ས་བཏགས་པ་གང་
ཡིན་པ་དེ་མེད་དོ། །དེའི་ཕྱིར་ཚོས་ཐམས་ཅད་རང་བཞིན་མེད་པར་སྐྱ་བ་འདི་ནི་སྟོང་པ་ཉིད་ཀྱི་དོན་ལོག་པར་
མཐོང་བ་མ་ཡིན་ནོ། །

གང་གི་ཕྱོགས་ལ་ཡོད་པ་དང་། །མེད་དང་ཡོད་མེད་ཡོད་མིན་པ།
དེ་ལ་ཀུན་ཀ་བུ་བ་ནི། །ཕྱིན་རིང་དུ་ཡང་བརྟོད་མི་ནུས། །དཔུ་མ་བཞི་བཀུ་བ་ལེའུ ༡༧ ཚིགས་བཅད་ ༣༤

དེའི་ཕྱིར་ཡང་དག་ཉིད་དུ་ན། །འདོས་པོ་གང་ཡང་གྲུབ་པ་མེད།

དེའི་ཕྱིར་དེ་བཞིན་གཤེགས་རྣམས་ཀྱིས། །ཚོས་རྣམས་ཐམས་ཅད་མ་སྐྱེས་གསུངས།། ༧༨ ||
ཡང་དག་པར་ན་དངོས་པོ་ཕྲ་རབ་ཀུང་ཡོངས་སུ་གྲུབ་པར་མི་འཛིན་ཏེ། དེ་ལྟར་བསྟན་པའི་ཚུལ་གྱིས་གཅིག་
དང་དུ་མའི་རང་བཞིན་དང་བྲལ་བའི་ཕྱིར་རོ། །དེའི་ཕྱིར་ཡང་དག་པར་ན་གང་གི་སྐྱེ་བ་དང་། སྟོན་དུ་འགྲོ་
བའི་གནས་པ་དང་། མི་རྟག་པ་དང་། དེ་ལ་བརྟེན་པའི་ཚོས་གཞན་ཡང་ཡོད་པར་འགྱུར་རམ། དེ་ལྟ་བས་ན།
བློ་གྲོས་རྒྱ་མཚོས་བསྟན་པ་ལས་འདི་སྐད་གསུངས་ཏེ།

གང་དག་སྟེང་ཅིང་འཁྱིལ་འབྱུང་བ། །དེ་དག་དངོས་ཉིད་ཅི་ཡང་མིན།
གང་དག་དོ་བོ་ཉིད་མེད་པ། །དེ་དག་གང་དུ་འབྱུང་བ་མེད། །

ཞེའོ། །རྒྱང་པོའི་རྒྱལ་གྱི་མདོ་ལས་ཀྱང་།
གང་ཞིག་སྐྱེ་བར་འགྱུར་བ་ཡི། །ཚོས་དེ་གང་ཡང་མི་དམིགས་ན།
འབྱུང་བ་མེད་པའི་ཚོས་རྣམས་ལ། །ཁྱིས་པ་དག་ནི་འབྱུང་བར་འདོད། །

ཞེས་གསུངས་སོ། །དཀོན་མཆོག་འབྱུང་གནས་ཀྱི་མདོ་ལས་ཀྱང་།
གང་ལ་རང་བཞིན་ཡོད་པ་མ་ཡིན་ཏེ།
རང་བཞིན་མེད་པས་གནན་རྐྱེན་དེ་ལྟར་འགྱུར།
རང་བཞིན་མེད་པས་གནན་གྱིས་དེ་ལྟར་བསྐྱེད།
རྒྱ་འདེ་བའི་བར་གཞིགས་པས་བསྐྱན་པ་ཡིན། །   འགྱུར་མི་འདུར་དཔུ་མ་ཚིག་གནས་ལ་དྲ་ས་སྲར་མ་ཕོག་གུངས
༡༢ ན་ཡོད།

ཞེས་གསུངས་སོ། །དེའི་ཕྱིར་ཡབ་སྲས་མཐལ་བའི་མདོ་ལས་ཀྱང་།

རྟེན་ཅིང་འབྲེལ་པར་འབྱུང་བ་ལ་འཇུག་པས་ཆོས་ཀྱི་དབྱིངས་ལ་འཇུག་པ་བསྟན་ཏེ། བཙོམ་ལྡན་འདས་དེ་ལ་
མ་རིག་པ་ནི་མ་རིག་པ་ཉིད་ཀྱིས་མ་མཆིས་སོ། །དེ་ཅིའི་སླད་དུ་ཞེ་ན། འདི་ལྟར་མ་རིག་པ་ནི་རང་བཞིན་དང་
བྲལ་བ་སྟེ། ཆོས་གང་ལ་ཡང་རང་བཞིན་མ་མཆིས་པ་དེ་ནི་དངོས་པོ་མ་མཆིས་པའོ། །གང་ལ་དངོས་པོ་མ་
མཆིས་པ་དེ་ནི་ཡོངས་སུ་མ་གྲུབ་པའོ། །གང་ཡོངས་སུ་མ་གྲུབ་པ་དེ་ནི་མི་སྐྱེ་བའོ། །གང་མི་སྐྱེ་བ་དེ་ནི་མི་
འགག་པའོ། །གང་མ་སྐྱེས་མ་འགགས་པ་དེ་འདས་པ་ཞེས་གདགས་པར་བགྱི་བ་མ་ལགས། མ་འོངས་པ་དང་
ད་ལྟར་བྱུང་བ་ཞེས་གདགས་པར་བགྱི་བ་མ་ལགས་སོ། །གང་དུས་གསུམ་དུ་མི་དམིགས་པ་དེ་ནི་མིང་མ་མཆིས་
པ། མཚན་ཉིད་མ་མཆིས་པ། གདགས་སུ་མ་མཆིས་པ་སྟེ། གཞན་དུ་མ་ལགས་ཀྱི་མིང་ཚམ་དང་། བརྗ་ཚམ་
དང་། ཐ་སྙད་ཚམ་དང་། ཀུན་རྫོབ་ཚམ་དང་། བརྗོབ་པ་ཚམ་དང་། གདགས་པ་ཚམ་དུ་སེམས་ཅན་རྣམས་
གཟུང་བའི་དོན་དུ་བགྱི་བ་མ་གཏོགས་པར་མ་རིག་པ་དེ་ནི་དོན་དམ་པར་དམིགས་སུ་མ་མཆིས་སོ། །

ཆོས་གང་དོན་དམ་པར་དམིགས་སུ་མ་མཆིས་པ་དེ་ནི་གདགས་སུ་མ་མཆིས་པ་ཐ་སྙད་དུ་བགྱིར་མ་མཆིས་པ་
བརྗོད་དུ་མ་མཆིས་པ་སྟེ། བཙོམ་ལྡན་འདས་གང་མིང་ཚམ་ཞེས་བགྱི་བ་ནས་གདགས་པ་ཚམ་གྱི་བར་དེ་དག་ཀྱང་
ཡང་དག་པར་མ་ལགས་པ་ཞེས་རྒྱ་མཆེ་འབྱུང་ངོ་། དེ་ལྟར་བྱས་ན།

ཆོས་ཀྱི་འཁོར་ལོ་བསྐོར་བ་ན། །གཟོད་ནས་ཞི་ཞིང་མ་སྐྱེས་དང་།

རང་བཞིན་མྱ་ངན་འདས་པ་ཞེས། །ཆོས་རྣམས་མགོན་པོ་ཁྱོད་ཀྱིས་བསྟན། །

ཅེས་བྱ་བའི་ཚིགས་སུ་བཅད་པ་འདི་ལེགས་པར་བཤད་པར་འགྱུར་ཏེ། འདི་ནི་ཆོས་ཐམས་ཅད་དུས་གསུམ་
མཉམ་པ་ཉིད་དུ་ཡོངས་སུ་བསྟན་ཏེ། །གཟོད་མ་ནི་མ་འོངས་པའི་དུས་ཏེ་རང་བཞིན་དང་བྲལ་བའི་ཕྱིར་དེར་ཞི་
བའོ། །ད་ལྟར་བྱུང་བའི་དུས་ན་ཡང་མ་སྐྱེས་ཏེ། རང་བཞིན་དང་བྲལ་བའི་ཕྱིར་རོ། །འདས་པའི་དུས་ན་ཡང་
རང་བཞིན་གྱི་པོ་བོ་ཉིད་ཀྱིས་མྱ་ངན་ལས་འདས་པ་སྟེ། རང་བཞིན་དང་བྲལ་བ་ཉིད་ཀྱི་ཕྱིར་རོ། །

ཡབ་དང་སྲས་དང་མཐལ་བའི་མདོ་ལས། ཇི་སྐད་དུ། ཆོས་འདི་དག་ཐམས་ཅད་ནི་དུས་གསུམ་དུ་མཉམ་པ་
ཉིད་ཀྱིས་མཉམ་པ་སྟེ། འདས་པའི་དུས་ན་ཡང་ཆོས་ཐམས་ཅད་རང་བཞིན་དང་བྲལ་བའོ། །མ་འོངས་པ་མ་
ལགས། ད་ལྟར་བྱུང་བ་མ་ལགས་སོ། དེ་ཅིའི་སླད་དུ་ཞེ་ན། རང་བཞིན་མ་མཆིས་པ་དེ་ནི་འདས་པ་ཞེས་

གདགས་པར་བགྱི་བ་མ་ལགས། མ་འོངས་པ་དང་ད་ལྟར་བྱུང་བ་ཞེས་གདགས་པར་བགྱི་བ་མ་ལགས་སོ་ཞེས་འབྱུང་ངོ་། །སྐྱེ་བ་མེད་པ་ལ་སོགས་པ་ཡང་། ཡང་དག་པའི་ཀུན་རྫོབ་ཏུ་གཏོགས་པ་ཡིན་དུ་ཟིན་ཀྱང་།

དམ་པའི་དོན་དང་མཐུན་པའི་ཕྱིར། །འདི་ནི་དམ་པའི་དོན་ཞེས་བྱ།

ཡང་དག་ཏུ་ན་སྐྱེས་པ་ཡི། །ཚོགས་རྣམས་ཀུན་ལས་དེ་བྱོལ་ཡིན།། ༡༠ །།

དོན་དམ་པ་ནི་དངོས་པོ་དང་དངོས་པོ་མེད་པ་དང་། སྐྱེ་བ་དང་མི་སྐྱེ་བོ་དང་། སྟོང་པ་དང་མི་སྟོང་པ་ལ་སོགས་པ་སྤྲོས་པའི་དྲ་བ་མཐའ་དག་སྤངས་པའོ། །སྐྱེ་བ་མེད་པ་ལ་སོགས་པ་ནི་དེ་ལ་འདྲག་པ་དང་མཐུན་པའི་ཕྱིར་དམ་པ་ཞེས་ཏེ་བར་འདོགས་སོ། །

ཡང་དག་ཀུན་རྫོབ་རྣམས་ཀྱི་སྐྱེས། མེད་པར་ཡང་དག་ཁད་པ་ཡི།
སྟེང་དུ་འགྲོ་བར་བྱ་བ་ནི། མཁས་ལ་རྟད་བ་མ་ཡིན་ནོ། །

ཅིའི་ཕྱིར་དངོས་སུ་དོན་དམ་པ་མ་ཡིན་པར་བསྟན་པ།

སྐྱེ་བ་ལ་སོགས་མེད་པའི་ཕྱིར། །སྐྱེ་བ་མེད་ལ་སོགས་མི་སྲིད།
དེ་ཡི་ངོ་བོ་བཀག་པའི་ཕྱིར། །དེ་ཡི་ཚིག་གི་སྒྲ་མི་སྲིད།། ༡༡ །།

ཡུལ་མེད་པ་ལ་དགག་པ་ཡི། །སྒྱུར་བ་ལེགས་པ་ཡོད་མ་ཡིན།
རྣམ་པར་རྟོག་ལ་བརྟེན་ནས་ཡང་། །ཀུན་རྫོབ་པར་འགྱུར་ཡང་དག་མིན།། ༡༢ །།

སྐྱེ་བ་ལ་སོགས་པ་མེད་ན་དེ་བཟློག་པའི་སྐྱེ་མི་འཕད་དོ། །དེ་བས་ན་ཡུལ་མེད་པ་ལ་དགག་པའི་ཕྱིར་སྐྱེ་བ་ཡང་མེད་པས་སྐྱེ་བ་མེད་པ་ལ་སོགས་པ་མི་སྲིད་དོ། །དེ་ལྟ་སྟེ་རང་གི་མཚན་ཉིད་ནི་སྐྱེ་འདི་དག་གི་ཡུལ་མ་ཡིན་མོད་ཀྱི་ངོ་ཀུང་ཕོག་མ་མེད་པའི་དུས་ཀྱི་བག་ཆགས་ལས་བྱུང་བའི་རྣམ་པར་རྟོག་པ་ལ་སྣང་བའི་དང་ཅན་གྱི་ཡུལ་ཉིད་དུ་བདག་གིར་བྱས་ཏེ། ཚོས་ཅན་འདི་ཉིད་ལ་བརྟེན་ནས་སྐྱེ་བ་ལ་སོགས་པ་རྣམ་པར་རྟོག་པ་ལ་སྣང་བའི་དོན་འདི་ཅི་གནས་དག་འདོད་པའི་དོན་ལ་བརྟེན་ནས། ཡོན་ཏེ་མ་ཡིན་ཞེས་ཡོད་དམ་མེད་པ་སེམས་པར་བྱེད་ཀྱི་སྐྱེ་བ་ལ་སོགས་པ་རྣམ་པར་རྟོག་པ་ལ་སྣང་བའི་དོན་འདི་ནི་སྟོང་པར་མི་བྱེད་ཏེ། དེ་ཉིད་བློ་ལ་སྐྱེན་པར་བྱ་བའི་ཕྱིར། སྣ་སྟོར་བའི་ཕྱིར་རོ་ཞེན། རྣམ་པར་རྟོག་པ་ཡང་རྣམ་པར་ཞེས་པའི་དོ་བོ་ཉིད་ཡིན་པས་དེ་དབུད་པ་ཉིད་ཀྱིས་བསལ་ཞིན་ནམ། གཞན་ཡང་དེ་ལྟ་ན་ཀུན་རྫོབ་ཅེས་བུ་བའི་རྣམ་པར་རྟོག་པའི་བློ་ལ་བརྟེན་པའི་ཕྱིར་མ་སྐྱེས་པ་ལ་སོགས་པ་ནི་ཀུན་རྫོབ་པར་འགྱུར་གྱི་དོན་དམ་པར་མ་ཡིན་ཏེ། གེན་ལ་སོགས་པའི་སྐྱེའི་དོན་བཞིན

ནོ། །གཞན་ཡང་དངོས་པོ་མ་གྲུབ་ན་དེ་ལ་བསྟོས་ནས་རབ་ཏུ་བརྟགས་པ་བདག་གི་དེ་ལྟོན་དངོས་པོ་མེད་པ་ལ་སོགས་པ་ཡང་མེད་དོ། །འདི་སྐད་གསུངས་ཏེ།

གལ་ཏེ་དངོས་པོ་མ་གྲུབ་ན། །དངོས་པོ་མེད་པར་འགྱུབ་མི་འགྱུར།

དངོས་པོ་གཞན་དུ་འགྱུར་ན་ནི། །དངོས་པོ་མེད་ཅེས་སྐྱེ་བོ་སྨྲ། ཞེའོ་

དེ་སྐད་དུ།

ནོ་མར་ཚོ་ལ་སོགས་མེད་པ། །དེ་ན་སྟ་ན་མེད་ཅེས་བྱ།

ནོ་ལ་འོ་མ་མེད་པ་ནི། །ཞིག་ནས་མེད་པའི་མཚན་ཉིད་ཡིན། །

མགོ་ཡི་ཡན་ལག་སྦྱོང་བ་དང་། །སྐྱེ་དང་སྲུ་བ་རྣམས་སྒྲུབས་པ།

དེ་ཕོངས་དུ་ལ་སོགས་དངོས་སུ། །དེ་ནི་གཏན་མེད་བརྗོད་པ་ཡིན། །

བ་ལང་ལ་ནི་རྟ་སོགས་མེད། །དེ་ནི་གཅིག་ལ་གཅིག་མེད་བརྗོད། །

ཅེའོ། །སོ་སོག་ཏུ་གྱུར་པ་དངོས་པོ་མེད་པར་གྱུར་པ་ཡང་། དངོས་པོ་མེད་པ་ཉིད་དུ་དངོས་པའི་རྣས་དྲངས་ནས། རྣམ་པར་བཞག་སྟེ། སོ་གཞན་ལ་སོགས་པ་དང་། བུ་ལ་སོགས་པ་ཡོད་པར་མ་ངེས་ན་སོ་གཞན་གྱི་བུ་ལ་སོགས་པར་རྣམ་པར་རྟོག་པར་མི་འགྱུར་རོ། །དེ་བས་ན་བྲོ་གྲོལ་རྒྱ་མཚོའི་མའི་ལས་བསྐྱེན་པ། ཆེནས་པ་ཆོས་གང་ཡོངས་སུ་མ་གྲུབ་པ་དེ་ཡོད་པ་ཉིད་དུ་ཞེའམ། མེད་པ་ཉིད་དོ་ཞེས་ཁས་མི་ལེན་ཏོ་ཞེས་ལེགས་པར་བཤད་པར་འགྱུར་རོ། །ལུང་ཀར་གཞིགས་པ་ལས་ཀྱང་།

ཡོད་པའི་རྣས་དྲངས་མེད་པ་སྟེ། །ཡོད་པ་འང་མེད་པའི་རྣས་དྲངས་སོ།

དེ་བས་མེད་པས་བསམས་མི་བྱ། །ཡོད་པ་ཉིད་དུ་འང་མི་རྟོག་གོ ། || ལེའུ་ ༡ ཚིགས་བཅད ༧༩

གང་ལ་ཅི་ཡང་མི་སྐྱེ་བ། །ཅི་ཡང་འགག་པར་མི་འགྱུར་ཏེ།

འཇིག་རྟེན་རྣམ་པར་དབེན་མཐོང་བ། །དེ་ལ་ཡོད་དང་མེད་པ་མེད། || ལེའུ་ ༡ ཚིགས་བཅད ༡༥

ཅེས་གསུངས་སོ། །དེ་ལ་དོན་ནི་འདི་ཡིན་ཏེ། ཡོད་པའི་རྣས་དྲངས་ནས་མེད་པ་རྣམ་པར་བཞག་སྟེ། དཔེར་ན་ཞིག་ནས་མེད་པ་རྣམ་པ་གསུམ་ལྟ་བུའོ། །མེད་པའི་རྣས་དྲངས་ནས་ཡོད་པ་སྟེ། དཔེར་ན་སྐྱེ་བ་སྟ་ན་མེད་པ་ལྟ་བུའོ། །

སྟ་ན་ཡོད་པ་སྐྱེ་འགྱུར་ན། །སྐྱེས་པ་ལ་ཡང་ནི་སྐྱེ་བར་འགྱུར། །

ཞེའོ། །དེ་ལྟ་བས་ན། བློ་གྲོས་བཟང་པོས་གང་གསུངས་པ།

གང་དག་བདག་དངོས་གཞན་དངོས་དང་། །དངོས་དང་དངོས་མེད་མི་མཐོང་བ།

དེ་དག་རབས་རྒྱས་བསྟན་པ་ལ། །ཡང་དག་མཐོང་བ་མ་ཡིན་ནོ། །རྩ་བ་ཤེས་རབ་ ༡༥ ༨

གང་དག་དངོས་རྣམས་བརྟེན་བྱུང་ནས། །རྟུ་ཡི་རྣ་བ་ལྟ་བུར་ནི།

ཡང་དག་མ་ཡིན་ལོགས་མིན་པར། །འདོད་པ་དེ་དག་ལྟས་མི་འཕྲོག །རིགས་པ་དྲུག་ཅུ་པ་ ༩༦

ཐམས་ཅད་དག་མིན་མི་དག་པ་དང་། །ཅི་ཡང་མེད་དེ་དག་དེ་བཞིན།

དངོས་ཡོད་དག་དང་མི་དག་པར། །འགྱུར་ན་དེ་ནི་ག་ལ་ཡོད། །སྟོང་ཉིད་བདུན་ཅུ་པ་ ༥༨

གང་ཅི་བརྟེན་པ་ཐམས་ཅད་ནི། །ངོ་བོ་ཉིད་ཀྱིས་སྟོང་རིགས་བྱུ།

སྟོང་ཞེས་བྱ་བ་དེ་ཡང་སྟོང་། །འདི་ལྟར་མི་སྟོང་ཡོད་མ་ཡིན། །

སུ་ལ་སྟོང་ཉིད་མི་འབྱུང་བ། །དེ་ལ་ཅི་ཡང་འབྱུང་བ་མེད། །རྩ་བ་ཤེས་རབ་ ༡༥ ༡༩

ཅེས་བྱ་བ་འདི་ལེགས་པར་གསུངས་པའོ། །

དེ་བས་ན་ཀླུའི་རྒྱལ་པོ་རྒྱ་མཚོས་ཞུས་པ་ཆེན་པོ་ལས།

སྟོན་མཐའ་སྟོང་ཞེན་ཕྱི་མའི་མཐའ་ཡང་སྟོང་། །སྐྱེ་དང་འཇིག་དང་གནས་པའི་དངོས་པོ་སྟོང་།

འདི་ནི་དངོས་པོ་ཡོད་མིན་དངོས་མེད་མིན། །

ཞེས་གསུངས་སོ། །

ཡོ་ན་དེ་ནི་རྟོགས་གྱུར་པས། །དེ་ཡི་རང་བཞིན་མཛད་སྒྱུ་ཕྱིར།

མི་མཁས་རྣམས་ཀུན་དངོས་རྣམས་ཀྱི། །དངོས་པོ་འདི་འདུ་ཅེས་མི་རྟོགས།། ༧༣ ॥

དེ་རྟོགས་ན་དེའི་རང་གི་ངོ་བོ་མི་རྟོགས་པ་ནི་མི་རིགས་ཏེ། བུམ་པས་དབེན་པའི་ས་གཞི་དམིགས་ན། དེའི

བདག་ཉིད་གྱུར་པ་བུམ་པས་དབེན་པ་རྟོགས་པ་བཞིན་ནོ། །དངོས་པོ་རྣམས་ནི་སོ་སོའི་སྐྱེ་བོའི་ལྟ་བ་དགར་པོ

མ་ཡིན་པ་ཐ་སྙད་རྣམས་ཀྱིས་ཀུན་དངོས་པོ་ལ་སྒོགས་པའི་རྣམ་པ་མེད་པ་ལ་སྐྱེ་བཏགས་པས། སྐྱེ་བཏགས་པ

ཡང་དག་པ་ཇི་སྐད་དུ་སྨྲོས་པ་མཐའ་དག་དང་བྲལ་བ་ཁོ་ན་ཡིན་པར་རྟོགས་ན་ཅིའི་ཕྱིར་དེ་ལྟ་ཡིན་པར་མི

རྟོགས་ཤེ་ན།

མ་ཡིན་ཕྱོག་མེད་རྒྱུད་ཕྱི་བར། །དངོས་པོར་སྨྲ་བཏགས་དབང་བྱས་པ།

དེའི་ཕྱིར་སྟོག་ཆགས་ཐམས་ཅད་ཀྱིས། །མཚན་སུམ་རྟོགས་པར་མི་འགྱུར་རོ།། ༡༤ །།
ཐོག་མ་མེད་པའི་སྲིད་པར་སྐྱེས་པ་དངོས་པོ་ལ་མཚན་པར་ཞེན་པའི་དུག་གིས་དཀྲུགས་པའི་བློ་ཅན་དག་གིས་
མཚན་སུམ་ཆད་དུ་རྟོགས་པ་རྣམས་པ་ཆོ་དུ་ཁྱུད་པར་མི་ནུས་ཏེ། འདུ་བ་གཅིག་ནས་གཅིག་ཏུ་ཁྱུད་པ་དམིགས་
པས་བློ་སྐྱེ་བ་དག་གིས་སྐད་ཅིག་མ་ཉིད་མི་རྟོགས་པ་བཞིན་ནོ། །གཞན་ཡང་འདི་ནི་ལོ་མཆན་མི་ཆེ་སྟེ། འདི་
ལྟར་ཐུམ་པ་དང་བ་ཡང་ཉིད་ལ་སོགས་པས་འབིན་པའི་བ་ལང་ལ་སོགས་པའི་ཕྱིས་གསལ་བར་མཐོང་ཡང་།
སེར་སྐྱ་དང་གཟིགས་མ་ལ་སྒྱུད་པའི་ལུགས་ཀྱིས་བློ་གྲོས་ཤིན་ཏུ་ཕྱིན་ཅི་ལོག་ཏུ་གྱུར་པ་དག་དེ་ལྟར་རྟོགས་པར་
མི་བྱེད་དོ། །

ཨོན་སུ་དག་གིས་དེ་རྟོགས་ཤེ་ན། བཤད་པ།

དེ་ལ་བློ་བཏགས་གཅོད་བྱེད་པ། །ཤེས་པར་བྱེད་པའི་གཏན་ཆིགས་ཀྱིས།

རྗེས་སུ་དཔོག་རྣམས་ཤེས་པར་བྱེད། །རྣལ་འབྱོར་དབང་རྣམས་མཚན་སུམ་གསལ།། ༡༥ །།
དངོས་པོ་ལ་སོགས་པར་བློ་འདོགས་པ་བསལ་བ་བསྐུབ་པ་ཕྱོགས་གཅིག་ཆམ་ཞིག་ཏེ་སྐད་བསྟན་པ་དག་གིས་
ཐོས་པ་བསམ་མ་ཐོབ། བསམ་པ་ལས་བྱུང་བའི་ཆོས་རབ་ཏུ་རྣམ་པར་འབྱེད་པ་བསགས་པ་དག་སྒོས་པ་དང་ཕྲལ་
ཆེས་པར་བྱེད་དོ། །རྣལ་འབྱོར་པའི་དབང་ཕྱུག་རྣམས་ནི་ཆོས་ཐམས་ཅད་ཀྱི་རང་བཞིན་མཉམ་པ་ཉིད་དུ་རྣམ་
པར་ཕྱེ་བའི་ཏིང་ངེ་འཛིན་གྱི་སོགས་པ་ལས་བྱུང་བའི་ཡེ་ཤེས་རྣམ་པར་རྟོག་པའི་དྲི་མ་དང་བྲལ་བ་ཉིད་ཀྱིས་ནན་
དང་ཕྱིའི་དངོས་པོ་མ་བཏགས་པ་དགའ་བ་སྟིང་པོ་མེད་པ། རྒྱ་ཉིང་གི་སྟིང་པོ་ལྟ་བུ་ཐམས་ཅད་ཏེ་ལྟར་བློ་
འདོགས་པའི་ས་བོན་ཡང་ཕྱིས་མི་སྐྱེ་བ་ལྟར་ཕྱགས་སུ་ཆུད་དེ།

སྟིང་རྗེ་ཆེན་པོ་ལ་འཇུག་པའི་མདོ་ལས།

ཏེ་ལྟར་ཆུ་ཤིང་རློན་པའི་སྡོང་པོ་ལ།
ཤེས་བྱ་བ་ལ་སོགས་རྗེ་སྐད་གསུངས་བར་ལ་བུ་བོ། །ཆེད་དུ་བརྗོད་པ་ལས་ཀྱང་།

གང་ཞིག་ལུ་དྲྭ་ར་དག་ལ་མི་ཏོག་ལྟར། །སྲིད་པ་དག་ལ་སྲིང་པོ་མེད་པར་སེམས་བྱེད་པ།
དགེ་སློང་འདི་ནི་ཕ་རོལ་མིན་པའི་ཕ་རོལ་སོན། །སྦྲུལ་གྱིས་རྣས་པ་ཡི་པགས་པ་རྗེས་པ་བརྗེ་བ་
བཞིན། ། ཚོམས་ ༡༢ ཚིགས་ ༤༤

ཞེས་གསུངས་སོ། །ཚོས་ཐམས་ཅད་རང་བཞིན་མེད་པར་ཁས་བླངས་ན། ཕྱོགས་ཀྱི་ཚོས་ལ་སོགས་པ་རང་ལ་
མ་གྲུབ་པའི་ཕྱིར་རྟེས་སུ་དཔག་པ་དང་། རྟེས་སུ་དཔག་པར་བྱ་བའི་ཐ་སྙད་མི་འགྲུབ་པ་མ་ཡིན་ནམ། དེའི་
ཕྱིར་རྟེས་སུ་དཔོག་པ་པོ་སེ་རེ་སྐྱར་གཏན་ལ་དབབ། གལ་ཏེ་ཡང་ཚོས་ཐམས་ཅད་རང་རང་བཞིན་མེད་པར་སྒྲུབ་
པའི་གཏན་ཚིགས་ས་བཟོད་ན། དེའི་གཏན་ཚིགས་མེད་པར་མི་འགྲུབ་པའི་ཕྱིར་འདོད་པའི་དོན་མི་འགྲུབ་
བོ། །ཅི་སྟེ་བཟོད་ན་ནི་གཏན་ཚིགས་ཡོད་དེ། དེ་ལྟར་ན་ཡང་ཚོས་ཐམས་ཅད་རང་རང་བཞིན་མེད་པར་མི་འགྲུབ་
པས་འདོད་པའི་དོན་མི་འགྲུབ་བོ། །འདི་ནི་ཀྱི་ན་སྟེ། འདི་ལྟར།

    གཞན་གྱིས་བསྐྱེད་པའི་བུ་ག་གི། །ཚོས་ཅན་སྟངས་ནས་མ་ཁས་པ་དང་།
    བུད་མེད་ཁྱིས་པའི་བར་དག་ལ། །གྲུགས་པར་གྱུར་པའི་དངོས་རྣམས་ལ།། ༧༦ ॥
    བསྐྱབ་དང་སྐྱབ་པའི་དངོས་པོ་འདི། །མ་ལུས་ཡང་དག་འཐུག་པར་འགྱུར།
    དེ་སྐྱ་མིན་ན་གཞི་མ་གྲུབ། །ལ་སོགས་ལ་ན་ནི་རེ་སྐྱང་གདབ།། ༧༧ ॥
    བདག་ནི་སྐྱང་བའི་རང་ཅན་གྱི། །དངོས་པོ་དགག་པར་མི་བྱེད་དེ།
    དེ་སྐྱ་བས་ན་སྐྲུབ་པ་དང་། །བསྐྱབ་བུ་བཞག་ལ་འཁྲུགས་ལ་མེན།། ༧༣ ॥

རྟེས་སུ་དཔག་པ་དང་རྟེས་སུ་དཔག་པར་བྱ་བའི་ཐ་སྙད་ཐམས་ཅད་ནི་ཁར་ཆུན་མི་མཐུན་པའི་མཐུན་བསྐྱེད་པ་
ཚོས་ཅན་ཐ་དད་པའི་ཡོངས་སུ་བཅད་སྟེ། མཁས་པ་དང་བུད་མེད་དང་ཁྱིས་པའི་བར་གྱི་མིག་དང་རྣ་བ་ལ་
སོགས་པའི་ཤེས་པ་ལ་སྣང་བའི་དང་ཅན་གྱི་ཕྱོགས་སྐྱ་ལ་སོགས་པའི་ཚོས་ཅན་ལ་བརྟེན་ནས་འཇུག་གོ །
དེ་སྐྱ་མིན་ན་ནི་དུ་བ་དང་། ཡོད་པ་ལ་སོགས་པའི་མེ་དང་མི་དྲག་པ་ཉིད་ལ་སོགས་པ་བསྒྲུབ་པར་འདོད་པ་ཐམས་
ཅད་གཏན་ཚིགས་ཀྱི་གཞི་འགྲུབ་པར་མི་འགྱུར་ཏེ། བསྒྲུབ་པའི་ཚོས་ཅན་ཡན་ལག་ཅན་དང་། རམ་མ་བའི་
ཡོན་ཏན་ལ་སོགས་པའི་རོ་བོ་རྣམས་མ་གྲུབ་པའི་ཕྱིར་རོ། །

དེ་སྐྱ་ན་ཚོས་གཞི་ག་དང་སྒྲུན་པའི་ཕྱིར་དཔེའི་ཚོས་ཅན་ཡང་མ་འགྲུབ་པ་ཉིད་དོ། །གལ་ཏེ་གྲུབ་པ་དང་གྲུབ་
པའི་ཐ་སྙད་འདི་སྐྱ་བུ་འདི་གཞན་དག་ཀྱང་ཁས་ལེན་ན་ནི་མཁས་པ་བཀལ་བའི་གྲུགས་པ་འདི་ཅི་དགོས་ཏེ།
འདི་སྐྱར་རང་གི་ཕྱོགས་ལ་མི་སྐྱ་བར་གཞན་གྱི་ཕྱོགས་ཀྱི་ཤེས་པ་འདི་ཉིད་བཟོད་དུ་ཟད་དོ། །

བོ་བོ་ཡང་མིག་ལ་སོགས་པའི་ཤེས་པ་ལ་སྣང་བའི་དང་ཅན་གྱི་དངོས་པོ་ནི་མི་སེལ་གྱི། ཤེས་རབ་དང་ཡེ་ཤེས་
ཀྱིས་དཔྱད་ན་ཆུ་ཞིང་གི་སྟོང་པོ་བཞིན་དུ་སྟིང་པོ་བག་ཙམ་ཡང་མི་སྐྱང་བས་དོན་དམ་པར་མི་འདོད་དོ། །དེ

142

ལྡར་ན་སྡུང་བའི་དོན་མ་བཀག་པ་ཉིད་ཀྱིས་མཚོན་པར་ཞེན་པ་མེད་པའི་སྒྲུབ་པ་དང་། སྒྲུབ་པའི་ཐ་སྙད་འཛུག་
པས་ཚོས་ཐམས་ཅད་རང་རང་བཞིན་མེད་པར་སྒྲུབ་པ་ལ། གནོད་པ་ཅི་ཡང་མེད་དོ། །དེ་སྐྱད་དུ།

༼ འཛིན་པ་སྤྱལ་ལ་མི་བརྟེན་ན། །ཐ་སྙད་རབ་ཏུ་འབྱུང་འགྱུར་ལ། །

ཐ་སྙད་རྣམས་ལ་མཁས་གྱུར་ན། །བསྟན་བཅོས་དོན་ལ་རྨོངས་པ་མེད། །

དོན་དམ་པའི་ཚུལ་ལ་སྡུང་བས་དབང་སྒྱུར་བ་གང་དག་འདི་ལྟ་སྟེ། ཚོས་ཐམས་ཅད་རང་བཞིན་མེད་པར་སྒྲུབ་
ནི་མེད་པ་ཉིད་དུ་སྤྱི་པོ་ནས་དབང་སྒྱུར་བ་ཞེས་སྒྲུབ་པ་དང་།

དེ་སྐྱར་རྒྱུ་དང་འབྲས་བུ་སྒྱུར་འདེབས་པ། ལོག་སྐྱས་དཀར་ཕྱོགས་དུང་འཕྲིན་དང་ཚོས་ཀྱི། ལོ་ཏྲིག་མེར་བ་
ནམ་མཁའི་མེ་ཏོག་འདི། །ཤེགས་འདོང་རྣམས་ཀྱིས་རྒྱུང་རིང་སྤྱང་བར་བྱ། །

ཞེས་སྒྲུ་བ་དེ་དག་གི་ཕྱིར་འདི་བརྗོད་དེ།

དེའི་ཕྱིར་ཕྱོག་མེད་སྲིད་རྒྱུད་ནས། །དངོས་དང་དངོས་མེད་རྟོག་སོགས་ཀྱི།
རིགས་དང་མཐུན་པའི་ས་བོན་ཉིད། །རྗེས་སུ་དཔག་པར་བྱ་བ་ཡིན།། ༩ ༠ ||
འདི་ནི་དངོས་པོའི་མཐུ་སྟོབས་ཀྱིས། །འབྱུང་བ་མ་ཡིན་དེ་མེད་ཕྱིར།
དངོས་པོ་རྣམས་ཀྱི་བདག་ཉིད་དེ། །རྒྱུ་ཆེན་རབ་ཏུ་བཀགས་པ་ཡིན།། ༩༠ ||
རིམ་གྱིས་འབྱུང་ཕྱིར་སྐྱོ་འབྱུར་མིན། །ཧྲག་བྱུང་མ་ཡིན་ཧྲག་མ་ཡིན།
དེ་བས་གོམས་འདི་དེ་ཉིད་ཕྱིར། །དང་པོ་རང་གི་རིགས་ལས་སྐྱེས།། ༩༢ ||

འདི་སྐྱར་དོན་དམ་པར་ན་དངོས་པོ་འདི་དག་ཐམས་ཅད་ནི་སྐྱེས་པ་ཐམས་ཅད་དང་བྲལ་བ་ཡིན་ན་དེ་ལྟ་བུ་དེ་
དག་ལ་བློ་དགར་བ་མ་ཡིན་པ་རྣམས་ཀྱི་དངོས་པོ་དང་། དངོས་པོ་མེད་པ་ལ་སོགས་པར་རྣམ་པར་རྟོག་པ་
རྣམས་འབྱུང་སྟེ། དེ་དག་ཀུན་ཕྱོག་མ་མེད་པའི་ལས་དང་། སྲིད་པ་ལ་སོགས་པའི་རྒྱུན་ནས་རིགས་མཐུན་པའི་
ས་བོན་ནི་རྒྱུགནན་མེད་དོ། །དེ་དག་ནི་དམིགས་པའི་སྤྱོས་ཀྱི་འབྱུང་བ་མ་ཡིན་ཏེ། དངོས་པོ་དང་དངོས་པོ་
མེད་པ་ལ་སོགས་པའི་བདག་ཉིད་ཀྱི་དངོས་པོ་རྣམས་ཀུང་རྒྱུ་ཆེན་བཀགས་པའི་ཕྱིར་རོ།

དེ་ལ་གལ་ཏེ་རང་གི་རིགས་མཐུན་པའི་ས་བོན་གྱི་རྒྱུ་མེད་དུ་ཟིན་ན། དེ་ལས་སྐྱ་མ་གནན་ཅི་ཞིག་ཡོད། ཨོ་
ན་སྐྱེ་བའི་རྒྱུ་མེད་པའམ། རྒྱ་ཧྲག་པ་ལས་སྐྱེས་པའམ། བདག་ཉིད་ཧྲག་པ་ཡོད་དེ། ཇི་སྐྱར་སྒོ་བྱར་འབྱུང་བར་
སྐྱ་བ་དང་། དབང་ཕྱུག་ལ་སོགས་པའི་རྒྱུ་ལ་འཆེལ་བ་དང་། ཤེས་པ་ཡོད་པ་ཧྲག་ཅེས་ཁས་ལེན་པ་ལྟ་

བུའོ། །ཞེན། དེ་ལྟ་ཡང་མ་ཨིན་ཏེ། དེ་དག་རིམ་གྱིས་འབྱུང་བའི་ཕྱིར་རོ། རྒྱུ་ལ་མི་ལྟོས་པ་དང་དུག་ཏུ་ཉེ་
བར་གནས་པའི་རྒྱུ་དང་། རང་བཞིན་རྣམས་ནི་རིམ་གྱིས་འབྱུང་བ་དང་འགལ་ལོ། །

དེ་བས་ན་དངོས་པོ་ལ་སོགས་པར་རྣམ་པར་རྟོག་པའི་ཕྱིར་ཚེ་འདི་ལ་དང་པོ་འབྱུང་བ་དག་གུང་འདུ་བ་ལ་གོ-མས་
པའི་བག་ཆགས་ལས་སྐྱེ་བར་རྟེས་སུ་དཔག་སྟེ། སྐྱེས་པ་རྣམས་གོང་ནས་གོང་དུ་རྒྱུད་དུ་དང་འཕྲིང་དང་ཆེན་པོ་
ལ་སོགས་པའི་དྲེ་བྲག་གི་ཐ་དད་པ་གོམས་པའི་སྟོབས་ལས་འབྱུང་བ་དངོས་པོ་ལ་སོགས་པ་རྣམ་པར་རྟོག་པ་
བཞིན་ནོ། །དེའི་ཕྱིར་ཕྱོག་མ་མེད་པའི་སྲིད་པ་གནན་གྲུབ་བོ། །

འདིས་ནི་མ་འོངས་པའི་སྲིད་པ་རྟེས་སུ་དཔག་པ་ལ་ཡང་འཕང་ཞིན་ཏེ། འདི་ལྟར་འདོད་ཆགས་མ་བྲལ་བའི་འཆེ-
བའི་སེམས་ནི་བདག་དང་བདག་གི་ཆགས་པའི་ཕྱིན་ཅི་ལོག་གི་བག་ཆགས་དང་འ་བྲེལ་བའི་ཕྱིར་སེམས་གནན་
གྱི་མཚམས་སྦྱོར་ནུས་ཏེ། དེ་སྟོན་གྱི་སེམས་སྐྱེས་པ་དང་འདྲ་བས་སྐྱབ་པ་གསལ་ལོ། །

དེའི་ཕྱིར་དུག་ཆད་ལྟ་བ་རྣམས། །གཞན་འདི་ལ་རིང་དུ་གནས། །
སྟོག་དང་རྟེས་སུ་འཇུག་པ་ཡང་། །ཞ་བོན་སྐྱུ་གུ་ལྟག་སོགས་བཞིན།། ༢༣ །།

དོན་དམ་པར་རྟག་པ་དང་ཆད་པ་དག་གི་སྐྲབས་མེད་པ་ཉིད་དེ། དེ་གཉིས་ནི་དངོས་པོ་ལ་བརྟེན་པ་ཨིན་ལས།
དངོས་པོ་མེད་ན་དེ་དག་ལྟག་ལ་ཡོད། གུན་རྟོབ་ཀྱི་བདེན་པ་ལ་བརྟེན་ནས་ནི་སྲ་མ་ས་མའི་སྐྱད་ཅིག་ལོག་ནས།
སྐྱད་ཅིག་གཞན་དང་གཞན་འབྱུང་བས་དངོས་པོ་རྣམས་ལ་ཕོག་མ་དང་ཐ་མ་མེད་དེ། ཕྱི་རོལ་པ་ལ་དག་འདོད་པ་
དང་འདུ་བས་དེ་གཉིས་ཞིན་དུ་ཡོད་པར་མི་འགྱུར་རོ། །

འདིར་གསུངས་པ། ཡོད་ན་དངོས་པོ་རྟག་འགྱུར་ལ། །མེད་ན་ངེས་པར་ཆད་འགྱུར་ཏེ། དངོས་ཡོད་གཉི་གར་
འགྱུར་བས་ན། །དེའི་ཕྱིར་དངོས་པོ་ཁས་མི་བླང་། །གང་ཕྱིར་དངོས་པོ་རང་འབྱུང་བ། །དེའི་ཕྱིར་ཆད་པར་
འགྱུར་མ་ཨིན། །གང་ཕྱིར་དངོས་པོ་ལྟོག་འགྱུར་བ། །དེའི་ཕྱིར་རྟག་པར་འགྱུར་མ་ཨིན། །གང་དག་བུང་རྒྱབ་
བརྟེན་པའི་ཕྱིར། །དོན་དུ་མེད་པར་ཁས་མི་འཆེ། །མི་སེམས་སྟོང་པར་མི་བྱེད་པ། །དེ་དག་ཇི་ལྟར་མེད་པར་
འདོད། །ཅེའོ། །དཀོན་མཆོག་སྤྲིན་ལས་ཀྱང་། ཇི་ལྟར་ན་བྱང་རྒྱབ་སེམས་དཔའ་ཐེག་པ་ཆེན་པོ་ལ་མགས་པ་
ཨིན་ཞེན། འདི་ལ་བྱང་རྒྱབ་སེམས་དཔའ་བསྒྲུབ་པ་ཐམས་ཅད་ལ་ཡང་སྟོབ་ལ། སྟོབ་པ་ཡང་མི་དམིགས།
བསྒྲུབ་པའི་ལམ་ཡང་མི་དམིགས་གང་སྟོབ་པ་དེ་ཡང་མི་དམིགས་ཏེ། རྒྱུ་དེ་དང་རྐྱེན་དང་གཞི་ནེས་ཆད་པར་ལྟ
བར་ཡང་མི་འགྱུར་ཞེས་གསུངས་སོ། །ཡང་དེ་ཉིད་ལས། རིགས་ཀྱི་བུ་འདི་ལ་བྱང་རྒྱབ་སེམས་དཔའ་དཔའ་ཡང

དགའ་བའི་ཤེས་རབ་ཀྱིས་གཟུགས་ལ་རྟོག ཚོར་བ་དང་། འདུ་ཤེས་དང་། འདུ་བྱེད་རྣམས་དང་། རྣམ་པར་
ཤེས་པ་ལ་རྟོག་སྟེ། དེ་གཟུགས་ལ་རྟོག་པ་ན་གཟུགས་ཀྱི་སྐྱེ་བ་མི་དམིགས་སོ། གུན་འབྱུང་བ་མི་དམིགས་
སོ། །འགོག་པ་མི་དམིགས་སོ། ཚོར་བ་དང་། འདུ་ཤེས་དང་། འདུ་བྱེད་དང་། རྣམ་པར་ཤེས་པའི་སྐྱེ་བ་མི་
དམིགས། གུན་འབྱུང་བ་མི་དམིགས། འགོག་པ་མི་དམིགས་སོ། དེ་ཡང་དོན་དམ་པར་སྐྱེ་བ་མེད་པར་དཔྱོད་
པའི་ཤེས་རབ་ཀྱིས་ཡིན་གྱི། ཐ་སྙད་ཀྱི་རང་བཞིན་གྱིས་ནི་མ་ཡིན་ནོ་ཞེས་ཡོངས་སུ་བསྟན་པ་ཡིན་ནོ། །
རྣམ་པར་གྲོལ་བ་ཡང་གཞུང་འདི་ཉིད་ལ་སྐྱ་ཉིད་དེ། འདི་ལྟར། ཚོས་ལ་བདག་མེད་མ་མཁས་ན། །རང་
བཞིན་མེད་པ་གོམས་བྱས་པས། ཕྱིན་ཅི་ལོག་ལས་བྱུང་བ་ཡི། །ཉོན་མོངས་སྐྱིས་པ་མེད་པར་སྐྱོང་། ༢༥ །།
རྫ་བ་སྐྱོན་མའི་ཉིང་དེ་འཛིན་ལས་ཏེ་སྐྱད་དུ། ཤེས་གང་ཆགས་པ་དང་། གང་ལ་ཆགས་པ་དང་། གང་གིས་
ཆགས་པའི་ཚོས་དེ་ཡང་དག་པར་རྟེས་སུ་མ་མཐོང་དོ་ཞེས་རྒྱ་ཆེར་གསུངས་སོ། །འདིར་(རྟོགས་པ་དུག་ཏུ་ཡར་
)ཡང་གསུངས་པ། དངོས་པོར་འཛིན་ལེན་ཡོད་ན་ནི། །འདོད་ཆགས་ཞེ་སྡང་མི་བཟད་འབྱུང་། ལྟ་བ་མ་རུངས་
ཡོངས་སུ་འཛིན། །དེ་ལས་བྱུང་བའི་རྩོད་པར་འགྱུར།། ༢༧ དེ་ནི་ལྟ་བ་ཀུན་གྱི་རྒྱུ། །དེ་མེད་ཉོན་མོངས་མི་
འབྱུང་སྟེ། དེ་བས་དེ་ནི་ཡོངས་ཤེས་ན། །ལྟ་དང་ཉོན་མོངས་ཡོངས་སུ་འབྱུང་།། ༢༨ གང་གིས་དེ་ཤེས
འགྱུར་ཞེ་ན། །རྟེན་ཅིང་འབྱུང་བ་མཐོང་བས་ཏེ། བརྟེན་ནས་སྐྱེས་པ་མ་སྐྱེས་ཞེས། །ཡང་དག་གཞིག་པ་
མཚོག་གིས་གསུངས།། ༢༩ ཤེའོ། །གཞན་ཡང་རང་བཞིན་མེད་པའི་ཆུལ་ལ་གང་མི་འཁྲུ་དོ་ཞེས་རྩོལ་བའི་
ཉོན་མོངས་པ་དང་། ལས་དང་། སྐྱེ་བའི་ཀུན་ནས་ཉོན་མོངས་དེ་གང་ཡིན། །རྣམ་པར་བྱང་བ་ནི་གང་ཡིན།
ལས་དང་འབྲས་བུར་འབྲེལ་བ་དང་། རྟེས་སུ་དངག་པ་དང་། རྟེས་སུ་དངག་པར་བུ་བའི་ཐ་སྙད་ལ་སོགས་པ་
ནི་གང་ཡིན། མ་རིག་པ་དང་འདུ་ཤེད་ལ་སོགས་པ་སྲིད་པའི་ཡན་ལག་རྣམས་ཀྱི་རྒྱུ་དང་འབྲས་བུའི་དངོས་པོ་
དང་། གཉེན་པོ་གོམས་པར་བྱས་པ་ཤིན་ཏུ་ཉམས་སུ་ལེན་ལས་ཉོན་མོངས་པ་དང་མི་མཐུན་པའི་གནས་འབྱུང་
བ་དང་། དགེ་བ་དང་མི་དགེ་བའི་ལས་ཀྱི་རྣམ་པར་སྨིན་པ་སྟུག་པ་དང་མི་སྟུག་པ་འབྱུང་བ་དང་།

དངོས་གང་ཡང་དག་ཇེ་བཞིན་པ། །དེ་ནི་དེ་འདྲའི་ཐབས་སེམས་ཀྱི།

རྒྱུ་ཡིན་དེ་ལས་དེ་ལྟའི་དངོས། །དེ་བས་དེ་བསྐྱེད་དུགས་ཅན་བློས།།   རྣམ་འགྲེལ་མངོན་སུམ་ལེའུ་ ༢༡

ཞེས་བུ་བ་དེ་ལྟ་བུ་ནི་བསྐྱེད་པར་བུ་བ་དང་། སྐྱེད་པའི་དངོས་པོ་མ་ཡིན་ནམ་གལ་ཏེ་དེ་ལྟ་ན་
ཡང་པོ་མ་བུ་ཅིག་ཅར་ཀུན་ག་ངར་བ་ཐམས་ཅད་ཀྱི་ལན་གདབ་པ་འདི་ནས་པར་རྱངས་ཤིག །

རྒྱུ་དང་འབྲས་བུའི་དངོས་པོ་ནི། །ཀུན་རྫོབ་ཏུ་ནི་མ་བརྫིགས་པས།

ཀུན་ནས་ཉོན་མོངས་རྣམ་བྱང་སོགས། །རྣམ་པར་བཞག་ལ་འཁྲུགས་པ་མེད།། ༦༩ །།

གལ་ཏེ་རྣམ་པར་གནས་པ་འདི་དོན་དམ་པར་ཁས་ལེན་ཅིང་རང་དུ་འབད་ན་དེའི་ཚེ་ཚོགས་ཕྱུ་མོ་ལ་སོགས་པ་ནས་རྣམ་པར་ཤེས་པ་ལ་ཐུག་པའི་བར་དག་གཅིག་ཨཔམ་དུ་མའི་རང་བཞིན་དུ་སྐྱབས་ཤིག །སྟོང་པ་ལྟར་བརྫོད་པ་རྣམས་ཀྱི་ལན་ཡང་ཐོབ་ཅིག །འདི་ལྟར་འདི་མ་ལུས་པ་བདེན་ཞིན་བརྟན་པ་མ་ཡིན་ཏེ། མི་སྐྱ་བའི་ཚོས་ཅན་ཙོ་ཞེས་རེས་པར་ཁས་ལེན་ཏེ། །འདི་སྐྱད་ཅེས་ཀྱང་གསུངས་ཏེ།

རྣམ་པར་དབེན་དོན་མི་ཤེས་ལ། །ཐོས་པ་ཚམ་ལ་འཇུག་བྱེད་ཅིང་།

གང་དག་བསོད་ནམས་མི་བྱེད་པ། །སྐྱེས་བུ་བ་ཞཔའེ་དག་བརྫུག ། རིགས་པ་དྲུག་ཅུ་པ་ ༣༦

ལས་ཀྱི་འབྲས་བུ་ཡོང་པ་དང་། །འགྲོ་བ་དག་ཀྱང་ཤེས་ཏུ་བརྫོད།

དེ་ཡི་རང་བཞིན་ཡོངས་ཤེས་དང་། །སྐྱེ་བ་མེད་པ་དག་ཀྱང་བསྟན།། རིགས་པ་དྲུག་ཅུ་པ་ ༣༣

འཇིག་རྟེན་དབང་དུ་རྒྱལ་བ་རྣམས། །ང་དང་ང་ཡི་ཤེས་གསུངས་ལྟར།

ཕུང་པོ་ཁམས་དང་སྐྱེ་མཆེད་རྣམས། །དེ་བཞིན་དགོས་པའི་དབང་གིས་གསུངས།།

རིགས་པ་དྲུག་ཅུ་པ་ ༣༥

ཤེས༌སོ། །ཡང་དམིགས་པ་ཅན་གང་དག་ན་རེ་ལྟ་བ་འདི་ནི་བསོད་ནམས་དང་ཡེ་ཤེས་ཀྱི་ཚོགས་ཡོངས་སུ་བགང་བ་འབད་པར་ཏེ་ལྟར་འགྱུར་བ་ཡིན་ནམ། གལ་ཏེ་འཁོར་གསུམ་ཡོངས་སུ་དག་པར་འགྱུར་རོ་ཞེན། དེ་ཡང་རིགས་པ་མ་ཡིན་ཏེ། འདི་ལྟར་མཚོད་པ་དང་ཐན་གདགས་པར་འདོད་ལས་གང་ཁྱིན་ནེ་དང་པ་ཤིན་ཏུ་སྐྱེ་ཀྱི་གང་གིས་སྐྱིན་པར་བྱ་བ་དང་། སྐྱིན་པ་པོ་དང་། ཤེན་པ་པོ་དང་དམིགས་པ་ལ་གནས་པས་ནི་མ་ཡིན་ནོ། །འདི་ལྟར་ཅི་ཡང་མེད་པའི་ཕྱིར་སྐྱིན་པར་བྱ་བ་ལ་སོགས་མི་དམིགས་སམ། ཞོན་ཏེ་ཡུལ་མ་ཡིན་པའི་ཕྱིར་མི་དམིགས། ཕྱོགས་དང་པོ་ལ་ནི་གང་གིས་ཅི་ལ་པེ་གང་ལ་གང་གིས་ཅི་ལ་ཡང་བྱིན་པ་མེད་ལས་བསོད་ནམས་མེད་པར་འགྱུར་རོ། །བྱང་རྒྱལ་སེམས་དཔའ་རྣམས་ཀྱིས་སེམས་ཅན་གྱི་དོན་གྱི་ཕྱིར་དལ་བ་གང་ཡིན་པ་དེ་ཡང་སེམས་ཅན་མེད་པའི་ཕྱིར་དོན་མེད་པར་འགྱུར་རོ། །

སྐྱིན་པར་བྱ་བ་དང་སྐྱིན་པ་པོ་དང་ལེན་པ་པོ་རྣམས་ནི་དེ་བཞིན་གཤེགས་པ་རྣམས་ཀྱིས་གཟིགས་ཏེ། དེ་བས་ན་ཡུལ་མ་ཡིན་པའི་ཕྱིར་མི་དམིགས་སོ་ཞེས་བྱ་བ་ཡང་མི་འཐྱུང་ངོ་། །གཞན་སྐྱིན་པར་བྱ་བ་ལ་སོགས་པ་དང་། ལེན་པ་པོ་དང་སྐྱིན་པ་རང་གི་སེམས་དང་སེམས་ལས་བྱུང་བ་དེ་དག་རང་གིས་རིག་པར་བྱེད་ན་དེ་ཇི་ལྟར་

146

ཡུལ་མ་ཡིན། ཡང་སྐྱེས་པ། སྐྱེན་པ་གང་ཞིག་ཕན་གདགས་དང་། །མཆོད་པའི་ཕྱིར་ཡང་སྐྱེན་བྱེད་པ། དེ་ནི་
ཉིན་ཏུ་དད་པར་བྱེད། །མཐོང་མེད་གནས་པས་མ་ཡིན་ནོ། །མེད་པའི་ཕྱིར་ནི་མི་དམིགས་སམ། །ཚོན་ཏེ་ཡུལ་
མིན་ཕྱིར་རམ་ཅི། མེད་ན་བསོད་ནམས་འཇིག་པར་འགྱུར། །དག་པའི་དོན་ཡང་མེད་པར་འགྱུར། །གསུམ་
ཆར་རྒྱལ་བས་གཞིགས་པས་ན། །དེ་བས་ཡུལ་མིན་མ་ཡིན་ནོ། རང་གི་སེམས་དང་སེམས་བྱུང་གང་། །དེ་
དག་རང་གིས་རིག་པར་བྱེད། །ཅེས་རྩོལ་བ་དེ་ལ་སོགས་པ་ཐམས་ཅད་ཀྱང་དེ་ལྟོ་མཐོང་བ་ལྟར་མཛོན་པར་
ཞེས་པ་མ་ཡིན་པས། བཀྲལ་བར་བསྟན་པ།

 འདི་ལྟར་རྒྱུ་དང་འབྲས་བུ་ཡི། །ཚོས་འདི་རྣམ་པར་བཞག་པས་ན།
ཚོགས་རྣམས་ཏུ་མ་མེད་པ་ཡང་། །གཞུང་འདི་ཉིད་ལ་རུང་བ་ཡིན།། ༢༥ ॥
རྣམ་པར་དག་པའི་རྒྱུ་ལས་ནི། །འབྲས་བུ་རྣམ་པར་དག་པ་འབྱུང་།
ཡང་དག་ལྷས་བྱུང་རྒྱལ་ཁྲིམས་ཀྱི། །ཡན་ལག་ལ་སོགས་རྣམ་དག་བཞིན།། ༢༦ ॥
དེ་བཞིན་རྣམ་དག་མ་ཡིན་ལས། །འབྲས་བུ་རྣམ་དག་མ་ཡིན་འབྱུང་།
ལོག་ལྟའི་སྟོབས་ལས་བྱུང་བ་ཡི། །ལོག་པར་གཡེམ་ལ་སོགས་པ་བཞིན།། ༢༧ ॥
འབྲས་བུ་ཐམས་ཅད་ནི་རྒྱུའི་རྟེ་སུ་འགྲོ་བ་དང་། སྟོག་པ་དང་མཐུན་པར་བྱེད་པས་དེ་རྣམ་པར་དག་པ་དང་།
རྣམ་པར་མ་དག་པ་གཉིས་ཀྱིས་རྣམ་པར་དག་པ་དང་རྣམ་པར་མ་དག་པར་འགྱུར་ཏེ། དཔེར་ན། ཤེགས་པར་
བྱུང་པ་དང་། ཉེ་པར་བྱུང་པའི་ལས་རྣམས་ཀྱི་འབྲས་བུ་རྣམ་པར་སྐྱེན་པ་ཡོད་པ་དང་མེད་ཅེས་ཟེར་བ་ལྟ་བུ་
སྟེ། ཡང་དག་པ་དང་ལོག་པར་ལྟ་བས་མཛོན་ཏུ་དྲངས་པའི་ཚུལ་ཁྲིམས་ཀྱི་ཡན་ལག་དང་། བཀ་ཡོད་པའི་
ཡན་ལག་ལ་སོགས་པ་དང་། འདོད་པ་ལ་ལོག་པར་གཡེམ་པ་ལ་སོགས་པ་བཞིན་ནོ། །འདིས་ཅི་ཞིག་འགྲུབ་
ཅེ་ན། བསྟན་པ།

ཚོན་མའི་གནོད་པ་ཡོད་པས་ན། །དངོས་པོ་དངོས་པ་ཡོད་པ་ནི།
སྐྱིག་རྒྱུ་ལ་སོགས་ཞེས་པ་བཞིན། །ཕྱིན་ཅི་ལོག་པར་ཡོངས་སུ་རྟོག ༢༢ ॥
ཡང་དག་པར་ན་དངོས་པོ་ཐམས་ཅད་ནི། གཅིག་དང་དུ་མའི་རང་བཞིན་དུ་མི་འཐབ་པས་ཡོད་པ་ལ་གནོད་པའི་
ཚོན་མ་ནི་སྐྱེར་བཤད་ཟིན་ཏོ། །རིག་པར་བྱ་བ་དང་རིག་པར་བྱེད་པའི་མཆན་ཉིད་དང་ཡུལ་ཉིད་ལ་གནོད་པའི

ཚད་མ་ཡང་སྒྱུར་བགད་ཟིན་ཏོ། །དེ་ལྟ་བས་ན་འདི་ཡང་དག་པར་ཡོད་དོ་ཞེས་མངོན་པར་ཞེན་ཏེ། སྨྲིག་རྒྱུའི་
ཚོགས་ལ་ཆུར་ཞེས་པ་བཞིན་ནོ། །གང་གི་ཕྱིར་དེ་ལྟར་གྱུར་པ།

དེའི་ཕྱིར་དེའི་མཐུན་བྱུང་བ་ཡི། །ཡ་རོལ་ཕྱིན་པ་བསྐྱབ་པ་ཀུན།

བདག་དང་བདག་གིར་ལོག་པ་ལས། །བྱུང་བ་བཞིན་དུ་སྟོབས་ཆུང་ངོ།། ༢༩ །།

ཇི་ལྟར་ཕྱི་དང་ནང་གི་སྐུ་སྟེགས་ཅན་རྣམས་ཀྱི་སྣིན་པ་དང་། རྒྱལ་ཁྲིམས་ལ་སོགས་པ་ནན་ཏན་བྱེད་པ།
འདིག་ཚོགས་ལ་ལྟ་བ་ལས་བྱུང་བ་ནི་དེ་མ་ཐག་ཏུ་དྲུན་མེད་པ་ཡང་དག་པར་རྟོགས་པའི་བྱང་རྒྱལ་ཀྱི་ཡན་ལག་
ཏུ་མི་འགྱུར་ཏེ། སྟོབས་ཆུང་བ་དེ་བཞིན་དུ་དམིགས་པ་ཅན་རྣམས་ཀྱི་ཡང་སྟོབས་ཆུང་སྟེ། ཕྱིན་ཅི་ལོག་ལས་
བྱུང་བར་ཏེ་ཐག་མེད་པའི་ཕྱིར་རོ། །

དངོས་པོར་དམིགས་པ་མེད་པ་ལས། །བྱུང་བ་འབྲས་བུ་ཆེན་པོ་སྟེ།

རྒྱས་པའི་རྒྱ་ལས་བྱུང་བའི་ཕྱིར། །ས་བོན་བྱུང་བའི་མྱུག་སོགས་བཞིན།། ༣༠ །།

ཡོད་པ་དང་རིག་པར་བྱ་བ་མི་འཇབད་པའི་ཕྱིར། ཡང་དག་པར་ན་རིག་པར་བྱ་བ་ལ་སོགས་པ་མི་དམིགས་
སོ། །རྒྱས་པའི་རྒྱའི་ཕྱིན་ཅི་མ་ལོག་པའི་ཕྱིར་ཏེ། གང་ཟག་ལ་བདག་མེད་པར་ལྟ་བ་བཞིན་ནོ། །དེ་ལས་བྱུང་
བ་སྨྲིན་པ་ལ་སོགས་པ་ནི་སྟོབས་དང་ལྡན་པའི་རྒྱལ་སྲོ་དུ་དྲངས་པའི་ཕྱིར། འབྲས་བུ་ཞིན་ཏུ་རྒྱ་ཆེ་བ་མངོན་
པར་སྐྱབ་ནུས་པར་འགྱུར་ཏེ། ས་བོན་ལས་བྱུང་བའི་མྱུག་གུ་ལ་སོགས་པ་བཞིན་ནོ། །

འདི་ནི་ཚོགས་ཡང་དག་པར་སྐྱོད་པ་ལས་གསུངས་ཏེ། ཚོས་ཐམས་ཅད་ནི་དམིགས་པ་མེད་པ་སྟེ། དེ་ལ་རྣམ་པར་
ཞེས་པ་མི་འཇུག་གོ་ཞེའོ། །ཡང་དེ་ཉིད་ལས། བཅོམ་ལྡན་འདས་ཚོས་ཐམས་ཅད་མི་མཐོང་བ་ནི་ཡང་དག་
པར་མཐོང་བའོ། །ཞེས་གསུངས་སོ། །རྒྱལ་བ་སྐྱེད་མ་ལས་ཀྱང་། རབ་འབྱོར་འདི་ཅི་སྙམ་དུ་སེམས། ཤར་
ཕྱོགས་ཀྱི་ནམ་མཁའི་ཚད་གཟུང་བར་སྣུན་འམ། རབ་འབྱོར་གྱིས་གསོལ་པ། བཅོམ་ལྡན་འདས་དེ་ནི་མ་ལགས་
སོ་ཞེས་བྱ་བ་ནས། རབ་འབྱོར་དེ་བཞིན་དུ་བྱང་རྒྱབ་སེམས་དཔའ་གང་མི་གནས་པར་སྦྱིན་པ་ཡོངས་སུ་གཏོང་
བ་དེའི་བསོད་ནམས་ཀྱི་ཕུང་པོ་ཡང་ཚད་གཟུང་བར་སྣུ་བ་མ་ཡིན་ནོ་ཞེས་བྱ་བའི་བར་དུ་གསུངས་སོ། །ཡང་དེ་
ཉིད་ལས། རབ་འབྱོར་འདི་ལྟ་སྟེ། དཔེར་ན། མིག་དང་ལྡན་པའི་མི་ཞིག་མུན་པར་ཞུགས་ནས། ཅི་ཡང་མི་
མཐོང་བ་དེ་བཞིན་དུ་གང་དངོས་པོར་ལྟུང་བ་ལས་སྦྱིན་པ་ཡོངས་སུ་གཏོང་བས་བྱང་རྒྱབ་སེམས་དཔར་ལྟའོ། །

རབ་འབྱོར་འདི་ལྟ་སྟེ། དཔེར་ན། ནམ་ལངས་ཤེ་མ་ཕྱར་ནས་མིག་དང་ལྡན་པའི་མི་ས་གཟུགས་རྣམ་པ་སྣ་
ཚོགས་དག་མཐོང་བ་དེ་བཞིན་དུ་གང་དངོས་པོར་མ་ལྷུང་བས་སྨྲིན་པ་ཡོངས་སུ་གཏོང་བའི་བྱང་ཆུབ་སེམས་
དཔའ་ལྷའི་ཤེས་གསུངས་སོ། །

མཆོད་པ་དང་། ཕན་འདོགས་པར་འདོད་པས་སྨྲིན་པ་དེ་འཕོར་གསུམ་དག་པར་བྱིན་ན་དེ་ཉིད་རྣོ་གྲོས་དང་ལྡན་
པ་རྣམས་ལ་ཤིན་ཏུ་དང་བའི་གནས་སུ་འགྱུར་ཏེ། འདི་ལྟར་དངིགས་པ་མེད་པ་འདི་ནི་ཕྱིན་ཅི་མ་ལོག་པ་སྟེ།
དེ་ཡང་གཏི་མུག་མེད་པའི་དགེ་བའི་རྩ་བའོ། །བསོད་ནམས་དང་འབྲེག་པ་དང་ངལ་བ་དོན་མེད་པར་ཐལ་བར་
ཡང་མི་འགྱུར་བ་ནི་རྒྱུ་དང་འབྲས་བུའི་དངོས་པོ་ནི། །ཀུན་རྟོབ་ཏུ་མ་བརྟགས་པས་ཤེས་པས་བསྟན་ཟིན་ཏོ།
གསུམ་ཆར་ཡང་གཟིགས་ཤེས་བྱ་བ་ཡང་ཀུན་རྟོབ་པ་ཉིད་དོ། །རང་རིག་པ་ཡང་ཀུན་རྟོབ་ཀྱི་བདེན་པར་
གཏོགས་པ་ཉིད་དེ་གཅིག་དང་དུ་བའི་རང་བཞིན་དུ་བཏགས་མི་བཟོད་པའི་ཕྱིར་ཤེས་བྱ་བས་གཏན་ལ་ཕབ་ཟིན་
ཏོ། །དེའི་ཕྱིར་བཅོས་ཟིན་པ་ཡང་མི་འཆའོ། །གང་དག་གིས་ཀྱི་དང་འབྲས་བུའི་དངོས་པོར་དག་བཙན་ལས་
ཁོལ་བ་ནར་པ་ཐམས་ཅད་ཀྱི་ལན་བཏབ་པར་འདོད་པའི་ཀུན་རྟོབ་ཀྱི་དངོས་པོ་དེ་དག་གང་ཡིན་པ་དེ་དྲུང་
པར་བྱའོ། །

ཅི་སེམས་དང་སེམས་ལས་བྱུང་བ་ཙམ་གྱི་བདག་ཉིད་པོ་ནམ་ཅིའི་ཕྱིར་བདག་ཉིད་ཀྱང་ཡིན་ཞེན། དེ་ལའ་
ཅིག་ནི་ཕྱོགས་ཕྱི་མ་ལ་བརྟེན་ཏེ་བསྟན་བཅོས་ལས་སེམས་ཙམ་མོ་ཞེས་གསུངས་པ་ནི་ཕྱིན་པ་པོ་དང་ཟ་བ་པོ་
དགག་པའི་ཕྱིར་རོ་ཞེས་སྟུ་བ་ལྟ་བུའོ། །གཞན་དག་སེམས་པ་ནི།

        རྒྱུ་དང་འབྲས་བུར་གྱུར་པ་ཡང་། །ཤེས་པ་འབའ་ཞིག་ཁོ་ན་སྟེ།
        རང་གིས་གྲུབ་པ་གང་ཡིན་པ། །དེ་ནི་ཤེས་པར་གནས་པ་ཡིན།། (༥) །།

རང་གིས་གྲུབ་པའི་དོ་བོ་པོར་ནས་ཤེས་པའི་དོ་བོ་གཞན་ཉོག་པ་མེད་དོ། །རང་གིས་གྲུབ་པའི་རང་བཞིན་ཡང་
སྟེ་ལམ་དང་སྐྱ་མ་ལ་སོགས་པའི་གཟུགས་བརྙན་བཞིན་ནོ། །གཟུགས་ལ་སོགས་པའི་ཕྱི་རོལ་ཏུ་འཛིན་པ་རྣམས་ཤེས་
པ་ལས་གུན་ན་ཡོན་པར་གུས་ན་ཡང་མིག་ལ་སོགས་པ་བཞིན་དུ་མ་ཉམ་པ་དང་མི་མཉམ་པའི་ཚོ་རབ་ཏུ་དེ་
བའི་རྒྱུ་མེད་པས་རིག་པར་མི་འགྱུབ་བོ། །དེ་ལྟ་བས་ན་དེ་དག་མྱོང་བ་ནི་ཐ་དད་པ་མ་ཡིན་པའི་སྟོན་པོ་ལ་
སོགས་པའི་རྣམ་པ་སྙང་བ་སྟེ། སྙང་བའི་དོ་བོ་ཡིན་པས་ཚི་ལམ་དང་སྐྱ་མ་ལ་སོགས་པའི་སྙང་བ་བཞིན་ནོ། །

གལ་ཏེ་ཤེས་པའི་རྣམ་པ་སྐྱེད་པའི་དོན་གནན་ཞིག་འབྲས་བུ་ལས་གུན་ན་ཡོད་པར་རྟེས་སུ་དཔོག་ན། དེ་ལྟ་ན་
ཡང་མཚོ་ཆེ་སུམ་དུ་གྱུབ་པར་མི་གྱུར་གྱི་རྟེས་སུ་དཔག་པར་ཟད་དོ། །དེ་ལྟ་ན་ཡང་འདི་མེད་པར་གྱུབ་པ་སྟེ། དེ་མ་
ཐག་པའི་རྐྱེན་ངེས་པར་ཡོད་པ་དང་། དུལ་ཕྲ་མོ་ལ་སོགས་པ་བཀག་པའི་ཕྱིར་རོ། །དེ་ལྟར་བྱས་ན་སྐྱག་པོ་
བགོད་པ་དང་། དགོངས་པ་ངེས་པར་འགྱིལ་པ་ལ་སོགས་པ་ལས་འབྱུང་བ་ཐམས་ཅད་དང་མཐུན་པ་ཡིན་
ནོ། །ལྷུར་གཞིགས་པ་ལས།

༄ ཕྱི་རོལ་གཟུགས་ནི་ཡོད་མ་ཡིན། །རང་གི་སེམས་ནི་ཕྱི་རོལ་སྣང་། །༡༠ ༢༢༩
ཞེས་བསྟན་པ་འདི་ཡང་ལེགས་པར་བཤད་པ་ཡིན་ནོ་སྙམ་དུ་བསམ་མོ། །བློ་ཡི་མ་ཐུ་མི་རྒྱུན་བ་དང་སྒྲག་པར་
བཅོན་པ་དག་གིས་ཀུང་སེམས་དེ་ལ་གཅིག་དང་དུ་མའི་རང་བཞིན་དུ་བརྟགས་ན། དོན་དམ་སྟེང་པོ་མི་མཐོང་
བས། ཡང་དག་པར་འདོད་པ་མ་ཡིན་ནོ། །དེའི་ཕྱིར།

སེམས་ཙམ་ལ་ནི་བརྟེན་ནས་སུ། །ཕྱི་རོལ་དངོས་མེད་ཤེས་པར་བྱ།
རྒྱལ་འདིར་བརྟེན་ནས་དེ་ལ་ཡང་། །ཤིན་ཏུ་བདག་མེད་ཤེས་པར་བྱ།། ༼༩ ॥
སེམས་ཙམ་གྱི་རྒྱལ་ལ་བརྟེན་ནས། མཆུངས་པར་སྤྱན་པ་དང་བཅས་པའི་སེམས་ལས་ཕྱི་རོལ་དུ་འདོད་པ་
བདག་དང་བདག་གི་དང་། གཟུང་བ་དང་འཛིན་པ་ལ་སོགས་པ་རང་བཞིན་མེད་པར་ཚོགས་མེད་པ་ལོ་ནར་
ཏོགས་སོ། །རྒྱལ་འདི་ནི་རང་འབྱུང་ན་མེད་ལས་སེམས་དེ་རང་བཞིན་མེད་པར་ཏོགས་སུ་ཟིན་ཀྱང་། མཐའ་
ཐམས་ཅད་སྐྱངས་པ་དབུ་མའི་ལམ་འདི་ཏོགས་ན། །གཉིག་དང་དུ་མའི་རང་བཞིན་དང་བྲལ་བས་རང་བཞིན་
མེད་པ་ཤིན་ཏུ་ཏོགས་སོ། །དེའི་འཇིག་རྟེན་ལས་འདས་པའི་ལེའུ་ལས་ཀྱང་། གྱི་རྒྱལ་བའི་སྲས་དག་གནན་
ཡང་ཁམས་གསུམ་པ་ནི་སེམས་ཙམ་དུ་ཏོགས་ཏེ། དུས་གསུམ་ཡང་སེམས་ཙམ་དང་མཆུངས་པར་ཏོགས་སོ། །
སེམས་དེ་ཡང་མཐའ་དང་དབུས་མེད་པར་ཁོང་དུ་ཆུད་དོ་ཞེས་བསྟན་པ་འདི་ལེགས་པར་བཤད་པར་འགྱུར་ཏེ།
སྐྱེ་བ་དང་འཇིག་པའི་མཐའ་དང་གནས་པའི་མཚན་ཉིད་ཀྱི་དུས་མེད་པའི་ཕྱིར་མཐའ་དང་དབུས་མེད་
པའོ། །ཚོས་ཡང་དག་པར་སྐྱད་པ་ལས། བཅོམ་ལྡན་འདས་ཚོས་ཐམས་ཅད་ནི་ཀུན་བཏགས་པའི་སྙིང་པོ་སྟེ།
སེམས་ཙམ་དུ་བས་པ་རྫས་མ་མཆིས་པར་སྐྱ་མ་ལྤར་ཐུ་བ་མ་མཆིས་པ་ཞེས་འབྱུང་ངོ་། །

སེམས་ཙམ་ལ་ནི་བརྟེན་ནས་སུ། །ཕྱི་རོལ་དོན་ལ་མི་ཏོག་གོ
ཡང་དག་དམིགས་པར་གནས་ནས་སུ། །སེམས་ཙམ་ལས་ཀྱང་ཤིན་ཏུ་བརྒྱ། །ལང་གཤེགས། ༡༠ ༢༢༤

སེམས་ཙམ་ལས་ནི་བརྫས་ནས་ཀྱང་། །སྣང་བ་མེད་ལས་ཧིན་ཏུ་བརྫ། །

སྣང་མེད་གནས་པའི་རྣལ་འབྱོར་པ། །དེ་ཡིས་ཐེག་པ་ཆེ་པོར་མཐོང་། ། ལང་གཤེགས ༡༠ ༢༥༧

འདུག་པ་སྤྱན་གྱིས་གྲུབ་ཅིད་ཞི། །སློན་ལས་དག་གིས་རྣམ་པར་སྤུངས། །

ཡེ་ཤེས་དག་པ་བདག་མེད་པ། །སྣང་བ་མེད་ལ་མི་མཐོང་ངོ་། ། ལང་གཤེགས ༡༠ ༢༥༢

རྒྱུ་དང་རྐྱེན་ནི་རྣམ་ལོག་དང་། །རྒྱུ་ཡང་ངེས་པར་བཀག་པ་དང་། །

སེམས་ཙམ་རྣམ་པར་བཞག་པ་ནི། །སྐྱེ་བ་མེད་པར་ངས་བསྟན་ཏོ། ། ལང་གཤེགས ༩ ༡༽

དངོས་པོ་རྣམས་ཀྱི་ཕྱིར་དངོས་མེད། །སེམས་ཀྱང་ཡོངས་སུ་གཟུང་མ་ཡིན། །

ལྟ་བ་ཐམས་ཅད་སྤངས་པའི་ཕྱིར། །སྐྱེ་བ་མེད་པའི་མཚན་ཉིད་དོ། །

ཞེས་གསུངས་སོ། །འདིར་ཡང་གསུངས་པ།

འདི་ལ་སྐྱེ་བ་ཅི་ཡང་མེད། །འགག་པར་འགྱུར་བ་ཅི་ཡང་མེད།

སྐྱེ་བ་དང་ནི་འགག་པ་དག །ཤེས་པ་འབའ་ཞིག་ཉིད་ནོ། །

འབྱུང་བ་ཆེ་ལ་སོགས་བཤད་པ། །རྣམ་པར་ཤེས་སུ་ཡང་དག་འདུ། །

དེ་ཤེས་པས་ནི་འཕྲལ་འགྱུར་ན། །ལོག་ལས་རྣམ་བརྟགས་མ་ཡིན་ནམ། ། ལང་གཤེགས ༢༥

ཞེའོ། །

ཆུལ་གཅིས་ཤིག་དར་བཞིན་ནས་སུ། །རིགས་པའི་སྒྲུབ་སྐྱོགས་འདུ་བྱེད་པ།

དེ་དག་དེའི་ཕྱིར་རྟེ་བཞིན་དོན། ཐེག་པ་ཆེན་པོ་བ་ཉིད་འཕྲོབ།། །༢ །།

དངོས་པོའི་སྟོབས་ཀྱིས་ཞུགས་པའི་རྟེས་སུ་དཔག་པ་ལ་འདུག་པ་ལ་རྣམས་ཆུལ་གཅིས་བརྟོད་པས་བསྟས་པ། དེ་བཞིན་གཤེགས་པ་རྣམས་གསེགས་ཤིད་གཤེགས་པའི་ཐེག་པ་ཆེན་པོས་དངོས་པོ་མཐའ་དག་རང་བཞིན་མེད་པར་ཁོང་དུ་ཆུད་པར་བྱེད་དེ། ཤིད་དུ་ཆེན་པོ་ལ་ཞོན་པ་དག་ཁ་བསྒྱམས་པའི་སྒྲུབ་སྐྱོགས་ཤེགས་ལ་པར་བཟུང་བ་བཞིན་དུ་དོན་དང་ལྡན་པའི་ཐེག་པ་ཆེན་པོ་ཤེས་བྱ་བ་ཡང་དག་པ་ཐོབ་པར་བྱེད་དོ། །

ལང་གར་གཤེགས་པ་ལས། ཆུལ་གཅིས་ཀྱིས་བསྒུས་པའི་ཐེག་པ་ཆེན་པོ་དེ་མཆོར་བསྟན་པ་འདི་སྟེད་དེ།

ཆོས་ལ་དག་དང་རང་བཞིན་དང་། །རྣམ་པར་ཤེས་པ་བཀྱུད་ཉིད་དང་། །

བདག་མེད་གཉིས་ཀྱི་དངོས་པོ་ནི། །ཐེག་པ་ཆེན་པོ་ཐམས་ཅད་འདུས། །

ཞེས་འབྱུང་ངོ་། །ཚུལ་རྣམ་པ་འདི་གཉིས་ནི་རྣམ་འགོད་དང་། ཁྱབ་འཇུག་དང་། མིག་མི་བཟང་ལ་སོགས་
པས་རྣམ་པ་མང་དུ་བཤད་ལ། ཐེག་པ་ཆེན་པོ་འདི་ལ་ཉེ་བར་ཉེ་བར་ཏུ་གྱུར་པ་ཅི་ཡོད་དམ། འདི་ལྟ་སྟེ། བདུད་རྩི་
ཐིགས་པ་གསང་བ་ལས་བསྟན་པ། རྣམ་རིག་ཙམ་ཞི་དག་ཏུ་རྣམ་པར་དག །འདི་ལྟར་སངས་རྒྱས་དག་ཏུ་གྲོལ་
པ་ཡིན། སྤྲུང་དང་དོར་བ་མེད་ཅེས་རབ་བརྟགས་པ། ཆངས་པ་སྐུ་ངན་མེད་པར་དག་གནས་ཚོས། །
ཞིའོ། །ཞག་ལྷ་ལ་ནས་བྱུང་བ།

  མེད་ཆམ་ལས་ནི་རབ་འདས་ཤིང་། །དོརས་དང་དདོས་མེད་རྣམ་སྤངས་པ། །
  དབྱུང་དང་བསྒྲུ་ལས་རེས་གྲོལ་བ། །དེ་ནི་ནོ་རང་ལྷུ་བུ་ཞེས་བྱུ། །
  དདོརས་ལ་དདོས་ཉིད་ཡོད་མ་ཡིན། །དདོས་མེད་ལ་ཡང་དདོས་ཉིད་མིན། །
  དདོས་དང་དདོས་མེད་རྣམ་གྲོལ་བ། །གང་གིས་ཤེས་དེ་རིག་བྱེད་རིག །
ཅེའོ། །ཞི་བའི་མཛེས་སྟོར་ལས་བྱུང་བ། །

  བུ་གཅིག་ཆངས་པ་མཆོག་ཏུ་བའེན། །རིག་པའི་དབང་ཕྱུག་མ་མཐའ་ཡས། །
  འབའར་ཞིག་ཡོན་པ་ཉིད་སྐྱབ། །དེ་ཡང་ཞིག་པར་རབ་ཏུ་བརྟོ། །
ཅེའོ། །ཡ་དང་བུའི་སྤྱར་བ་ལས་བརྟོ་ནོ། །དང་སྟོང་ཆེན་པོ་སེར་སྐྱས་སྐྱས་པ། །
  ཡོན་ཏན་རྣམས་ཀྱི་རང་བཞིན་མཆོག །མཐོང་བའི་ལམ་དུ་གྱུར་མ་ཆོག །
  མཐོང་བའི་ལམ་དུ་གང་གྱུར་དེ། །སྐྱ་མ་ལྷ་བྱར་ཤིན་ཏུ་གསོག །
ཅེའོ། །དེ་བས་ན་འདི་ལ་དེ་བཞིན་གཤེགས་པའི་སྙེས་པ་བྱེད་པ་ཕུན་མོང་མ་ཡིན་པ་ཅེ་ཡོད། དེ་ནི་དེ་ལྷ་མ་
ཡིན་ཏེ། ཆོས་ཐམས་ཅད་རང་བཞིན་སྟོང་པར་བསྟན་པ་ནི། དེ་བཞིན་གཤེགས་པ་ཉིད་ཀྱི་སེང་གེའི་སྒྲ་སུ་
སྟེགས་བྱེད་ཀྱི་གྲུང་པོ་ཆེ་དང་། རེ་དགས་ཀྱི་ཚོགས་རྣམས་སྐྲག་པར་བྱེད་པའོ། །
འདི་ལྟར་ལ་རོལ་སུ་སྐྱེགས་བྱེད་བདག་ན་སོགས་པ་ལ་ལྷ་བུ་ལ་མཛོ་བར་ཞེན་པ་ཐམས་ཅད་ནི་ཉི་ཆོ་བོ་ན་ལ་
སྟོན་པ་ཉིད་བརྟོད་དེ། འདི་ལྷ་སྟེ་གནས་བ་བའི་རྗེས་སུ་འབྱུང་བ་དག་ནི། བདག་དང་པ་ནི་གཅིག་པུ་ཁོན་
རྣམ་པར་ཤེས་པར་ཆམ་གྱི་བདག་ཉིད་ཡིན་དེ། ནམ་མཁའི་ཆེན་པོ་དང་འདུའོ་ཞེས་བརྟོད་དེ། དེ་ལ་རྣམ་འབྱོར་
ལ་གོམས་པས་གཤུག་མ་དང་གཤུག་མ་མ་ཡིན་པའི་མ་རིག་པ་དང་བྲལ་ནས་བྲལ་བ་ལ་སོགས་པ་ཆག་ན་དེའི་
ནམ་མཁའན་ནམ་མཁའ་ཆེར་པོ་འདུ་བཞིན་དུ་སྟོག་ཀྱང་དེར་འདུ་ན་རབ་ཏུ་སྐྱ་བ་དག་གིས་དེ་སྟོག་དང་ཡོན་

152

ཅན་དང་། འབྱུང་བ་ཉིད་ལ་སོགས་པ་དངོས་པོ་མཐའ་ཡས་པ་རྣམ་པར་བརྟགས་སོ། །འཇིག་རྟེན་འདི་ནི་སྐྱ་
མའི་རང་བཞིན་ཏེ་གཉིས་སུ་མེད་ཀྱང་རྟེ་ལས་སྐྱེས་པ་བཞིན་དུ་སྐྱ་ཚོགས་ཀྱི་ངོ་བོར་སྣང་ངོ་། །
འདིར་སྨྲས་པ། བུམ་པ་ལ་སོགས་ཞིག་པ་ནི། །རྟེ་ལྟར་ཉམས་མཁར་འདུ་འགྱུར་བ། དེ་བཞིན་སྒྱོག་ཀྱང་བདག
འདིར་འདུ། །གཟུགས་དང་འཕྲས་བུ་རབ་ཏུ་བརྗོད། །

དེ་དང་དེ་ནི་ཐ་དད་ཀྱང་། །ནམ་མཁའ་ལ་ནི་ཐ་དད་མེད།
དེ་བཞིན་སྒྱོག་ཀྱང་རེས་པ་ཡིན། །

རྗེ་ལྟར་བྱིས་པ་རྣམས་ལ་ནི། །ནམ་མཁའ་དེ་མས་དེ་ཅན་འགྱུར།
དེ་བཞིན་མི་མཁས་རྣམས་ལ་ཡང་། །བདག་ནི་དེ་མས་དེ་ཅན་འགྱུར། །

རྗེ་ལྟར་སྨྲན་ཁྱངས་མ་རྟོགས་ཏེ། ཐག་པ་སྤྲུལ་གྱི་རྒྱུན་ལ་སོགས།
དངོས་པོར་རྣམ་པར་བརྟགས་པ་ལྟར། །དེ་བཞིན་བདག་ཀྱང་རྣམ་པར་བརྟགས། །

རྗེ་ལྟར་ཐག་པ་རེས་རྟོགས་ན། རྣམ་པར་རྟོག་པ་རྟོགས་འགྱུར་ཏེ།
ཐག་པ་གཅིག་ཉིད་གཉིས་མིན་པ། །དེ་ལྟར་བདག་ཀྱང་རེས་པ་ཡིན། །

སྒྱོག་ལ་སོགས་པ་མཐའ་ཡས་པའི། དངོས་པོ་དེ་རྣམས་རྣམ་པར་བརྟགས།
གང་གིས་དེ་དག་ཉིད་སྟོངས་པ། །དེ་ནི་ལྟ་དེའི་སྐྱ་མ་ཡིན། །

སྒྱོག་ཏུ་རིགས་པས་སྒྱོག་ཅེས་བརྗོད། །འབྱུང་བ་ཡིན་ཞེས་དེ་རིགས་རྣམས།
ཡིན་ཏན་རིག་རྣམས་ཡོན་ཏན་སྐྱ། །ཡང་དག་ཡིན་ཞེས་དེ་རིགས་རྣམས། །

གཉིས་མིན་ཡིད་ནི་སྐྲ་ལ་མ་ན། །གཉིས་སུ་སྣང་སྟེ་ཕྱེ་ཆོམ་མེད། །
དེ་བཞིན་གཉིས་ཀྱིས་མ་ལོག་ཆེ། །གཉིས་མིན་གཉིས་སྣང་ཕྱེ་ཆོམ་མེད། །

རྒྱུ་དང་མི་རྒྱ་གང་ཅིའང་རུང་། །གཉིས་སུ་སྣང་བ་འདི་ཡིད་ཡིན། །
ཡིད་ནི་མེད་པར་གྱུར་པ་ན། །གཉིས་སུ་དམིགས་པར་མི་འགྱུར་རོ། །

བདག་ནི་བདེན་པར་རྟོགས་གྱུར་པས། །གང་ཚེ་ཀུན་ཏུ་མི་རྟོག་པ། །
དེའི་ཚེ་ཡིད་ནི་མི་འགྱུར་ཏེ། །གཟུང་བ་མེད་པས་དེ་འཛིན་མེད། །

ཅེའོ། །བདག་ཏྭག་པ་ལ་སྩྭ་བ་གཉིས་སུ་མེད་པར་བརྟོད་པའི་རྒྱལ་འདི་ཐམས་ཅད་ཀྱང་སྣར་སྣང་ནས་ཉེན་
ཏེ། །གཞན་ཡང་གཅིག་གྲོ་ལ་ན་ཐམས་ཅད་གྲོ་ལ་བར་འགྱུར་རོ། །ཞོན་ཏེ་མ་གྲོ་ལ་ན་གྲོ་ལ་བར་འདོད་པ་ཡང་མ་
གྲོ་ལ་བར་གྱུར་ཏེ། །ཐ་དད་པ་མེད་པའི་ཕྱིར་རོ། །གཞན་དུ་ན་མི་མཐུན་པའི་ཆོམ་གནས་པས་ཐ་དད་པ་ཉིད་དུ་
འགྱུར་རོ། །

རྣལ་འབྱོར་གྱོམས་པའི་རྣལ་འབྱོར་པས། །ཅི་ཞིག་བརྟོག་ཅིག་ཅིང་ཅི་ཞིག་གྱུབ། །
དེ་ཡི་བདག་ཉིད་ཕྱིན་ཅི་ལོག །སྐྱུང་བར་ནུས་པ་མ་ཡིན་ནོ། །

ཞེས་པ་ཡང་དག་བསྐྱེད་དུ་མིན། །དེ་ཉིད་དག་ཏུ་གནས་ཕྱིར་རོ། །
དེ་ཕྱིར་རྣལ་འབྱོར་བསྐྱོམས་པ་འདི། །འབྲས་བུ་མེད་པར་འགྱུར་བ་ཡིན། །

བར་སྐྱབས་ཀྱི་ཚིགས་སུ་བཅད་པ་དགའོ། །
ཡེ་སྐྱིད་པའི་དངོས་པོ་རྟག་པ་དང་གཅིག་ཏུ་དཀགག་པ་སྣར་བརྟོད་པ་ཉིད་ཀྱིས་བྱམ་པ་དང་རྣམ་མཁའི་དཔེ་ཡང་
མ་གྱུབ་བོ། །གཅིག་འདུ་ན་ཐམས་ཅད་ཀྱང་འདུ་བར་འགྱུར་བ་དང་། །ཞོན་ཏེ་མ་ཡིན་ན་འདོད་པར་ཡང་མི་
འགྱུར་ཏེ། །ཐ་དད་པ་མེད་པའི་ཕྱིར་རོ་ཞེས་བུ་བའི་ཡང་བཀལ་ཞིང་བཏག་པ་དང་མཐུན་པ་ཉིད་དོ། །

དེ་ལྟོ་ན་མཐོང་བ་བསྐྱོམས་པས་གྲོ་བུར་གྱི་ཉེན་མོངས་པ་དང་བྲལ་བ་ཡང་རང་བཞིན་གྱིས་འོད་གསལ་བའི་
སེམས་སྐྱད་ཅིག་གིས་འཇིག་པའི་ཚོས་ཅན་ལ་འཇུད་དོ། །གཞན་དུ་ན་ལྟ་ཕྱིའི་གནས་སྐབས་སུ་དག་པ་དང་མ་
དག་པར་འགྱུར་ཏེ། ཐ་དད་པ་མེད་པའི་ཕྱིར་རོ། དེས་ན་དམ་བཅས་པ་དང་། འབྲུལ་པ་དང་མ་འབྲུལ་པ་རྣམ་
པར་བཞག་པ་ལ་ཐ་དད་པར་བརྗོད་པ་ཡང་སྐྱད་ཅིག་པ་བརྟེན་པ་ཉིད་ལ་རིགས་ཏེ། སྐྱེ་བུ་ཧྲག་པ་གཅིག་ཕུའི་ཏོ་
ལོ་ལ་འཚོལ་བར་གྱུར་པའི་གནས་སྐྱབས་འདི་དག་གིས་ལན་གདབ་པར་མི་ནུས་པའི་ཕྱིར་རོ། །
ཤེས་པའི་སྐྱེས་བུ་ཧྲག་པ་དང་གཅིག་ཕུའི་རང་བཞིན་ལ་གཉིས་ཀྱིས་ལོག་པ་དང་གཉིད་ཀྱིས་མ་ལོག་པའི་གནས་
སྐྱབས་འཛིག་པ་ལ་ཡང་གནས་སྐྱབས་ཐ་དད་པ་མི་རིགས་པའི་ཕྱིར་རོ། །དེ་བས་ན།

རིག་བྱེད་མཐའ་ལས་དེད་རྣམས་ཀྱིས། །སྲི་ལམ་སྐྲ་མ་ཅི་འདུ་དང་།
དེ་ཞེའི་གྱོང་ཁྱེར་ཅི་འདུ་མཐོང་། །དེ་ལྟར་འཇིག་རྟེན་འདི་དག་མཐོང་། །
འགོག་པ་མེད་ཅིང་སྐྱེ་བ་མེད། །བཅིངས་མེད་ཅིང་སྐྱོལ་པོ་མེད། །
ཐར་འདོད་མེད་ཅིང་ཐར་པ་མེད། །འདི་ནི་དོན་དམ་ཉིད་ཡིན་ནོ། །
ཚགས་དང་འཇིགས་དང་ཁྲོ་བྲལ་བ། །རིག་བྱེད་མཐར་ཕྱིན་ཐུབ་རྣམས་ཀྱིས། །
སྟོས་པ་ཉེར་ཞི་གཉིས་མེད་པའི། རྣམ་པར་མི་རྟོག་འདི་མཐོང་རོ། །

དེ་དག་གིས་གང་བརྗོད་པ་དེ་ནི་བདེ་བར་གཤེགས་པ་ས་གསུངས་པ་སྟོལས་པའི་ཚོགས་ཐམས་ཅད་ལས་གྲོལ་བ།
དོན་དམ་པའི་བདེན་པ་ལ་བརྟེན་པ་ལ་མངོ་རོ། །ཐུག་པ་དང་གཅིག་ཕུའི་བདག་བཀག་པ་འདེས་ཉེ་དབང་གི་
ཕུགས་གྱུང་བསལ་ཟིན་ཏོ། །

ཡེ་ཤེས་པའི་སྐུ་ལ་ཡང་ཁྱབ་པ་དང་། ཧྲག་པའི་བདག་དང་རྣམ་མཁའ་ལ་སོགས་པ་བསལ་ལས་བསལ་ཞིན་
ཏོ། །ཡེ་ཤེས་པ་དེ་ཡང་ཧྲག་པ་ཉིད་དང་། ཁྱབ་པ་ཉིད་དང་། བྱེད་པ་པོ་ལ་སོགས་པ་ཡང་དག་པ་ཉིད་དུ་
བརྗོད་པའི་ཕྱིར་རོ། །སེར་སྐྱས་བརྗོད་པ་སྟིང་སྟོབས་དང་། ཧྲལ་དང་། མུན་པ་མཆམ་པའི་གནས་སྐྱབས་ཀྱི་
མཚན་ཉིད་གཙོ་བོ་དམ་པའི་རང་བཞིན་བརྗོད་པ་ཡང་སྒྱར་སྟོས་པའི་ཁྱབ་པ་དང་ཧྲག་པའི་དངོ་པོ་བསལ་བ་
ཉིད་ཀྱིས་བསལ་ཞིན་ཏོ། །

རང་གི་སྟེ་ལ་གང་དག་ཚོས་ཐམས་ཅད་དངོས་པོ་ལ་སོགས་པའི་མདོའི་ཚོས་འཆད་པ་ན་སྐྱང་པ་དང་། ཤུང་བའི་
དོན་ལ་སོགས་པ་འཆད་དེ། དངོས་པ་རྣམས་དན་པ་ཡིན་པས་དངོས་པོ་མེད་པ་སྟེ། དབུས་དང་ད་ལྟར་གྱི་

གནས་སྐབས་ན་མི་བཏུན་པའི་ཕྱིར་རོ། །ཡང་ན་དངོས་པོ་དག་ནི་དངོས་པོ་མེད་པ་མང་བས་དངོས་པོ་མེད་པ་
སྟེ། སྟོན་དང་ཕྱི་མའི་མཐར་མ་སྐྱེས་པ་དང་། འདས་པའང་རང་བཞིན་མེད་པའི་ཕྱིར་རོ། །

བཏད་པ་འདི་ཡང་གལ་ཏེ་སྐྱར་དཔྱད་པ་བྱས་པའི་སྐྱངས་པས་གནན་གྱི་དབང་ཡང་དག་པར་ཡོད་པར་གྱུར་ན་
ནི་ཁོ་བོའི་སེམས་རངས་པར་འགྱུར་རོ། །གཞན་དུ་ནི་ཉེ་བྲག་ཏུ་སྐྱ་བ་དང་། གནས་མ་བུ་པའི་ཚུལ་གྱི་རྗེས་སུ་
འབྲངས་ནས། འདི་ནི་སྐྱར་གྱངས་ཅན་ལ་སོགས་པའི་ལུགས་ཀྱི་དངོས་པོ་དགག་པ་ཡིན་ནོ་ཞེས་འདི་བཏད་མི་
ནུས་པ་ཅི་ཡོད། ཡང་ན་བཏད་པ་འདི་ནི་འདུལ་བའི་སྐྱེ་བོ་བློ་མི་ཞིབ་པའི་སྐྱག་པ་བསལ་བའི་ཕྱིར་ཏེ། དེ་དག་
ཏུ་ཟད་དོ་ཞེས་བྱ་བ་ནི་མི་སེམས་སོ། །

དེ་ལྟ་བས་ན་ཕྱུབ་པའི་རྒྱལ་པོས་ཉི་ཚེ་བ་མ་ཡིན་པའི་སྟོང་པ་ཉིད་བསྟན་པ་ལོན་མུ་སྟེགས་བྱེད་ཀྱི་ཚོགས་ཐམས་
ཅད་དང་ཕུན་མོང་མ་ཡིན་པ་འདི་ནི་མཇེས་པ་ལོན་ཡིན་ཏེ། རྩ་བ་སྐྱོན་མའི་ཉིད་ར་འཛིན་ལས་འདི་སྐྱད་དུ།

ཚོས་རྣམས་ཐམས་ཅད་དག་ཏུ་རང་བཞིན་སྟོང་།

ཞེས་བྱ་བ་ལ་སོགས་པ་གསུངས་པ་ལྟ་བུའོ། །འདིར་ཡང་བཏོད་པ།

ཤིན་ཏུ་ཕྲ་བའི་དངོས་ལ་ཡང་། །གང་གིས་སྐྱེ་བར་རྣམ་བརྟགས་པ།
མ་བཟས་པ་མ་ཡིན་དེ་ཡི་སེ། །རྒྱེན་ལས་གྱུང་པའི་དོན་མ་མཐོང་། རྟོགས་པ་བདུག་ཅུ་པ་ ༡༣
གལ་ཏེ་དོན་ག་ཅིག་ཡོད་གྱུར་ན། །ཅི་ཡི་ཕྱིར་ན་རང་བཞིན་མེད།
མདོ་སྟེ་མང་དང་འགལ་བར་འགྱུར། །འདིག་རྟེན་མི་མཐུན་ཉིད་དུ་འང་འགྱུར། །
ཁྱབ་དང་དབང་ལ་སོགས་མ་མྱོང་། །དཔག་ཏུ་མེད་པར་གནས་པའི་རྒྱ།
འཇིག་རྟེན་སྐྱེ་བོར་གྱུར་བས་ཀྱང་། །ཤིན་ཏུ་སྐྱོང་པ་མ་ཡིན་པ། །༩༤ །།
ཡང་དག་བདུད་ཅི་དག་པ་འདི། །ཕྱགས་རྗེ་དག་པའི་རྒྱ་ཅན་གྱི།
དེ་བཞིན་གཤེགས་པ་མ་གཏོགས་པ། །གཞན་གྱི་ལོངས་སྤྱོད་མ་ཡིན་ནོ།། །༩༥ །།

རྩ་བའི་ལོན་ཟེར་ལྟར་དག་པ་གང་ཟག་དང་ཚོས་ལ་བདག་མེད་པ་རང་བཞིན་ཉི་ཚོ་བ་མ་ཡིན་པ་བདུད་ཅེ་འདི་
ནི་སྐྱོབ་པ་ཤིན་ཏུ་གསོལ་ལ་ཏེ། རྣམ་པ་ཐམས་ཅད་ཀྱི་མཆོག་དང་ལྡན་པའི་ཞེས་རབ་དང་། ཕྱགས་རྗེ་དུལ་ཕྱུ་
རབ་འདུས་པའི་སྐྱ། ཉོན་མོངས་པ་དང་ཞེས་བྱའི་སྐྱོབ་པའི་ཕྱང་པོ་མ་ལུས་པ་དང་བྲལ་བ། ཐམས་ཅད་ཀྱི་
མཆོག་འཁོར་བ་ཏེ་སྐྱོད་པར་བཞགས་སོ། །

འདི་ལྟར་འདི་ནི་བདག་མེད་པ་དང་པོ་རྟོགས་པ་ས་བློ་རྣམ་པར་དག་པ་ཉན་ཐོས་དང་། རང་སངས་རྒྱས་རྣམས་ཀྱི་ཡང་ས་མ་ཡིན་ན། ལོག་པ་བདག་ཏུ་ལྟ་བ་ལ་ཞེན་པ་ལྟ་ཅེན་པོ་དང་། ཁྱབ་འཇུག་དང་། ཚངས་པ་ལ་སོགས་པའི་ས་མ་ལྟ་ཅི་སྨོས།

དེ་ཕྱིར་ལོག་པར་བསྐྱེན་པ་ཡི། །ཁྱབ་མཐར་འཆེལ་བའི་བློ་ཅན་ལ།

དེ་ལུགས་རྟེས་འདུག་བློ་ཅན་རྣམས། །སྙིང་རྗེ་ཉིད་ནི་རབ་ཏུ་སྐྱེ།། ༤༤ ༎

བདག་དང་གཞན་གྱི་ལུས་ལ་སྲུག་བསྐལ་གྱི་རྒྱུན་བཀྲལ་བ་མི་ལྡང་བར་རྟེས་སུ་འཤེལ་བའི་རྒྱུར་འགྱུར་བ། ལོག་པར་བསྐྱེན་པའི་ཚེས་འདུལ་བ་ཕྱིན་པ་རྣམས་དང་། དེའི་རྟེས་སུ་འགྲོ་བ་རྣམས་ལ་དེ་ལོན་ཞེན་པ་འདི་ལྟ་བུ་ཚེལ་བས་དེ་ལོན་མཚོག་གཏན་ལ་ཕབས་ནས་བའི་བར་གཅིག་པའི་བསྐྱེན་པ་སྙིང་རྗེ་རིགས་ཀྱི་ཁྱིག་ལས་ལེན་པ། སྐྱེས་བུ་ཕྱིར་ཁྱེར་བ། ཐོག་པ་དང་ཕུལ་བ་རྣམས་ཀྱི་སྙིང་རྗེ་ཅེན་པོ། མི་མཐུན་པའི་ཕྱོགས་རྒྱུན་དུ། དང་ཡང་མ་འདེས་པ་སྐྱེ་སྟེ། གཞན་སྲུག་བསྐལ་དང་བྲལ་བར་འདོད་པ་ནི་སྙིང་རྗེ་ཅེན་པོ་ཡིན་ནོ།

དེ་དག་གི་སྲུག་བསྐལ་དང་། དེའི་རྒྱུ་རབ་ཏུ་འཕེལ་ན་སྐྱེ་བར་འགྱུར་ཏེ། བུད་ཤིང་བསྐྱེན་ན་མེ་ཆེ་འབར་བ་བཞིན་ནོ། །དོན་དམ་པ་ལ་རྣམ་པར་སྟང་བ་དག་ནི་སྲུག་བསྐལ་རྒྱུའི་མཚོག་ལ་གནས་པ་ཡིན་ཏེ། འདི་དག་རྟེ་ལྟ་བུར་དུ་བ་དག་ནི་དེ་ལྟར་བདག་དང་གཞན་གྱི་དག་མ་ཡིན་ཏེ། དེ་དག་ནི་རྣུ་གིས་བསྐྱེད་ནས་རྒྱུའི་རྒྱུ་འབྱུང་བྱུང་བ་ལྟ་བུར་ཤིན་ཏུ་མི་ཧྲག་པ། བདག་ལ་ཕན་པ་ཅུང་ཟད་ཀྱང་མི་ནུས་པའི་ལུས་རྣམས་ཅན་གུངས་ཡོན་པ་གཅིག་གསོད་པར་ཟད་ཀྱི། འདི་དག་ནི་འཁོར་བ་རྟེ་སྙིང་པར་བཤགས་པ། བདག་དང་གཞན་ཕུན་སུམ་ཚོགས་པས་མཛེས་པ། གྲངས་ལས་འདས་པའི་རྒྱལ་བ་དང་འཕེལ་པའི་ཚོས་ཀྱི་སྐྲ་ལ་གནོད་པ་སྟེ། དེའི་ས་བོན་ཚོས་ཀྱི་དེ་ལོན་ལ་མོས་པ་ལ་གནོད་པ་ཕྱེད་པར་ཞུགས་པའི་ཕྱིར་རོ། །དེ་ཉིད་ཀྱི་ཕྱིར་དག་པའི་ཚོས་སྟོང་པའི་རྣམ་པར་སྐྱེན་པ་ཞེན་ཏུ་མི་བཟད་པ་རྣམ་པ་མང་པོ་མོའི་སྟེ་ལས་བརྗོད་དོ། །ཡང་གསུངས་པ།

ཤེན་ཏུ་རྒྱ་ཆེར་རབ་ཟབ་ལ། །སྙིང་ལུག་ཤེན་ཏུ་མ་སྤྱངས་ལ།

བདག་གཞན་དག་དག་གདི་ལྷག་མིས། །ད་ལྟར་ཐེག་པ་ཆེ་ལ་སྐྱོད།

ཚུལ་ཁྲིམས་ལས་ནི་ཉམས་བླ་ཡི། །ལྷ་ལས་ཅེས་ཀྱང་མ་ཡིན་ཏེ།

ཚུལ་ཁྲིམས་ཀྱིས་ནི་མཐོ་རིས་འགྲོ། །ལྷ་བས་གོ་འཕང་མཚོག་ཏུ་འགྱུར། ། ༡༣ ༡༡

གདི་ལྷག་དབང་གིས་བསྐྱིབས་གྱུར་ཏེ། །གང་ཞིག་ཡང་དག་གེགས་བྱེད་པ།

དེ་ལ་དགོ་བའི་འགྲོ་བ་མེད། །ཐར་པ་མེད་པ་སྐྱོ་བ་ཅི་དགོས། །༡༣ ༡༠

གཏོད་པའི་ས་བོན་གྱུར་པ་ཡི། །སྲུ་སྟེགས་བྱེད་མང་མཐོང་ནས་ནི།

ཚོགས་འདོད་སྐྱེ་བོ་ལ་རྣམས་ལ། །སྙིང་རྗེ་མི་འགྱུར་སུ་ཞིག་ཡོད། །

ཅེ་འོ། །ཟླ་བ་སྐྱོན་མའི་ཏིང་ངེ་འཛིན་ལས། །དང་པོ་བཏོད་པའི་བྱུད་པར་ལས་དེ་སྐྱད་གསུངས་པ་བཞིན་
ནོ། །འདི་ལྟར་གནས་ཀྱི་ལུགས་འདི་ལ་བརྟགས་ནེ་ཉེ་མའི་འོད་ཟེར་ཤིན་ཏུ་འཇེབས་པ། གངས་རི་ཁ་བའི་
དྲ་གྱུགས་ལ་བབ་ན་འདུ་པར་འགྱུར་བ་ལྟ་བུར་གདིང་མི་ཆགས་ལས་བདག་ལེགས་སུ་འདོད་པ་རྣམས་འདི་ལ་
མ་ཞེན་པར་བྱ་ཆེད་ཆེར་འཛིན་ཏོ། །

གཞན་ཡང་བོ་བོ་བདག་ཅག་དང་། གཞན་གྱི་གཞུང་ལུགས་རྒྱ་ཆེར་དཔྱད་པས་རྟེན་ཅིང་འབྲེལ་པར་འབྱུང་བ་
སྟོན་པའི་ཚོགས་ཐབས་ཅད་བྱལ་བ་འདི་དེ་བོ་ན་བསྟུས་པ་དང་། དོན་དམ་པ་གཏན་ལ་དབབ་ལ་ལ་སོགས
པར་དཔྱད་ཟིན་གྱིས། ཤིན་ཏུ་རྒྱས་པར་འདོད་པ་དག་གིས་དེ་དག་ལས་ཁོང་དུ་ཆུད་པར་གྱིས་ཤིག །

བློ་ཆོར་ལྡན་ལས་ལུགས་གཞན་ལ། །ཇི་ལྟར་སྙིང་པོ་མེད་མཐོང་བ།

དེ་ལྟར་དེ་དག་སྐྱོབ་པ་ལ། །ཀུས་པ་ཤིན་ཏུ་སྐྱེ་བར་འགྱུར།། ༡༤ །།

གཞན་གྱི་ལུགས་ནི་རིགས་དང་ལྗུན་པའི་སྐྱེ་བོ་ལ་ཡང་ལུགས་པའི་ཡུལ་རགས་ལ་ལ་ཡང་འབྱུལ་པར་མཐོང་བ།
དེ་བཞིན་གཤེགས་པའི་དགའ་གཤུང་རབ་ཕོག་མ་དང་། བར་དང་། ཐ་མར་དགེ་བ། གསེར་བཙར་པོ་སྲ་བྱར་བ་སྲིག
པ་དང་། བཏང་པ་དང་། བཟར་བ་དང་འདུ་བའི་མཚོན་སྲུམ་དང་། རྗེས་སུ་དཔག་པ་དང་། རང་གི་ཚིག
རྣམས་ཀྱི་གཏོ་པར་མ་གྱུར་པ་ནི་འཚོར་བ་རྣམས་དང་མ་འདྲེས་པའི་ཡེ་ཤེས་ཀྱི་དེ་བོ་ན་ཤིན་ཏུ་འཐིབ་པོ་འཕྱུག
པ་མེད་པར་མཐོང་ནས་མི་དང་ལྷ་ཡུལ་པའི་འདྲེན་པ་མཐའ་དག་གི་ཚོང་པ་གྱི་འཕྱིབ་ལས་ཞབས་གཉིས་མཛེས
པར་བྱས་པ་དང་ལྡན་པའི་འཆིག་རྗེན་གྱི་ལྷ་མ་བདག་ཤེས་པ་སུ་ཞིག་མཆོན་པར་མ་ཞེན་པའི་ཀུལ་གྱིས་སྐྱབ་ལ་
སྙིང་པོར་བྱེད་པའི་དད་པ་མི་སྐྱེད། དེའི་ཕྱིར་དེ་ལྟར།

ཡང་དག་ཤེས་ཚོལ་སློན་བཏང་སྟེ། །དོན་དེ་རྣམ་པར་ངེས་བྱས་ནས།

ལྷ་དང་འཕིབས་གནས་འདྲིག་རྟེན་ལ། །སྙིང་རྗེ་ཀུན་ནས་བསྐྱེད་ནས་སུ། །

འགྲོ་དོན་བྱེད་པ་པར་གྱུར་བ། །བྱང་ཆུབ་བློ་རྒྱས་མཁས་པ་ནི།

བློ་དང་སྙིང་རྗེས་བཀྱུན་པ་ཡི། །ཐུབ་པའི་བཏུལ་ཞུགས་ཡང་དག་སློད། །

ཡང་དག་དད་པའི་རྟེས་འབྲང་བ། །རྟོགས་པའི་བྱང་ཆུབ་སེམས་བསྐྱེད་ནས།
ཐུབ་པའི་བཅུལ་ཞུགས་བ་བློངས་བྱས་ཏེ། །དེ་ནི་ཡང་དག་ཤེས་ཚོལ་བརྩོན། །
བློ་མིག་ཞིབ་པའི་བློ་ལྡན་དག །ལམ་གོང་ནས་ནི་འཇུག་གྱུར་པ།
ལུང་དང་རིགས་པ་གསལ་ལྡན་པ། །དེ་ལྟར་ཕྱོགས་ཀ་ཅིག་བསྟན་པ་ཡིན། །
འདིར་ནི་ཀླུ་བ་དག་འདུའི་བསོད་ནམས་བདག་གིས་གང་ཐོབ་པ།
དེས་ནི་ཐུབ་མཆོག་ལུགས་ཀྱི་ཡང་དག་དགའ་ལྡན་འཇིག་རྟེན་ཀུན།
ལྷ་དང་མྱུན་པའི་དུ་བ་རབ་ཏུ་མང་པོ་རྣམ་པསལ་ནས།
སྲིད་པའི་འདོད་ཆགས་རབ་ཏུ་བསལ་ཏེ་བྱང་ཆུབ་ཐོབ་པར་ཤོག །
བདག་གིས་ཡུལ་གྱི་ལོངས་སྤྱོད་སྤྱང་བས་བརྒྱལ་བའི་མྱུན་བསལ་ཅིང་།
ཡང་དག་དམ་པར་རིག་ཅིང་ཡང་དག་རིགས་དང་འགྲོགས་པ་དང་།
གཞན་གྱི་དོན་ལ་གཅིག་ཏུ་གཞོལ་ཅིང་འཛམ་པའི་དབྱངས་ཀྱི་ཞབས།
གཙང་མ་བདུར་བརྟེན་ཅིང་ཤིན་ཏུ་བརྟན་པས་གུས་པར་ཤོག །
གསལ་བའི་ལུང་དང་རིགས་པ་དག་གིས་གང་ཞིག་འདིར་བརྟོད་པ།
རྒྱལ་བ་ཁྱུ་མཆོག་དམ་པའི་གསུང་གི་སྐྱོན་ཆེན་ཡང་དག་པར།
གདལ་བྱེད་འདི་ནི་ས་ལ་དགེས་པོའི་ཏོ་བོ་ཡང་དག་པ།
དེ་སྲིད་མི་འཛིར་དེ་སྲིད་རྣམ་པ་ཀུན་ཏུ་གནས་གྱུར་ཅིག །
རྒྱལ་བ་གང་དག་རྟེན་འབྲེལ་འབྱུང་། །རྟོག་པ་མི་བཟད་དུ་བ་ཀུན།
རྣམ་གྲོལ་གསུངས་པ་དེ་དག་ལ། །ཐུག་པར་རྒྱུན་དུ་ཕྱག་འཚལ་ལོ། །
དེ་ལྟའི་ཆུལ་དུ་དབུ་མ་ཡི། །རྒྱན་འདི་བདག་གིས་བྱས་པ་ནི།
རིགས་དང་མདོ་སྡེ་ཚོགས་ཀྱི། །རིན་ཆེན་བཀོད་པས་མཛེས་པར་བྱས། །
ཞིབ་པའི་བློ་ཡིས་འདི་རྟོགས་ནས། །ཀླུ་སྒྲུན་ལ་སོགས་བློ་ཐབ་རྣམས།
སྐྱེ་བོ་བློ་ཡི་ནོར་སྤུན་ཞིང་། །བཅུན་རྣམས་འཇིགས་མེད་སྐྱོམ་པར་ཤོག །
བཅུན་རྣམས་འདི་འཛིན་བྱེད་པ་དང་། །མཁས་ལ་རྟོན་པར་བྱེད་པ་ནི།

159

བདག་དང་གཞན་ལ་ཁྱབ་པ་མཆོག་གི། །ཡོངས་སུ་མགྲ་བར་རབ་ཏུ་བྱེད། །
དམིགས་པ་ཅན་ཀུན་སྟི་ཏོ་ལ་གྱིས། །རྟོག་པ་རྣམ་པར་བསལ་ཕྱུན་ནས། །
སྤྱོབས་པ་སོ་སོར་རིག་ལ་ཡིས། །ཞིན་ཏུ་མཐོ་བར་འགྱིང་བར་བྱེད། །
རབ་མོའི་ཆོས་ཀྱི་ཡད་དག་ཞིད། །སྟོན་པ་མཛད་པའི་ཐུབ་ཆེན་གྱི། །
གྲགས་པ་དག་ནི་ཕྱོགས་རྣམས་ཀྱི། །རབ་འབྱམས་ཀུན་ཏུ་རྒྱས་པར་བྱེད། །
ཆོས་ལ་བདག་མེད་རྣབ་པའི་ཕྱིར། །སྟོབ་དཔོན་སྟ་མ་སྟོང་སྟེང་གྱིས། །
སྒྲུབ་པ་རྣམས་ནི་སྤྱུར་མཛད་པ། །ཁྱབ་འདུ་བ་གང་ཡིན་རྣམས། །
མཁས་རྣམས་ཡད་དག་དག་པ་འདི། །ཞེས་ནས་ད་ནི་དེ་དག་ལ། །
འདོད་པས་དེ་མེད་དང་འབྱེལ་བ། །རྣམ་པར་ཉེས་པར་བྱེད་པར་ཕོག །
གང་དག་དེ་ལ་འཕྱས་བྱེད་པ། །འཕུ་བའི་བདག་ཉིད་དེ་དག་གུང་། །
དོགས་མེད་རྗེས་འགྲོ་ཕྱོག་ལྱན་གྱིས། །ཅིགས་མེད་ཆར་གཅོད་བྱེད་གྱུར་ཅིག །

དབུ་མའི་རྒྱན་འདི་ནི་སྟོབ་དཔོན་ཞི་བ་འཚོ་བདག་དང་གཞན་གྱི་གྲུབ་པའི་མཐའི་རྒྱ་མ་ཚོའི་པ་རོ་ལ་ཏུ་ཕྱིན་སོན་
པ། འཕགས་པ་དག་གི་དབང་ཕྱུག་གི་ཞབས་ཀྱི་པདྨ་རྟོག་པ་མེད་པའི་ཤེ་ཤུ་འབྱུ་སྟི་བོས་ཞེན་ལས་མཛད་པ་
རྫོགས་སོ། །

རྒྱ་གར་གྱི་མཁན་པོ་ནི་ཡེཤྩ་པོ་ཊི་དང་། ཞུ་ཆེན་གྱི་ལོ་ཙ་བ་བནྡེ་ཡེ་ཤེས་སྡེས་བསྒྱུར་ཅིང་ཞུས་ཏེ་གཏན་ལ་ཕབ་
པའོ། །

160

BIBLIOGRAPHY

Western Sources

Blumenthal, James 2004. *The Ornament of the Middle Way: A Study of the Madhyamaka Thought of Santaraksita*. New York: Ithaca.

Dreyfus, Georges. *Recognizing Reality: Dharmakirti's Philosophy and Its Tibetan Interpretations*. New York: SUNY Press. 1997.

_____ "Would the True Prasangika Please 'Stand Up'? The Case and View of Ju Mipham," in Dreyfus and McClintock 2003, 317-347.

Dreyfus, Georges and McClintock, Sarah eds. *The Svatantrika-Prasangika Distinction: What Difference Does A Difference Make?*. Boston: Wisdom, 2003.

Duckworth, Douglas. *Jamgon Mipam: His Life and Teachings* Boston: Shambhala, 2011.

Dudjom Rinpoche. *The Nyingma School of Tibetan Buddhism*. Vol. I and II Trans. and ed. Dorje, Gyurme and Kapstein, Matthew. Boston: Wisdom,1991.

Friquegnon, Marie-Louise. *A Brief Introduction to the Philosophy of Santaraksita* New York: Cool Grove, 2012.

Friquegnon, Marie and Dinnerstein, Noe., eds. *Studies on Santaraksita's Yogacara Madhyamaka*. New York: Global Scholarly Publications, 2012.

Gold, Jonathan. *Paving the Great Way: Vasubandhu's Unifying Buddhist Philosophy*. New York: Columbia, 2015.

Ichigo, Masamichi. "Santaraksita's Madhyamakalankara" *Studies in the Literature of the Great Vehicle: Three Mahayana Texts*. Ed. Gomez, Luis O. Collegiate Institute for the Study of Buddhist Literature and Center for the Study for South and Southeast Asian Studies. Ann Arbor: The University of Michigan, 1989.

Jha, Ganganatha 196. *The Tattvasangraha of Shantarakshita with the Commentary of Kamalashila, 2* vols. Reprint Delhi: Motilal Banarsidass. 1989.

Khenchen Palden Sherab Rinpoche and Khenpo Tsewang Dongyal Rinpoche:

Door to Inconceivable Wisdom and Compassion. Boca Raton: Sky Dancer Press. 1996.

The Buddhist Path. Boston: Snow Lion, 2010.

Opening the Wisdom Door of the Madhyamaka School. Boston: Snow Lion, 2006.

Opening the WisdomDoor of the and Sautrantika School. Walton: Dharma Samudra, 2007.

Opening the Clear Vision of the Mind Only School. Walton: Dharma Samudra, 2007.

Tattvasiddhi and Madhyamakalamkara by Santaraksita with commentaries by Khenchen Palden Sherab and Khenpo Tsewang Dongyal. ed. with introduction by Marie Friquegnon. Trans Khenchen Palden Sherab, Khenpo Tsewang Dongyal, Marie Friquegnon in collaboration with Geshe Lozang Jamspal. New York: Cool Grove Press, 2017.

Turning the Wisdom Wheel of the Nine Golden Chariots. Dharma Samudra, 2009

Mipham, Jamgon Rinpoche:

Trans. Doctor, Thomas. *Speech of Delight: Mipham's Commentary on Santaraksita's Ornament of the Middle Way*. Ithaca: Snow Lion, 2004.

Trans. Padmakara translation group. *The Adornment of the Middle Way: Shankarakshita's Madhyamakalankara with Commentary by Jamgon Mipham*. Boston: Shambhala, 2005.

Nagarjuna:

The Fundamental Wisdom of the Middle Way: Nagarjuna's Mulamadhyamakakarika. by Nagarjuna and Jay L. Garfield. Oxford: Oxford University Press, 1995.

Nagarjuna's Middle Way: Mulamadhyamakakarika (Classics of Indian Buddhism) by Mark Siderits and Shoryu Katsura. Boston: Wisdom, 2013.

Nagarjuna's Seventy Stanzas: *A Buddhist Psychology of Emptiness,* by Nagarjuna and David Ross Komito. Ithaca: Snow Lion Publications, 1987.

Smith, E Gene. *Among Tibetan Texts: History and Literature of the Tibetan Plateau*. Somerville: Wisdom Publications. 2001.

Thurman, Robert A.F. *Tsong Khapa's Speech of Gold in the Essence of True Eloquence: Reason and Enlightenment in the Central Philosophy of Tibet*. Princeton: Princeton University Press. 1984.

Tillemans, Tom. "What are Madhyamikas Refuting? Santaraksita, Kamalasila et al. on Superimpositions (samaropa)" Unpublished paper presented at the American Philosophical Association-Central Division Annual Meeting in Chicago, April 26, 2002.

Westerhof, Jan. Nagarjuna's Madhyamaka: A Philosophical Introduction. Oxford: Oxford University Press, 2009.

Tibetan Sources

Chandrakirti: *dbu ma la 'jugpa* P5262 (Madhyamakavatara)

Dharmakirti: *tshad ma rnam 'grel gyitshig le 'ur byas pa* P 5709

Dignaga: *tshad ma kun las btus pa* P5700 (Pramanasamuccaya)

Kamalashila: *dbu ma gyan gyi dka' 'grel* (*Madhyamakalamkara-panjika*) Derge edition, Tengyur 3886

de kho nan yid bsdus pa'I dka 'grel (Commentary on the *Tattvasamgraha*) trans. by Jha, *Ganganatha in the Tattvasamgraha of Shantarakshita*. Delhi: Motilal Banarsidass, 1937.

Lang kar gshegs pa'I mdo (*Lankavatarasutra*)

Nagarjuna: *dbu ma rts aba shes rab* (*Mulamadhyamaka-karika*)

      Yab dang sras mjal ba'I mdo P760 (Pitaputrasamagamasutra)

      dKon mchog spin gyi mdo P876 (*Ratnameghasutra*)

Shantarakshita: *dbu ma gyan* (*Madhyamakalamkara*)

GLOSSARY

Abhidharma: words of the Buddha, forming one third of the Tripitaka. Teachings on discriminating knowledge by analyzing elements of experience and investigations, thus discovering the nature of existing things.

Advaita: Non-dual Vedanta school of Hinduism that believes all that exists is Brahman

alaya: ground consciousness which in Chittamatra sparks all awareness.

amrita: nectar

arhat: "foe destroyer." A disciple of Buddha who has attained Nirvana after conquering the four *kleshas* (defilements), and has 'conquered' (*hata*) his 'enemies' (*ari*).

asura: demi-god

autonomous inferences: arguments that stand alone leading to the conclusion that something is the case. This contrasts with Buddhapalita and Chandrakirti's preference for reduction ad absurdum arguments that merely show the absurdity of a position without asserting anything about it.

ayatanas:--basic ground of agreement: what must be agreed on between debaters if the argument is to progress successfully

Bhagavan: Buddha, (in Hinduism, Vishnu.)

bodhichitta: "awakened state of mind." The aspiration to attain enlightenment for the sake of all beings; wisdom and compassion.

Chandrakirti: Madhyamaka philosopher of the Prasangika school advocating

Charvaka: materialist, nihilist philosopher.

Chittamatra: Mind-Only school of Buddhist philosophy.

daka: male counterpart to dakini who fulfills the four activities. An emanation of the chief figure in the *mandala*.

dakini: female tantric deities who perform the enlightened activities to protect the Buddhist doctrine and practitioners.

Danasila: Kashmiri scholar cited in Taranatha (575-1634)

datura: cotton plant

Dergey: an edition of the Tibetan Buddhist canon.

dewa chenpo: great bliss.

dharma has many meanings. In this text it mainly means a religious point of view. In some contexts, it may mean elements.

dharmadhatu: "realm of phenomena." The nature of mind and phenomena, which lies beyond arising, dwelling, and ceasing. The suchness in which dependent origination and emptiness are inseparable.

dharmakaya: the body of enlightened qualities. One of the three *kayas*, devoid of constructs.

Dharmakirti: Indian Buddhist philosopher 600-660

dharmata: dhamadhatu

dhatu: an element or sense organ of the body.

Dignaga:-- A 6th century Indian philosopher/logician and a disciple of Vasubandhu. Believed in two types of inference, based on sensation and reasoning.

Early School ("Hinayana"/ Theravada)´: vehicles focusing on the four noble truths and the twelve links of dependent origin for individual liberation.

eighteen dhatus:
>   six external bases (bāhya-āyatana)
>   six internal bases (adhyātma-āyatana)
>   six consciousnesses (vijñāna)

>>   (1) Visual Objects (rūpa-āyatana)
>>   (2) Eye Faculty (cakṣur-indriya-āyatana)
>>   (3) Visual Consciousness (cakṣur-vijñāna

>>   (4) Auditory Objects (śabda-āyatana)
>>   (5) Ear Faculty (śrota-indriya-āyatana)
>>   (6) Aural Consciousness (śrota-vijñāna)

>>   (7) Olfactory Objects (gandha-āyatana)
>>   (8) Nose Faculty (ghrāṇa-indriya-āyatana)
>>   (9) Olfactory Consciousness (ghrāṇa-vijñāna)

>>   (10) Gustatory Objects (*rasa-āyatana*)
>>   (11) Tongue Faculty (jihvā-indriya-āyatana)
>>   (12) Gustatory Consciousness (jihvā-vijñāna)

>>   (13) Tactile Objects (spraṣṭavya-āyatana)
>>   (14) Body Faculty (kaya-indriya-āyatana)
>>   (15) Touch Consciousness (kaya-vijñāna)

>>   (16) Mental Objects (dharma-āyatana)
>>   (17) Mental Faculty (mano-indriya-āyatana)
>>   (18) Mental Consciousness (mano-vijñāna)

emanations: beings coming from a sacred source

essence taking practice: used in the production of medicine

ghandarva: celestial musicians

Great Ascetic: Buddha

great emptiness: ultimate reality beyond conception

gunas: qualities

gyur chag: a homage paid by translators

Haribhadra Suuri: Jain leader and author c. 459-529

Hoshang Mahayana: Mahayana Chinese monk who debated with Kamalash-ila. He believed that enlightenment could be reached by passive inactivity.

interdependent co-origination: The interdependence of all things at each moment of time, arising within the system of cause and effect.

Ishvara: the Lord (Hindu).

Jain/Jainas: a non-orthodox Indian philosophical school that believed in a diversity of selves (*purushsas*) that could be liberated from matter through meditation and ascetic practice.

Jaimini: ancient Nepali scholar who founded the Mimamsa school of Hindu philosophy. Lived about the 4th century BCE

Jinamitra-Kashmiri. He also passed on teachings concerning monastic dis-cipline and pith instructions. pandit who went to Tibet at the request of King Ralpachen to take part in translating texts in the Kangyur and Tengyur directly from Sanskrit into Tibetan

Jnanagarbha: Eighth century master from Nalanda who belonged to the Svatanrika Madhyamika school. He was a teacher of Shantarakshita.

kalpa: a very long period of time: four thousand three hundred and twenty millions of years.

Kama: Skt. love

Kanada: Indian natural scientist and philosopher who founded the Vaishe-shika school of Indian philosophy. An atomist.

Kapila: the legendary founder of the Samkhya school

Kasyapa: the disciple of the Buddha who inherited leadership of the sangha.

ketak: A grass eaten by the musk elephant.

kaya: the three kayas: dharmakaya, sambhogakaya, and nirmanakaya, are ground as essence, nature, and expression; as path are bliss, clarity, and nonthought; and as fruition are the three kayas of buddhahood.

klesha: "disruptive emotion." The five poisons: desire, delusion, anger, envy, and pride.

Kriya Yoga: first of the three outer tantras, emphasizing purity of action and cleanliness.

kun tags: mental exaggerations

Lankavatara Sutra: Mahayana Sutra. Teaching given by Lord Buddha to Mahamati in Lanka. Drawa on concepts of Yogachara and Buddha Nature

lata: Skt. vine.

lokyavada: way of the world/materialism/syn. carvaka

Madhyamaka: school of Mahayana Buddhism that stresses emptiness.

Mahamudra: practice of meditation used by the Kagyu school for the luminous and empty nature of existence.

Mahayana: great vehicle, course, or journey. Major division of Buddhism in which one strives toward Buddha rather than an arhat.

mandala: "center and surrounding." Symbolic representation of a tantric deity's realm of existence, a ritually protected space

Manjushri´: bodhisattva of wisdom.

matulunga: a type of citrus tree.

Mimamsa´: school of Hindu philosophy that held that the universe was an external container of the vedas.

mudra: seal; hand gesture ritual.

mulatantra: root tantra.

Nagarjuna: Madhyamika philosopher

Naiyayaikas: Indian school of philosophy bases on logic

Nalanda: Buddhist monastic university in ancient and medieval India

nirmanakaya: emanational body of Buddha

Naiyayika: the logic school of Buddhism

Nyaya: Vaisheshika: The combined logic and atomistic Hindu schools.

Padmasambhava: Indian guru who with Shantarakshita introduced Buddhist philosophy into Tibet

Palden Sherab, Khenchen Rinpoche: 1938-2010. Great Madhyamika Yogachara philosopher who founded Padmasambhava Buddhist Center with Khenpo Tsewang Dongyal Rinpoche.

Panjika: Commentary on the Madhyamakalamkara by Kamalashila

paramita: perfection; the six or ten virtues of Buddhism.

Particularities: the quality of being individual

pitaka: basket; there are three baskets of Buddhism: (1) sutra pitaka (sayings of Buddha), (2) vinaya (monastic law), and (3) abhidharma pitaka (philosophy).

prakrti: nature (According to Geshe Jamspal, the equilibrium of the *gunas*)

pramana: source of proof: direct perception, inference, and trustworthy testimony or scripture.

Pramanavartika: by Dharmakirti, Indian Buddhist philosopher 600-660, Treatise on valid means of knowledge

Pratyekabuddha: "Solitary Buddha;" one who reaches awakening without help and does not preach to others.

probandum: conclusion

probans: premises

Pudgala (*gan zag*): a person

Purusha artha: object of human pursuit: the four proper goals of human life: dharma (religion), artha (meaning), kama (love) and moksha (liberation)

rigpa: knowledge

Rinchen Zangpo: a great Tibetan translator

rupakaya: the realm of forms comprising the sambhogakaya and nirmanakaya.

Sadhana: tantric or esoteric practice.

samatha: serenity attained through the cessation of material desires.

sambhogakaya buddha: of the realm of bliss. Embodying all five or hundred buddha families and support for purification practices.

Sambhota: minister of King Trisongdetsen who created an alphabet for Tibetan

Samkhya: a school of Hindu philosophy that held that all phenomena came from *prakriti* (nature).

Samye: monastery/university in Tibet founded by Guru Padmasambhava, Shantarakshita, and King Trisongdetsen in the eighth century.

Sangha: In general, the Buddhist community. There are special meanings in tantra.

Sarvajnadeva: Kasmiri translator

Sarvastivàdins: members of the All-Exists school of Buddhism, that accepted the existence of past, present, and future; and denied the reality of self-consciousness.

sattva: one of the three *gunas*. Light. In Buddhism: being

Sautrantika: "adherents of the sutras;" early school of Buddhism, that believed reality is indirectly known through mental objects, and is atomistic in nature.

sems tsam pa: Mind-Only school.

sense consciousness: awareness through eye, ear, nose, and touch

Shang Yeshe De: translator at the time of Guru Padmasambhava

Shantigarbha: great Vidhadharas in the eighth century

Shariputra: a disciple of Lord Buddha

shravaka: Disciples of the Buddha who seek to be an arhat.

siddha: "Accomplished one." Buddhist adept who has attained siddhi.

siddhi: power or ability

sloka: verse

Sravaka: Disciple of the Buddha who seeks to be an arhat.

Subhagupta: 640-700 CE teacher. Contemporary of Asanga and Vasuband-hu. Believed external objects are crowds of atoms.

sugata: "Blissfully Gone," an enlightened being, particularly the historical Buddha Shakyamuni.

sunyata: Emptiness, without substantial independence, fundamental notion in Mahayana conception of Ultimate Reality.

sutra: Collection of the Buddha's discourses

tala: palmyra tree

tantra: a mystical treatise; Esoteric Buddhist or Hindu tradition and texts.

tathagatagarbha: "Womb or embryo of the Buddha." Innate potential for buddhahood.

Tattvasangraha: philosophical treatise by Shantarakshita

ten sciences: arts, grammar, medicine, logic, and inner science (religious theory and practice of astrology, poetics, prosody, synonmics and drama)

tendrel: system of independent co--origination.

thought constructions: relativistic understanding created by the mind

Trisongdetsen, King: king of Tibet in the eighth century who invited Shan-tarakshita to Tibet

Tsong Khapa: Tibetan saint and scholar (1357-1419) Founder of the Geluk-pa school of Tibetan Buddhism

uncompounded cessation: Vaibhashika view that uncompounded or analytic cessation which is the object of yogic perception acquired throgh medita-tion is free from every characteristic of compoundedness and constitutes an ultimate truth. (Padmakara, Mipham p. 166)

valid cognition: "Valid inference depends on the relative level on perception. And the perception of an object comes in the end to reflexive self-aware-ness, whereby the object is clearly experienced. Therefore, if a conventional valid cognition is posited, it cannot be without reflexive self-awareness." Padmakara Mipham p. 203

: Buddhist philosophical school that held that all things are composed of atoms.

Vaisheshika:: A Hindu philosophical school that believed reality to be com-posed of atoms.

Vajrasattva: A form of Buddha

Vajrayana: "Vajra vehicle." A form of Mahayana that uses special tech-niques for the attainment of enlightenment.

Vasubandhu: Fourth century Buddhist Mind-Only philosopher.

Vasumitra: One of the 500 arhats present at the synod of King Kanishta.

Vedanta: (purpose of the Vedas) The Vedanta was made up of three schools that had varying ideas of the relation of Brahman (the supreme god) to the world:

> (1) Advaita (non-dualist) Nothing really exists but Brah-man. Brahman is experienced as being, awareness and bliss, although Brahman is really beyond our understand-ing. Brahman is ultimately nirguna, without qualities. We know of Brahman through non- conceptual direct aware-

ness in jnana (knowledge) yoga. Sankara is the most famous of the Advaita. Ordinary knowledge is illusory, Maya, and the illusory god is Brahman saguna, the god with qualities.

(2) Vishistadvaita (qualifies non-dualism) God must be somewhat different from the world, or devotion (bhakti) would be impossible. Brahman is the soul of the world, and the world is the body of God. People are composed of a soul (in this case, Brahman/Atman), a subtle body which reincarnates, and a gross body. Ramanuja is the most famous philosopher.

(3) Dvaita (dualism) God and the world are distinct. Madhva is the most famous philosopher.

Vimalamitra: Indian Buddhist philosopher 8th century Taught Dzogchen in Tibet

Vinaya: monastic rules of conduct.

yana: vehicle or path.

Yogachara ("Practice of yoga," Chittamatra, or "Mind Only"): Major Mahayana school emphasizing the nature of consciousness.

APPENDIX

The Eight Absurdums

1) Sloka 53: "Raises epistemological questions about the viability of clearly experiencing objects if there are no actual images or aspects" [Blumenthal, p. 128] "Proponents of False Images [as Gyel-Tsab calls them] maintain that there are no real images and thus their view entails the *absurdum* that all perceptions of entities inseparable from images must necessarily be deluded. This is because although consciousness does not really perceive the images, it thinks it does." [Blumenthal p. 128]

2) Sloka 54: [The position of the Proponents of False Images entails] "...the incorrectness of experiencing images at all." [Blumenthal P. 128] "Consciousness could not correctly experience images at all, because there are no actual images." [Blumenthal, p. 128]

3) Sloka 55: The Incorrectness of direct experience: "...despite the fact that they claim images do not exist, they would also claim that images are not known directly. Because...Yogacarins maintain direct perception based on the fact that consciousness and objects are of the same nature." [Blumenthal, p. 129]

4) Sloka 56: "This is meant to demonstrate that because images are false and do not actually exist, it is absurd to maintain that the image would have the causal efficacy necessary for it to produce itself as an image known to consciousness." [Blumenthal, p. 130]

5) Sloka 57: [Like with Dharmakirti there are]"...only two relationships between related objects: causal relationships and relationships of identity" [Blumenthal, p. 131]

[Also} "They cannot have a causal relationship, because if images do not actually exist, they cannot, by definition. Have any causal efficacy. And images and consciousness cannot have a relationship of identity because according to the Proponents of False Images, consciousness has a real nature while images do not. [Blumenthal, p. 131]

6) Slokas 58 and 59: Gyel-tsab calls this the "absurdum of being occasionally arisen." "These Yogacarins say that images are unreal because they arise periodically or occasionally." [Blumenthal p. 132] Therefore since they do not exist, these yogacarins hold that they must arise without causes. Shantarakshita replies that they arise from interdependent co-origination. "For even if we allow that there is no outer aspect of water in the optical illusion, if there is no illusory aspect of water within consciousness, how can there be an experience of something that is completely nothing? It is impossible." [Mipham Rinpoche, Padmakara, p. 256]

7) Sloka 59: "...if images do not exist and yet objects are perceived by means of images, then since there could not exist a consciousness connected with images (being that images do not exist)consciousness could not experience objects either, This is because objects are never experienced without images, and thus consciousness would be merely self-consciousness without an object." [Blumenthal, p. 133]

8) Sloka 60: "Here Santaraksita argues that even if the perception or consciousness of objects is erroneous, it must still arise in dependence on others even if that which it depends on is an illusion." [Blumenthal,p. 133]

Abelson, R. "Comments on Self-Awareness" in *Studies in The Yogacara Madhyamaka of Santaraksita* ed. Marie Friquegnon and Noe Dinnerstein. New York: Global Scholarly Publications, 2012.

Blumenthal, James *The Ornament of the Middle Way: A Study of the Madhyamaka Thought of Santaraksita*. Ithaca: Snow Lion, 2004, p. 83

King Trisrong Detsen's book on logic: *Narthang Tengyur sgra sbyor ngo* vol. 212 folios 636-996 or 63v-99v

Also: Shantarakshita advised the king to invite Guru Padmasambhava from the Swat valley (present day Pakistan) to help. The guru arrived, and quickly put a stop to this interference. Shantarakshita, who had left for Nepal, returned to Tibet and completed the monastery without further difficulty (810 CE). It was modeled after Odantpuri monastery in India, and its design formed a symbolic mandala of the universe.

The king decided to transmit many forms of Buddhism, and invited scholars to translate the entire canon from Sanskrit into Tibetan. Some of the famous scholars who came were Jinamitra, Sarvajnadeva, Danashila, Vimalamitra and Shantigarbha. Seven young men were ordained as novice monks and were carefully observed to see if they could keep the vinaya (discipline) vows. They were successful, and many more were ordained. Samye quickly became a great center for scholarship, philosophy and translation, as well as medicine and science.

Shantarakshita wrote five major philosophical works, *Commentary on Jnanagarbha's "Distinction Between the Two Truths'* (Jnanagarbha was his teacher), the *Tattvasamgraha* (Compendium of views),the *Madhyamakalamkara* (Ornament of the Middle Way), The *Madhyamakalankaravritti*, his own commentary on the *Madhyamakalankara*), *Vipancitartha*, a commentary on the logician Dharmakirti, the *Tattvasiddhi* (the Attainment of Reality), *Paramarthaviniscaya (*the *Investigation of the Ultimate* (which has been lost in both Sanskrit and Tibetan), as well as ritual texts and prayers. He died suddenly in Tibet.

"Generally speaking he [Shantarakshita] argues as a Sautrantika when criticizing Vaibhashika views, as a Yogacarya when criticizing Sautrantika views, and as a Madhyamika when criticizing various Yogacarya positions While in the final analysis he maintains specific views and we can correctly say that he is a Madhyamika since he rejects the existence of an ultimate nature in phenomena, one might also be inclined to say he is a 'Yogacara-Madhyamika' in that he rejects the externality of objects conventionally. By the use of 'sliding scales of analysis,' I think Santaraksita's brand of Buddhist
philosophy, far from being exclusive, is much more inclusive of all systems of Buddhist thought. In fact...he utilizes multiple provisional views, not

only that of Yogacara, in an attempt to lead followers to a Madhyamaka position realizing the lack of any inherent nature in phenomena." [Blumenthal, 2004 pp 167-168]

"The Conventional Status of Conventional Awareness: What's at Stake in a Tibetan Debate?" in *Studies on Santaraksita's Yogachara Madhyamaka* ed. Marie -Louise Friquegnon and Noe Dinnerstein. New York: Global Scholarly Publications: New York, 2012. pp. 291-327

(Kamalashila *Panjika* MAP) We cannot have omniscience because of external disturbances. That is subjective obscurations. Also, our knowledge is limited because things are limited. These are the objective obscurations. Thus, one should pay homage to *buddhas* who cultivate the mind of high devotion, and dwell above the great ones (non-Buddhists such as Vishnu), and who traverse the paths and stages, starting from devotion to 'no more learning.'

Example of pervasion and counter-pervasion: If there is smoke, there is burning. There is smoke. Therefore, there is burning; If there is no burning, there is no smoke. There is no burning. Therefore, there is no smoke. If there is a cause, there will be a result. There is a cause, therefore there will be a result; If there is no result, there would have been no cause. There is no result, therefore, there was no cause.

"It is said [in the auto-commentary], 'When the uncompounded entity, that is, the analytic cessation (cognized by yogic perception acquired through meditation) which the s consider to be truly existent, is subject to rational inquiry, it is not found to be a truly existent, single entity. This is so because the same uncompounded object is related to a succession of cognitive instants in the manner of known and knower.'" Mipham Rinpoche in Padmakara p. 166
Labeled by Kamalashila MAP Ichigo's critical edition 1985,33 P5286
Madhyamakalamkarapanjika

Blumenthal's translation of sloka 5: "Since the nature of the [latter] object does not arise in the earlier [time] and [the earlier] object] does not arise at the latter time, uncompounded phenomena like consciousness must be objects known to arise momentarily." [Blumenthal, 2004 p. 68]

"But, if the object observed by the present consciousness existed also in the past, (in the absence of the present knowing subject), and if it exists later, on (when the present moment of consciousness has ceased) why is the cognitive subject of those earlier and later moments not also present? For if the objects observed in distinct moments are unrelated to the observing consciousness, it is nonsense to speak of the perception of outer objects. The only truly existent, single entity is one that is not the object of different instants of consciousness. For if such an entity existed, it would follow that it is not the object of momentary consciousness. Accordingly, it should be understood that it is impossible to establish uncompounded cessation as one truly existent entity." (Mipham Padmakara Translation Group, 2005 p. 168)

[Mipham Rinpoche, Padmakara, p. 176].
Also, Tsong Khapa points out that Shantarakshita's criticism applies equally to partless particles and space (as well as the meditative objects of the *arhat*) because since "they are also asserted to be known periodically by distinct consciousness, they would also be rejected in a similar way..." *dbU ma rgyan gyi zin bris* 58 [CF. Blumenthal, 2004, p. 70]

Universals and generalities (Skt. *vishesha,* Tib. *khad pa*) are being compared to eunuchs because none of them, as Dignaga and Dharmakirti demonstrated can function. CF. [Blumenthal, 2004, p. 70]
See also:
> What benefit is there whatever
> In seeking meaning by investigating what is useless.
> What benefit is there in lustful women investigating
> Whether or not a eunuch is beautiful.
> *Pramanavartika*.211
> [*Svarthanumana,* VV. 211 CD, 212 ab]

(Shubha Gupta) [MF a 11th cent. logician mentioned in *Anekaan ta-jaya-pa-taakaa-tika* attributed to Haribhadra Suuri c. 1277 AD in Satis Chandra Vidyabhusana *A History of Indian Logic: Ancient, Mediaeval and Modern Schools*]

See also: *Tattvasamgraha*, 1990:
> "Thus, seeing other atoms,
> If they are viewed to be in this way,
> Then how can extensive hills etc.
> Be formed by them?"

CF. also Kamalashila's commentary in *Tattvasamgraha* answering the opponent: p 945 (jha-commentary to 1990-1992)

See also *Tattvasamgraha* 1991

Wikipedia (skandha article)
> "The eighteen dhātus [ag] – the Six External Bases, the Six Internal Bases, and the Six Consciousnesses – function through the five aggregates. The eighteen dhātus can be arranged into six triads, where each triad is composed of a sense object, a sense organ, and sense consciousness. In regards to the aggregates: [23]
> The first five sense organs (eye, ear, nose, tongue, body) are derivates of form.
> The sixth sense organ (mind) is part of consciousness.
> The first five sense objects (visible forms, sound, smell, taste, touch) are also derivatives of form.
> The sixth sense object (mental object) includes form, feeling, perception and mental formations.
> The six sense consciousness are the basis for consciousness."

The Eighteen Dhātus

Six External Bases (bāhya-āyatana)
Six Internal Bases (adhyātma-āyatana)
Six Consciousnesses (vijñāna)

(1) Visual Objects (rūpa-āyatana)
(2) Eye Faculty (cakṣur-indriya-āyatana)
(3) Visual Consciousness (cakṣur-vijñāna

(4) Auditory Objects (śabda-āyatana)
(5) Ear Faculty (śrota-indriya-āyatana)
(6) Aural Consciousness (śrota-vijñāna)

(7) Olfactory Objects (gandha-āyatana)
(8) Nose Faculty (ghrāṇa-indriya-āyatana)
(9) Olfactory Consciousness (ghrāṇa-vijñāna)

(10) Gustatory Objects (*rasa-āyatana*)
(11) Tongue Faculty (jihvā-indriya-āyatana)
(12) Gustatory Consciousness (jihvā-vijñāna)

(13) Tactile Objects (spraṣṭavya-āyatana)
(14) Body Faculty (kaya-indriya-āyatana)
(15) Touch Consciousness (kaya-vijñāna)

(16) Mental Objects (dharma-āyatana)
(17) Mental Faculty (mano-indriya-āyatana)
(18) Mental Consciousness (mano-vijñāna)

See also Kamalashila's commentary to Text 2000 *Tattvasamgraha Jha* p. 949-950:

> "When Cognition is said to be 'self-cognisant", it is not meant that it is the *apprehender* or *cognizer* of itself; what is meant is that it shines, _becomes manifested,_ by itself,_ by its very nature,_ just like the Light diffused in the atmosphere."

This is as the nature of self-reflection, because by nature it is illuminating. It is the opposite of a chariot etc. which by nature lacks understanding [Khenchen Palden Sherab Rinpoche]. When one knows the real nature of the self, one knows that blue, for example, does not depend on anyone other than oneself (Khenchen Palden Sherab Rinpoche). The so-called lack of the object of knowledge is asserted to be self-awareness. Thus, one asserts the object of self-awareness is not without awareness.

Also: The nature of objects which are not awareness would be different from knowledge. How could they be known because there is no relationship between object and knowledge? The awareness which is the characteristic of the nature of knowledge does not exist in the object. In that case then for what reason could the knowledge [of the object] be known by itself, and then, similarly and directly experienced and known? This is not possible because you assert of the object two things, that knowledge and that to be known are a different nature.

"Santaraksita follows this question in his autocommentary with a multi-layered argument aimed at convincing his opponents to accept that objects do not exist external to the consciousness which perceives them: for it would be impossible to know these objects directly if they are distinct entities. In addition, with regards to the neither-one- nor- many argument, if consciousness is truly singular, then it would be incoherent to assert that it could know objects from which it is different because it would have to be related to objects of a different nature. He is, of course, not arguing for a truly single nature of the mind, but merely as the truly single nature of consciousness and the ability to know objects distinct from itself. This is an excellent example of how Santaraksita pitches arguments to opponents on their own terms and aims to gradually lead them to what he considers to be the correct view (i.e. that of the Madhyamaka)]." [Blumenthal, p. 89]

Geshe Lozang Jamspal: The nature of the object is not luminous understanding because the object is different from knowledge.
"Since consciousness is luminous and aware, it is knowable to itself. But how is consciousness able to know things that are by nature different from itself and that lack these qualities of clarity and awareness? They are completely alien to it. Clear and knowing experience, the defining feature of consciousness, is wholly absent from the non-mental things that are foreign to it. How then can consciousness, which is self-cognizing, have a direct experience and knowledge of other things? For indeed those who affirm the existence of external objects and the knowing mind do say that consciousness and the object to be cognized are two quite different natures. The so-called detection of the object (*yul yongs su gcod pa*) is an extraordinary feature of consciousness. This is like the mind's experience of happiness, and so on-which cannot be a feature of external objects. To the extent that something is experienced by consciousness or appears to consciousness, this same experience can only be due to the clarity and knowing of the mind. How can there be an awareness of anything in the absence of clarity and knowing?" [Mipham Rinpoche, Padmakara, p. 204]

TS 2079: Therefore that which is the subject of the dispute (i.e., self-cognizing cognition) is considered to be non-dual, since it is devoid of object and subject (*vedyakartrtvaviyogat*) because it is the nature of consciousness, like a reflection. [Trans by Blumenthal, 2004, p. 89]

See also TS 2080, 2081 and Kamalashila's commentaries on all three passages. [KTDR: "Consciousness is not mind, not matter, but it can know itself. Gyeltsan argues that if one claims self-cognition is productive, one must also claim that it has inherent existent. But this does not follow from Shantarakshita's view, because self-cognition is neither one nor many it cannot have inherent existence. I think the production is simply the result of interdependent co-origination." MLF] Refuting and Sautrantika because they say subject and object are different: [Since you are not accepting self-awareness, and believe subject and object are different, then how could the subject grasp the object if subject and object are distinct? This would not be logical]. (Khenpo Tsewang Dongyal Rinpoche)

It has the nature of experiencing objects but is not itself an object.

"We find an explicit declaration of the non-dual nature of consciousness and its objects according to Shantarakshita in Tattvasamgraha when he says:

'Therefore, that which is the subject of the dispute (i.e. self-cognizing cognition) is considered to be non-dual, since it is devoid of subject and object (*vedyarkartrtyavivogat*) because it is the nature of consciousness, like a reflection'" TS 2078

"Not relying on others to be illuminated, that which is self-illuminating, is called the self-cognizing of consciousness." [Blumenthal, p. 87]
Also:
"Since its nature does not exist in (external) objects,
Because you have asserted
That subject and object are different
Having this characteristic,
Ultimately [consciousness and its object] will remain separated."
[*Tattvasamgraha* 2002]

"But since the object is akin to a reflection, It's by such means that things can be experienced." [Mipham Rinpoche, Padmakara, p. 54]
Also:
[MLF: Clarity can clarify our unclear perceptions, it cannot clarify clarity

which is beyond conception.]

Also:

"Shantarakshita explains that according to this position, one directly experiences images of objects because the gross imputed object is like a mirror image of the gathered actual images of the external object....Shantarakshita states [in MAV] that the position of his opponent holds that the mirror-like image of the object which is known by the consciousness is in the nature of the object and that, therefore, the consciousness which knows the mirror-like image of the object also knows the object itself." [Blumenthal, 2004, p. 92]

"The gradual arising of thought
    Is like a firebrand whirled around
    Because of the speed
    It appears in the mind simultaneously."
    [*CF. Tattvasamgraha* 1246]

[CF. Blumenthal, p, 95] Gyel-tsab: "At the time that a multiplicity of images such as blue, yellow, white and red are known to a single consciousness, these images could not be substantially distinct from one another because they are all indistinct from the one partless consciousness. If you accept this, then having appeared as images of the object, it would be incoherent to accept the establishment of the object as substantially different from the [consciousness which apprehends the images of the object] because those images are not of a different substance.]

THIS IS THE HALF EGG VIEW: Also B's explanation that terms such as ½ egg were introduced by Gyel-tsab and the Geluks and not used by Shantarakshita. [Blumenthal, p.121]

    [COMPARE WITH]:
    Through the aspect of the sound, the word 'vine'
    Similarly arises very quickly by the operation of the mind.
    By the precision of simultaneity
    How would not the reverse arise?
    [*Tattvasamgraha* 1250]

Also: Blumenthal explains this last point in the following way:
[Shantarakshita argues] " ...[T]hat even a conceptualizing mind, which one could argue makes such mistakes out of ignorance, could not cognize in the way this opponent claims. This is the case because as with the way images arise and disintegrate moment-by-moment, so too does the conceptual consciousness perceiving them. If the consciousness does not abide for any duration of time, such a conceptual consciousness could not hold a direct perception of a succession of images arising over time in the mind and could not even erroneously consider them to exist simultaneously. It would only be possible if the images were enduring and thereby many could appear to a single consciousness. But then one falls back to the same fallacies as the NonPluralist, in addition to having to accept the true existence of images due to their enduring nature." [Blumenthal, 2004, p. 100]

"And even if the moments of consciousness [of sights and sound] do arise in a similarly rapid manner, since they do not result in the complete, instantaneous perception of the object, such an object cannot be posited as the cause of the apprehending consciousness. [Padmakara note 298: This belongs to the Sautrantika theory of perception. In the first moment, the object, sense organ, and the consciousness act as the cause; in the second moment, the mental aspect of the object is produced, (i.e. , the result, Khenchen Pema Sherab Rinpoche). For an effect is necessarily consequent upon a cause. Where there is no cause, there is no effect." [Mipham Rinpoche, Padmakara, 2010, p.211]

"In other words, the opponent wants to claim that the consciousness is momentary like the images it perceives, yet must also make the contradictory claim that consciousness also abides for some duration of time in order to erroneously piece together the distinct consecutive images and to come to the incorrect conclusion that they are perceived simultaneously." [Blumenthal, 2004 p. 101]

Also: MLF's note: Perception must take place in the present which is instantaneous. Thus, if the mind unites the successive images, the resulting simultaneous experience cannot be considered perception, but only a kind of afterimage produced by the instantaneous states of the sense organs and the consciousness.

"Just through the manifesting of the torch

The circle arises appearing all at once.
Because each appears clearly,
The boundaries are mistaken."
[*Tattvasamgraha* 1254]

"The mistake of an eye consciousness and the mistake of a mental consciousness are two totally different types of mistakes. An eye consciousness can make a mistake by seeing something that is not there such as an
hallucination...mental consciousness with its memory can join conceptual thoughts, but an eye consciousness cannot do that because an eye consciousness is only conscious of the present according to Santaraksita." [Blu-
menthal, p. 103]

Also: "That is to say, as long as there is a temporal sequence of appearance from the cognitive perspective, this will invalidate simultaneous
appearance. And when the appearance is simultaneous, it cannot possibly
be observed as occurring in temporal sequence. Therefore [the claim] that
in the cognitive perspective the sequential appears simultaneously, it can
never be established by direct perception. Moreover, since regardless of
the objects of cognition one turns to, it will not be outside of the [above]
condition no inference or example can be found [either]." [Doctor, p. 295]
Blumenthal: "In other words, the opponent wants to claim that the consciousness is momentary like the images it perceives, yet must also make
the contradictory claim that consciousness also abides for some duration of
time in order to erroneously piece together the distinct consecutive images
and to come to the incorrect conclusion that they are perceived simultaneously. According to Gyel-tsab's explanation of the argument Shantarakshita
is making, if conceptual consciousness were momentary, it could not even
erroneously piece together such images. This is because the previous momentary image known to a previous momentary consciousness would not
be able to abide for any duration so as to be erroneously conceptualized as
being known simultaneously with other related images." [2004, pp 101-
102]

Also: [Blumenthal, p. 101]

Gyel-tsab quoted by Blumenthal in defense of Shantarakshita p. 104: "The
subject, a non-conceptual consciousness, could not join the boundaries of
the former and later [images by means of memory] because it could not
apprehend past objects. {For this position to be coherent} there would first

have to be [past] objects clearly appearing to the subject, and a mind which joins the boundaries of the former and later [images] because it apprehends past objects, [yet it is impossible for there to be clearly appearing past objects]."

Also: "…[T]here are as many consciousnesses as there are images "Blumenthal, p. 104]

Also: "Consciousness does not appear as one, for it is said to observe entities that are endowed with sundry properties." [Mipham Rinpoche, Padmakara p. 217]

"The appearance of gross objects would not occur because its objects are substances which have qualities [*guna, yontan* etc.]" [Blumenthal, p. 109]

Also: "If an aspect can be subdivided into a multiplicity of parts, it cannot be a single entity. It might be objected that the infinitesimal particle, which cannot be subdivided, constitutes a single aspect that is observable. But, says Shantarakshita, however much he has searched for it, and with painstaking effort, he has certainly never come across an infinitesimal particle of white and so forth, by nature isolated and unmixed with other things, indivisible into its different directions and appearing to all cognitions. He says, in short, that the infinitesimal, partless particle can never be the object of experience. [Mipham Rinpoche, Padmakara, p. 16]

Also: "Now the mental consciousness that observes mental phenomena does not apprehend mental factors alone; it observes the entire group of mind and mental factors together. Consequently, the object of that which is posited as the mental or sixth consciousness is considered to be an amalgam of main mind and mental factors." [Mipham Rinpoche, Padmakara, p. 21]

"[Jains and Mimasakas] both say, for instance, that just as the nature of a many-colored onyx [*zi* stone] is one, so too is the nature of all the various aspects of different things. In other words, they bring together all the different aspects of different objects and simply assume that they form a single thing. But the different cognitions that apprehend a variety of different objects cannot be a single consciousness. If a variegated object is not apprehended as such by different apprehending objects of consciousness, how can consciousness be in accord with its object? And if there is a discrepancy between them, it is impossible to say that the object is known. These schools believe that all objects of knowledge form a single whole, and they use the onyx stone with its different colors as an illustration of what they mean. But if this were true, everyone would have the same knowledge."

[Mipham Rinpoche, Padmakara, p. 223]

Also: "Gyel-tsab's explanation echoes Shantarakshita's argument by explaining by inference the argument in the thirty-sixth stanza. He argues quite simply that since entities have parts and emit manifold images, like the rays of a gem, and consciousness apprehends an entire object, including its manifold images, simultaneously, that the consciousness itself cannot be of a truly single nature by virtue of its relationship with manifold objects or images." [Blumenthal, p. 111]

This criticism of the Charvaka bears a striking resemblance to Wittgenstein's critique of his own early logical positivism, arguing it is inconsistent because the statement of the verifiability principle is itself unconfirmable by sense observation. [MLF]

[Buddhist Text & Research Society – 1895 Journal - Volumes 3-5 - Page 15 - Google Books Result]

It is necessary to add here that according to Kapila the sense-organs have emanated from the Sattva qualities of the *Prakriti* ...
https://books.google.com/books?id=ubwoAAAAYAAJ

Shantarakshita points out the same error in the Vedantins #330-331 in *Tattvasamgraha*. when they try to relate a single unchanging absolute to a diversity. [One should infer that the absolute which is beyond conception may not be said to be either permanent or impermanent.]

"The error in the view of these philosophers is a slight one, -due only to the assertion of eternality (of Cognition); as diversity is clearly perceived in the cognitions of Colour, Sound and other things, -If all these cognitions were one, then, Colour, Sound, Taste and other things would be cognizable all at once; as in an eternal entity there can be no different states."

Padmakara Mipham p.228: "The Samkhyas may say that the weak gunas do not appear, with the result that consciousness does not detect them. But to this we would answer that it is only a consciousness that perceives an object in conformity with the way it actually is that can be said to know its object. If the consciousness does not accord with an object, it is unsuitable to say it apprehends that object."

"The Samkhyas say that the object of consciousness has the nature

of three gunas; nevertheless consciousness itself manifests as a single entity. But do the Samkhyas then believe that the object is perceived in such a way that the knowing subject is not in accord with its object? In that case, how can they claim that this consciousness is the knowing subject, the apprehender of a threefold object? This is impossible." [Mipham Rinpoche, Padmakara, p.228]
[Sound would have to appear as the same thing to everyone. Geshe Lozang Jamspal.]
[See also Blumenthal, p. 113.]

. "It may be thought that since extramental objects like space and so forth are partless, the consciousness perceiving them must be a single entity. This however is not the case. In fact, a consciousness cognizing a nonthing (i.e. a privation) such as space never has the direct, naked, experience of an object. For these nonthings are nothing more than conceptual representations or reflections arising in connection with their names." [Mipham Rinpoche, Padmakara, p. 234]

See also: "If there is a truly existent single consciousness, It must be devoid of all capacity to function (as Shantarakshita explained when dealing with truly existent, permanent entities.) But this cannot be said of any consciousness." [Mipham Rinpoche, Padmakara, p. 235]

"One could claim *the existence of some consciousnesses that do not appear* individually *as a diversity* of objects. Such existence *may be allowed for*, or may be assumed. *Yet*, except for being mere imputations, *they cannot be posited authentically* as true singularities, *for* with respect to these consciousnesses, *their* possessing or *having such characteristics* of a true singularity, of a true singularity *is seen* by reasoning, *to be* hopelessly *flawed*. If there were some consciousness of a true singularity, it would, just as stated in [the section on] permanent entities, turn out to be entirely devoid of any ability to perform a function, and would therefore not be suited to be a cognition" [Mipham Rinpoche: Thomas Doctor p. 349.]

Shantarakshita points out the same error in the Vedantins folios 330-331 in *Tattvasamgraha.* when they try to relate a single unchanging absolute to a diversity. [One should infer that the absolute that is beyond conception may not be said to be either permanent or impermanent.]

"The Samkhyas say that the object of consciousness has the nature of three gunas; nevertheless, consciousness itself manifests as a single entity. But do the Samkhyas then believe that the object is perceived in such a way that the knowing subject is not in accord with its object? In that case, how can they claim that this consciousness is the knowing subject, the apprehender of a threefold object? This is impossible."

[Mipham Rinpoche, Padmakara, p. 228:] "The Samkhyas may say that the weak gunas do not appear, with the result that consciousness does not detect them. But to this we would answer that it is only a consciousness that perceives an object in conformity with the way it actually is that can be said to know its object. If the consciousness does not accord with an object, it is unsuitable to say it apprehends that object."

Also: "There are no subtle entities which are not included among the accumulated things. Therefore how does one analyze a mind which is the knower of one object? How is a gathering of mental states the single object of a mind?" [MAV 58-59, Blumenthal, p. 117]

. [Shantarakshita is speaking as a Yogacharin here: Blumenthal, p. 117]

Also: Actually there are no aspects of feeler and felt. They appear though they do not exist. They are like illusions, dreams, castles in the air, circles of light created by whirling firebrands, phantoms, the moon reflected on the water, and so forth. All this is the Cittamatra position." [Mipham Rinpoche, Padmakara, p. 239]

"Since these Chittamatrins have already said that the aspects [of an appearance] are not different, they cannot now say that they are different-that some aspects are moving and some are not. It is hard to sidestep such a consequence." [Mipham Rinpoche, Padmakara, p. 242]

And: "Yet their teaching says they are not different, that they are of that [single nature.] If that is the case, then if one image is engaged in the action of moving, etc. or if one is the nature of yellow etc. then all [related] remaining images will also be like that. If that is not the case, then they must definitely be of various natures (i.e. not one)." [Blumenthal, 2004. p. 123]

LJ Those who hold this view assert that happiness and so forth; as well as] the aspects blue and so forth have the nature of experience/knowledge. There are many, and also, they are homogeneous, but they occur as heterogeneous. According to their theory without previous and former states, according two minds do not arise, no chance for this. Similarly, all sentient beings have only a single conscious continuity. [Otherwise] it is difficult to avoid contradicting scripture.

"If we perceive as many, how can we call it a single object?" Mipham p.243 Also: the appearance would be infinitely divisible like the atom. Thus consciousness, like the agate [*gzi*], [is but one, but] appears variegated. This cannot be accepted in the way spoken of in this doubtful system [as atomic].

"But even if we assume with the False Aspectarians that the aspects are non-existent, how is it possible that within consciousness, which the False Aspectarians consider to exist and to stand alone and unsupported like a pure crystal sphere, there manifest a variety of experienced features? If there are no aspects, is it feasible that consciousness should be generated in the likeness of what it observes? That is something for the False Aspectarians to think about." [Mipham Rinpoche, Padmakara, p. 249] "Gyel-tsab writes 'If one asserts that a variety of images would be truly in the nature of a singular consciousness [as the Non-Pluralists assert, it would be] like the system of the Vedantists and the Nirgranthas. If that truly singular consciousness to which various objects appear is asserted, then there is a pervasion, because if various objects appear [to it, it] would not be truly singular, like a heap of a variety of precious [gems]. There is also the appearance of various images to the consciousness. If you accept the singularity of images, then it would be impossible for many different images to appear, such as "visible" and "invisible" etc. and images of various sorts such as blue and yellow, etc. because the various images are truly singular.' Gyel-tsab echoes Shantarakshita's argument by pointing out that if the so-called Non-Pluralists wish to maintain, as they must, that the variety of images and the consciousnesses perceiving them are truly singular, then all the images perceived must have the same nature as the perceiving consciousness. Therefore, all the many images of an object must have the same nature since they are all singular and of one nature with the consciousness. For example, one object cannot be the nature of blue while another has the nature of yellow because that would require a perceiving consciousness with a manifold, not single, nature because it has parts (I.e. the part conscious of blue and the part conscious of yellow). Therefore, such a position entails internal contradictions." [Blumenthal, p. 126.]

[CF. Mipham Rinpoche, Padmakara, p. 247]
Also [CF. Mipham Rinpoche, Doctor 383]
   Eight absurdums see Appendix. "[T]o demonstrate fallacies in the as-

sertions of yogacharins who claim images are not real. [Blumenthal, p. 128]

If images are mere illusions, like flowers in the sky, direct perception of them, of something that does not actually exist, would be absurd. This is particularly true given that Yogacharas maintain direct perception based on the fact that consciousness and objects are of the same nature. Shantarak-shita expresses this succinctly in the following manner in the fifty-fifth root text stanza. [Blumenthal, 2004 p. 129]

And Mipham Rinpoche's Padmakara [p. 247]:

"Indeed there is no consciousness
That from the aspects stands apart."

Also: "'Aspect' cannot be classified as anything other than a feature of the clarity and knowing of the consciousness that cognizes individual objects. This is why it is never possible for consciousness to be something that stands apart from the aspect. It is therefore important to reflect carefully on the consequence that if the aspect has no existence whatever it cannot appear. Otherwise, if one fails to do so and considers, without more ado, that the aspects just do not exist, this position will eventually turn against one and one will stray very far from the subtle position of the Madhyamaka path. Therefore, the authentic Chittamatra is the system of the True Aspec-tarians (who are authors of excellent treatises). On the other hand, in saying that the outer object in not even truly existent as the mind, the False Aspec-tarians are a little closer to the understanding that things are empty of true existence and thus provide in a manner of speaking, a bridge to the Madhya-maka. Although in the correct ordering of things the False Aspectarians are, as a result, placed higher on the scale of views, nevertheless, because the system exhibits many inconsistencies on the level of the conventional truth, the conventional should be expounded according to the system of the True Aspectarians. Once this key point is grasped, it will be easy to understand the refutations that follow." [Mipham Rinpoche, Padmakara, p. 249]

Khenchen Palden Sherab Rinpoche: Raising a doubt: Thus, what you es-tablished, and the proof are in contradiction. You must doubt this. There-fore, for you the object of knowledge and the aspect have no relationship, because both are your mind. CF. root text: *If knowledge has no object, this is like a sky flower.*

Also: [Blumenthal, p. 129] "…Yogacharas maintain direct knowledge of objects is possible, and since objects are considered to be of the same nature as consciousness, the claim for the unreality of images must in fact be faulty. This is the case because images do not actually exist in their view and so they must not be of the same substance as consciousness which is real."

For a Yogacharin who denies the reality of images, it would be absurd for images and consciousness to have either of these two kinds of relationships, yet they are asserted nonetheless to be related according to this system. They cannot have a causal relationship, because if images do not actually exist, they cannot, by definition, have any causal efficacy. And images and consciousness cannot have a relationship of identity because, according to the Proponents of False Images, consciousness has a real nature while images do not. Shantarakshita explains this in the fifty-seventh MA stanza and the related auto commentary. [Blumenthal, 2004. p. 131]

Gyeltsab in commentating on Shantarakshita's sixtieth sloka: "Even if in reality there are no images, that since they are perceived, they still must be dependently arisen. And dependent phenomena are real, functional objects according to Yogacharas[/Chittamatras]. ' If one says that, although in reality there are no [images] of objects, images appear due to a mistake, then the subject, images, would be other-dependent because they depend on a mistake. This is the case because they (i.e. the images) arise from the force of a mistake.'" [Blumenthal, 2004, p. 134]

Also: Note [Mipham Rinpoche, Padmakara, p. 251]: "…non-existent things have no power to produce cognitions that resemble them."

Kamilashila says that the hold that another form is in the mirror. Jaimini (Mimamsaka) says that the form itself is perceived that way. The Sautrantika's hold that what is seen in the mirror is not knowledge at all, only illusion. Shantarakshita says that all three are mistaken, because the example is misleading. The reflection does not exist [ultimately] (Mipham Rinpoche).

In this life and in another life
And at this time and another time
All objects are perceived as external
And as existing in themselves at separate times.

The analyzed object of dream-like knowledge,
This object and dissimilar objects,
Are like a paradoxical torch which is
Quickly whirled about.

Memories/visions of homes etc. are
Clouds of cities of *gandharvas.*
They are [the mind of] one who is tormented by thirst,
Perceiving a mirage of water caused by light in a desert wilderness.

The Ten Sciences: "The arts, grammar, medicine, logic, inner science (i.e. religious theory and practice), astrology, poetics, prosody, synonymics, and drama." *The Nyingma School of Tibetan Buddhism Dudjom Rinpoche*, Vol. 2. Boston: Wisdom Publications, 1991, p. 167.

One should pay attention to the illusory experiences of beings as one would pay attention to a child's nightmare.

> "...entities have no nature like a reflected image. He {Shantarakshita} explains that the erroneous assessment of entities as having a truly existent nature is similar to the way we cognize an image of water in the desert due to the intense rays of the sun on a dry surface. Although there is cause for cognizing in this way, it is not correct to say that the conclusion which we tend to draw, that there is water, is correct. (see MAV 81) Similarly, it is not correct to draw the conclusion that objects which appear to us to have a truly established nature actually do. They are also like the images in mirrors: they do not actually exist in the way that they appear to exist." [Blumenthal, p. 136]

Note: [Blumenthal, p. 117]: There are no subtle entities which are not included among the accumulated things. Therefore how does one analyze a mind which is the knower of one object? How is a gathering of mental states the single object of a mind? [MAV 58-59]

Cessation: Kalupahana *p. 339: "We state that whatever is dependently arising, that is emptiness. That is dependent upon convention. That itself is the middle path.*

Jay Garfield's *Nagarjuna's Root Text Madhyamakacarika* [Chap. 24, Verse 18, p. 305]:

> *"Whatever is dependently co-arisen, This is explained to be emptiness. That being a dependent designation, That itself is the Middle Way."*

Thus said. If like that: Are similarly heuristically/intentionally spoken about:

> "Santaraksita does not explicitly delineate a distinction between real and unreal conventional truths as Kamalasila does in MAP. Kamalasila clearly distinguishes between dependently arisen functional entities which can be considered as real conventional truths, and mere conventional constructs, such as the creator God" asserted by the Samkhyas which are unreal conventional truths." [Blumenthal, p. 141]

See Mipham Doctor p. 479; Gyel-tsab Blumenthal, p. 144; See Nagarjuna's *Establishment of the Conventional* [*Vyaviharasiddhi tha snyad grub pa*]

This is similar to the modern notion (Wittgenstein) of non-vacuous contrast. Because on the conventional level, the meaning of hot (for example) must be in contrast to cold, otherwise we could not make sense of these terms at all, and clearly, we do.

"To the minds of immature beginners, emptiness and appearance or existence and nonexistence inevitably seem as if they were mutually exclusive, with one being the negation of the other. It is hard to realize how these form a union. Nevertheless, when the vase placed in front [of us] is investigated with the reasoning of the absence of one and many, it is seen to be, in essence, devoid of even a particle of established nature. That emptiness is not something that did not exist before and has only now occurred at the time of investigating. Therefore, although it appears to arise, cease, and disintegrate, the vase has not moved in the slightest from the state empty of nature. While being empty, it appears as it does, and so one must develop certainty that the actual condition is one of appearance and emptiness united." [Mipham Rinpoche, Doctor p. 481]

Aryadeva *Four Hundred Verses* Chap. 16, Verse __

Khenchen Palden Sherab Rinpoche's suggested changes:
"From the childish to buddhas their experience is different. Whatever their experience is, it is their own perception, and I do not object. On the absolute level contrary to Kapila etc. [Nyaya-s, exists], [Charvak-as, do not exist]-[Jains, things both exist and do not exist], and all of this is exaggeration. The buddhas [the speaker], do not see wrongly the nature of emptiness. These do not exist on the absolute level. Thus, seeing the nature of everything as emptiness is not incorrect."

"Santaraksita clearly wants to emphasize that he does not merely talk about the past and future when speaking of a lack of inherent existence of production, but also of the present, of the "time of arising." This eliminates any potential ambiguity about the lack of inherent existence necessitating a relationship to a specific time other that the present, because the lack of inherent existence is the same in all of the three times." [Blumenthal, 2004 p. 14]
On the ultimate level, things and nothing, birth and non-birth, emptiness and non-emptiness, etc., are all abandoned like a complex net of elaborations. Though nothing arises etc., since entering into [accepting] this is harmonious with the ultimate, it is designated as ultimate.
Without the staircase of perfect conventionality,
One should not go
To the roof of the house of the ultimate.
It is not suitable for the wise.
[*Madhyamakohrdaya* by Bhavaviveka Chap. 3, v. 12 *legs ldan 'gyed*]

[Blumenthal, 2004, p. 148]
Also: Nagarjuna *The Dispeller of Disputes*:

If objects are not established,
Then non-existent objects will not be established.
When the object changes into something else,
People say, "It does not exist."

Thus said
"In milk, yogurt etc. does not exist.

It does not exist previously [in the milk].
In yogurt, milk does not exist.
It has the characteristic of non-existence, being destroyed.

The protrusion of the head
Lacks any solid existence.
The characteristics of the horn of a rabbit etc.
Are said to be absolutely non-existent.
As to the cow, there is no horse.
They are mutually exclusive."

Thus trivially, the meaning is, none of these things exist. They are certainly non-existent. They are all brought together by association. The non-existence of things is the enemy of certainty.

Certainly, one can now establish that a barren woman having a son etc. is not certain [cannot happen]. If one considers the matter, it cannot exist. In this way from the *Ocean of Intelligence Sutra* it has been taught: "Brahma, that phenomenon which is completely [presumably] established as self-existent, has been well explained as non-existent. " In the *Lankavatara Sutra*, Chap. 3, Verse 14 [MLF: Since things don't exist, we can't be certain about anything.]

Also: "Mere existence is the counterpart, the simple negation, of true existence. It definitely belongs to the conventional or relative level. It is not the ultimate or natural condition of phenomena. Since, however, it is in agreement with ultimate truth (that is the authentic ultimate state of things), this mere absence of true existence, the conceptual opposite of true existence, is called 'ultimate truth', in much the same way that the name of result is given to its cause. This is the approximate or conceptual (*btags pa ba*) ultimate." [Mipham Rinpoche, Padmakara, p. 296]

Khenpo Tsewang Dongyal Rinpoche taught that the Svabhavakaya was completely beyond words. The Dharmakaya was the intelligence or wisdom aspect of the Svabhavakaya and could be indicated by words. On-line retreat April 20, 2020. This is similar to the true ultimate and the proximate ultimate.

"…[C]onsequently, even a nonthing (absence) is posited in dependence on its counterpart: a causally efficient thing. If there were no certainty that barren women and children existed, it would be impossible to derive any meaning from the expression 'a barren woman's child'. It is through the understanding that this expression evokes that one uses it as an example of nonexistence.

Conversely, existence depends on its counterpart, nonexistence. One speaks for example of the birth, or coming into being, of something because this did not exist in the past. If it existed already, its present existence would render impossible any ulterior entry into existence. If something that was already existent could come into being, it would never stop coming into existence (which is absurd). Therefore, existence and nonexistence, truth and falsity, emptiness and nonemptiness—all such things are only the positings of thought. None of these categories correctly corresponds to the ultimate nature, for the latter is beyond all conceptual elaborations." (Zhonumalen/ Kumarila, in [Mipham Rinpoche, Padmakara, p. 304-305])

> "The counterpart of existence is non-existence.
> The counterpart of non-existence is existence.
> Thus, one should not think of existence,
> Nor should one think of non-existence.
>
> Where nothing whatever arises,
> Nothing whatsoever will cease.
> Seen without imagining,
> Nothing is, and nothing is not."

It is said along with this: The meaning of this is that regarding existence, you can establish non-existence: Before something existed. Now it is destroyed. And one that is born, did not exist before.

For example, when viewing destruction, three aspects of non-existence can be shown. (1. Some things are mutually non-existent; 2. Before something is born, it does not exist; 3. When something is destroyed, it no longer exists; 4. Some things are mutually non-existent, like a cow and a horse. As the companion of existence, there is nonexistence [non-vacuous contrast]. For example, birth is previously non-existent. Similarly, if the previously existent were born, then that past being will again become.

If this is the case, as Nagarjuna said

[*Mulamadhyamakakarika,* Chap. 15, Verse 6]:

"Those persons who concerning things and other than things,
Perceive neither objects nor the non-existence of objects.
By these the essence of Buddha's teaching,
Is not perfectly perceived."
[See Doctor 517 Padmakara 309: CF. Mipham Rinpoche Padmakara p. 296 on proximate ultimate.]

"Consequently the explanatory methods of the Prasangikas and the Svatantrika converge. As far as the ultimate view, the absence of all conceptual constructs, is concerned, they are the same. But when distinctions are made in the postmeditation period, it is easier to divide the ultimate truth into two categories as the Svatantrikas do. When in meditative equipoise, one penetrates nonconceptual primordial wisdom, there will be no further need to divide it, and a great freedom from all conceptual constructs will be accomplished. If one understands this, one will grasp the vital point of the Madhyamaka. It is difficult to do so otherwise." [Mipham Rinpoche, Padmakara, p. 302]

"...Yogacharas [who claim subject and object are the same and images are unreal] maintain direct knowledge of objects is possible, and since objects are considered to be of the same nature as consciousness, the claim for the unreality of images must in fact be faulty. This is the case because images do not actually exist in their view and so they must not be of the same substance as consciousness which is real." [Blumenthal, p. 129]

"In the present context, this 'seeing' may be expressed negatively as when one says, "I did not see anything." or positively, as when one says, "I saw nothing." There is, however, no difference in meaning, because even the latter statement does not indicate that there is something (a nothing) to see. Likewise, there is no difference in meaning between the statements "The ultimate is beyond the reach of intellect," "The ultimate is not the object of the intellect," and "The ultimate is the object of no-thought." Since the state of no-thought is identified as the halting of all concepts and the absence of all duality between the perceiver and the perceived, it does not mean that the ultimate can be "detected" as the object of no-thought.

[Mipham Rinpoche, Padmakara, pp. 300-301]

"All is real; all is unreal
    All is both unreal and real;
    All is neither real nor yet unreal;
    Thus by steps the Buddha taught."
[Mipham Rinpoche, Padmakara, p. 309;
"Those who say that things arise dependently
    And like the moon reflected in a pool
    Do not exist and are not non-existent,
    Can never be assailed by other views."
[Mipham Rinpoche, Padmakara, p. 309]

    All apparent permanence is impermanent.
    What does not exist is similarly impermanent."
    [Chap. 24, Verse 14 *Mulamadhyamakakarika*]

"Phenomena are not real, yet nevertheless appear, and this is the union of the two truths and is a great wonder." [Mipham Rinpoche, Padmakara, p. 312]

Or Doctor p. 519 And 304-305 Padmakara (Mipham Rinpoche): "...[C]onsequently, even a nonthing (absence) is posited in dependence on its counterpart: a causally efficient thing. If there were no certainty that barren women and children existed, it would be impossible to derive any meaning from the expression 'a barren woman's child'. It is through the understanding that this expression evokes that one uses it as an example of nonexistence.

Conversely, existence depends on its counterpart, nonexistence. One speaks for example of the birth, or coming into being, of something because this did not exist in the past. If it existed already, its present existence would render impossible any ulterior entry into existence. If something that was already existent could come into being, it would never stop coming into existence (which is absurd). Therefore, existence and non-existence, truth and falsity, emptiness and nonemptiness—all such things are only the positings of thought. None of these categories correctly corresponds to the ultimate nature, for the latter is beyond all conceptual elaborations."

Quote from Nagarjuna, Mipham Rinpoche, Doctor,
p. 119.

"The reasoning of the intrinsic nature is beyond bias, and from that perspective, none of the objects apprehended by those fond of characteristics
are posited. When the ship of attachment to entity is crushed in the ocean
of emptiness beyond extremes, the merchants of the mind of [the realm of]
existence, obsessed with the net of the characteristics of various observations, may, shocked and confounded with fear, try to grasp for the support
of some object. Yet the support itself is unsupported—this is the intrinsic
nature." [Doctor, p. 501]

[CF. Padmakara p. 314:] "But the false theories of Kapila and Kanada are
far stranger. For when they clearly see the shapes of objects, such as cows
or pots-objects that are themselves empty of universals (*spyi*) such as "cowhood" or "pothood" -they consider to be real not the thing seen, but the
unseen universal instead! See also Dreyfus' *Recognizing Reality* pp. 52-59)

"He [Shantarakshita} explains in MAV that the difference between the perception of those of low intellect who are unenlightened and the perception
of unenlightened ones is that in addition to valid cognition of gross objects,
those of low intellect also impute inherent existence onto the objects they
perceive. Thus they impute an extreme perspective onto objects which do
not abide in either of the two extremes." [Blumenthal, 2004 p. 152]

Samadhiraj Sutra, Chap. 9, Verse 23: "This is not ordinary perception but
non-dualistic." trans. Joshua Cutler *Great Treatise on the Stages of the Path
to Enlightenment* by Tsongkhapa: *King of Concentration Sutra*

Shantarakshita means valid perception as non-dualistic.

The center of the plantain plant is not hard, but edible.

[Cf. Blumenthal, 2004 pp 154-156]: "…Shantarakshita responds by arguing that a common subject can be established since there are validly established entities known by all beings." Sloka 76.

Cf.. *Udaanavarga,* varga 18, Verse 22, trans. Franz Berhard, Band 1, Gottigen: Vanden Hoecht, Ruprecht, 1965.

Shantarakshita wants to refute the view that if all conventionalities are unreal then inference has to be unreal and invalid. But he would argue that relative to the system of convention, inference is valid.
[Mipham Rinpoche, Padmakara, p.327]: "This is a trashy argument."

[McClintock/Blumenthal, 2004 p.367 note 211]: "... Sara McClintock (2003) has argued that Shantarakshita is using "sliding scales of analysis" in which he utilizes autonomous inferences (*svatantranumana*) when analyzing lower views from a Yogachara perspective, and when analyzing the Sautrantika position from a Yogachara perspective, yet in his final shift (when finally analyzing Yogachara views from a Madhyamaka perspective he no longer uses autonomous inferences. If this is the case, and Shantarakshita is only using such a form of reasoning when it is acceptable from the perspective of the tenets whose acceptance he is in a sense feigning, then use in such a circumstance should not be problematic.

Possible similarity to the use and mention distinction in contemporary philosophy. The criterion used, inference, is not the sort of thing that exists or doesn't exist. It is a technique that is used, but it is not validly considered as an object. [MLF]

[Blumenthal, 2004 p. 156] and Khenchen Palden Sherab Rinpoche: Mipham: "Appearances are there, but empty. If there is no appearance there is no emptiness and visa versa."
This then, is how one should understand that phenomena appear, even though they do not truly exist.
[CF. Blumenthal, 2004, p. 158]

Shantarakshita offers a detailed explanation of his argument in the *MAV.* He argues that these imputed notions of entities and entitylessness which even exist in newborn babies do not arise as a result of external entities. This is verified by the fact that such entities have already been rejected in this text. Likewise, they are not sudden and are not permanent since there is nothing that is permanent. Since the consciousness of even newborn infants are already accustomed to common modes of consciousness, such as perceiving entities and entitylessness, they must arise from a previous instance of a

similar type of consciousness, and thus from one of a previous life." [Blumenthal, 2004 p. 160]
[Cf. Gyel-tsab Blumenthal. P. 161]
Shunyasaptati [70 *Stanzas on Emptiness*, stanza 21, Nagarjuna]:

"If existent, an entity will be permanent.
If non-existent, an object will certainly be eliminated.
If there would be an entity that existed, it should be both.
Therefore, entities cannot be accepted.
Entities evidently arise,
And because of that, this is not nihilism.
Because entities are changing [reversed]
This is not eternalism.
Those who rely on enlightenment
Do not assert non-existence on the ultimate level.
Those not thinking and not acting,
How could they be nihilistic?"
["Pramanasiddhi" Chap. of *Pramanavartika*]

"If a phenomena were to exist inherently it should be permanent. If a phenomenon were to disintegrate completely then you must accept the nihilistic view. If a phenomenon were to exist inherently it would either exist permanently or else undergo complete disintegration: it cannot occur in a way which is different from these two. Therefore, one should not assert that a phenomenon has inherent existence." *Nagarjuna's Seventy Stanzas: A Buddhist Psychology of Emptiness*. ed. David Komito. Trans. and commentary Geshe Sonam Rinchen, Tenzin Dorjee and David Ross. Ithaca: Snow Lion, 1987 p. 128

Vyavarharasiddhi [accomplishment of usage] probably Nagarjuna [only in Chinese].
And: "Gyal-tsab's commentary refers to the cause of the afflictive emotions as the grasping at true existence (*bten 'dzin*) and eliminates Shantarakshita's use of the term "lack of inherent existence" (*rang bzhin med*) later in the stanza in favor of the more general "emptiness" (*stong nyid*). Geluk critics say that Shantarakshita accepts inherent existence). These changes again lend themselves in subtle ways towards reading Shantarakshita's text through a framework which will contribute to later Geluk critiques in

other philosophical materials." [Blumenthal, 2004 p. 162-163]

And it is also said in the *Candrapradipasamadhirajasutra Royal Meditation of the Moon Lamp Sutra:* "This attachment and to that to which there is attachment and the one who is attached are not seen on the ultimate level."

Also nb CF. Mipham Rinpoche, Padmakara, p. 337 on primordial wisdom.

"Pramanasiddhi" chapter of *Pramanvartika* [Blumenthal, 2004, p. 162]: "Santaraksita's treatment of this topic here is explained in the context of demonstrating how 'liberation' is easier [if one understands the meaning of] this text. 'understanding the meaning of this text' means understanding the lack of inherent existence of all persons and phenomena, which Shantarakshita has gone to great lengths to logically establish here. It seems as though his argument claims that by cultivating a realization of emptiness, knowledge of the selflessness of (persons and) phenomena, such an *arya* eventually attains liberation from cyclic existence through the abandonment of afflictive emotion obstacles (*klesavarana; nyon sgrib*) and contrived erroneous views. This is a result of a process of deepening one's understanding of emptiness through meditation and familiarity. (Sloka 83)
[*Sixty Verses, Yuctishastrika*, 47-49]
[Mipham Rinpoche Tib Doctor p. 422]:

> Moreover, if as you say nothing is existing then one might disagree and ask then what is affliction, karma, the arising of extreme affliction? What is purification? What is the relation of cause and effect, of inference, what is inferred through conventions, ignorance, formations, and the limbs of existence [twelve links]? When one becomes familiar with the antidote one is able to experience that which is not harmonious and without defilements, beloved and non-beloved, [all of] which is the maturing of virtuous and unvirtuous karma, and that is itself the antidote.

"The two truths make one another clear. How could they be contradictory? Ripened virtuous and non-virtuous actions arise and result in what is beautiful and not beautiful. Everything arises completely like this."
[*Pramanavartika*, Chap. 2, 81, 80].

"Since the mind is purely determined By the actions of the [earlier minds,]

[The subsequent] minds cannot arise without the [previous moments of the mind.] Therefore [the mind] is dependent on the [preceding] minds [and not the body.]
[bodhiwisdom.org/wpcontent/uploads/2018/05
Pramanavartika-root of Pramanavartika]

"Santaraksita proceeds from here to establish the argument by positing a logical connection between the correct view of emptiness and right moral action. The link is to be argued that, if one does not see all phenomena as lacking true existence, then ultimately valid cognition is harmed because one knows objects as truly existent when they actually are not. As a result, strong grasping becomes prevalent, serving as a basis for all sorts of inappropriate actions and intentions." [Blumenthal, 2004 p. 165]

Also: "When Santaraksita speaks of 'masters who know selflessness of phenomena,' it is interesting to note that Gyel-tsab refers to them more specifically as 'arya bodhisattvas.' This is as opposed to Hinayana arhats who, according to the Geluk presentation of Svatantrika-Madhyamaka, only know the selflessness of persons. This is worth knowing because for Gelukpas both Hinayana arhats and bodhisattvas realize the selflessness of persons and phenomena. This subtle shift presents Santaraksita's views in accordance with the way they will be later be presented and criticized in other Gelukpa philosophical materials. Neither in MA nor in his autocommentary on this stanza does Santaraksita refer to such persons or imply that such persons are necessarily arya bodhisattvas.

"The second interesting shift worth pointing out here concerns the technical terms used to describe emptiness. Gyel-tsab's commentary refers to the cause of afflictive emotions as the grasping at true existence (bden 'dzin) and eliminates Santaraksita's use of the term 'lack of inherent existence' (rang bzhin med) later in the stanza in favor of the more general 'emptiness' (stong nyid)." (Geluk critics say that Shantarakshita accepts inherent existence.) [Blumenthal, pp 162-163]

[*Vajracchedika Sutra* P. 81). In *Mahayana-Sutra-Samgraha* Part 1 in Sanskrit Learning, Darbhanga, 1961 Buddhist Sanskrit Texts #17. Ed. By Dr. P. L. Vaidya. Pub. By the Mithila Institute of Post-Graduate Studies and Research] [Cf. Kamalashila, *Panjika* Derge folio 127b]

Also: "While in many cases, Santararsita's text has been quite dynamic in his utilization of an assortment of both Buddhist and non-Buddhist views to help illuminate his own view, at this point in the text he is explicit in incorporation of a Yogachara framework for understanding conventional truth. I think it is important to reflect on what has happened in the text up to this point in order to fully understand his Yogachara Madhyamaka synthesis. Santaraksita is engaged in a dynamic philosophical enterprise in this text in which the perspective of his philosophical analysis shifts depending on the perspective of his opponents. Generally speaking, he argues as a Sautrantika when criticizing Vaibhashika views, as a Yogachara when criticizing Sautrantika view, and as a Madhyamaka when criticizing various Yogachara positions, While in the final analysis he maintains specific views and we can correctly say he is a Madhyamika since he rejects the existence of an ultimate nature in phenomena, one might also be inclined to say he is a 'Yogachara-Madhyamaka' in that he rejects the externality of objects conventionally...By use of 'sliding scales of analysis', I think Santaraksita's brand of Buddhist philosophy, far from being excusive, is much more inclusive of all systems of Buddhist thought....he uses multiple provisional views, not only that of Yogachara, in an attempt to lead followers to a Madhyamaka position realizing the lack of any inherent nature in phenomena."

[Mipham Rinpoche, Tib Doctor p. 422]: "Moreover, if as you say nothing is existing then one might disagree and ask then what is affliction, karma, the arising of extreme affliction? What is purification? What is the relation of cause and effect, of inference, what is inferred through conventions, ignorance, formations, and the limbs of existence [twelve links]? When one becomes familiar with the antidote one is able to experience that which is not harmonious and without defilements, beloved and non-beloved, [all of] which is the maturing of virtuous and unvirtuous karma, and that is itself the antidote 79.

"Without consciousness there can be no appearance of things." [Mipham Rinpoche, Padmakara, p. 362]

[If you infer another form which is external to the mind which produces knowledge, then this is different from the result. Khenchen Palden Sherab Rinpoche].

Bhavaviveka argued against this. [Khenchen Palden Sherab Rinpoche].
[Mipham Rinpoche, Padmakara, 2005, p. 362]: "It may be objected that,

even granted that the experience of a mental aspect is necessarily conscious-ness, it can be inferred nevertheless that there must be a mental object that is casting its aspect on the mind. But because the subtle particles and so forth do not exist (even though they have been inferred), this is untenable. Even in those systems where the particle is considered to exist, the latter is not established by perception. It is hidden and that it exists is no more than an inference. Now the fact that the non-existent hidden object is (only) inferred, whereas one experiences things clearly (in the mind) lends consid-erable force to the argument that phenomena are merely established by the mind itself. Indeed, this position cannot be invalidated by any other view."

Also: Nagarjuna's argument about causality is applied here, because causality is mental, and is only habitual patterns which arise in the mind like magic. There is no creation. [Khenchen Palden Sherab Rinpoche]

What we see as real is a projection of our minds.

[Reference not found]. Mentioned in p. 49 in *Vijnaptimatratasiddhi*, Vasu-bandhu, Gaganathajha-Granthamala series, pub director Research Institute Varanasi 1972.

Mind should be understood to be without circumference or center. This teaching is explained very well. Because [all things are] beyond the extreme of birth destruction, and remaining, there is no limit or center. In the *Dharmasangiti* it is said, "Oh Buddha, all elements have an imagined essence. The totality of things is mental, insubstantial, and like illusions, rooted in non-existence." *Lankavatara:* 10, 256---p. 246-247 Suzuki:

"By relying on mind
One does not imagine external objects.
Staying completely within perfect perceptions,
One even goes beyond mind only.
Going beyond even mind only,
Even to the view of the non-existence of appearances,
The yogi who abides in non-appearance,
Sees the great vehicle.
Without accomplishing by peacefully spontaneous engaging,

And completely purified by pure aspiration,
Without the excellent wisdom of selflessness
Reality cannot be seen.
Removing cause and conditions,
Even the remaining cause [mind] is an obstruction,
In the stipulation of Mind Only [things] arise unborn
As I have taught."
[*Lankavatara Sutra*, Verse 16, 88]

There are no external things
Also, the mind is not grasped.
Because of giving up all views
This is the characteristic of birthlessness.
Thus, it is said. Because of this it is also said:
There is not any birth.
There are no blockages.
Arising and cessation,
Are only mind.
Explaining the primary elements etc.,
As included in consciousness,
By knowing that, they are dispersed.
Are they not just wrongly imagined?

All the tathagatas are gone, going, will be gone.
[*De bzhen gshags pa rnams gshegs pa 'gyur pa.*]

From the *Lankavatara Sutra*: The Mahayana which is combined into two systems is the only concise teaching of the essence of the Mahayana sutras.

"The five dharmas, intrinsic existence
And the eight consciousnesses themselves,
Are entities with two selflessness [of dharma and persons] nature,
All included in the Mahayana."

Thus said. The two views as discussed by Brahma, Vishnu and Shiva are explained in many ways.

In the *Guhya Amrita Bindu* [*Secret Drops of Nectar*] it is stated: What is special in the great vehicle? [Even non-Buddhists say]:

"As to only mind which is completely pure,
One who is enlightened is permanently liberated.
Imagined without accepting and rejecting,
Brahma always remains without sorrow."

All the tathagatas are gone, going, will be gone. [*De bzhen gshags pa rnams gshegs pa 'gyur pa*].

Name, reason, conceptualization (controlled by others), suchness and perfect knowledge.

[Even in the *Upanishads* they say that Buddha is always pure, always liberated LJ]

From *Five Days* by Vishnu [Hindu work-they are saying we have no need for Madhyamaka because we already have these ideas.]:

"Having completely transcended mere names,
Having abandoned entity and non entity,
Thus free from evolving and dissolution,
This is the so-called son of the wealth deity. [Vishnu]"

Therefore, the King of the Sages, taught only the beautiful vast complete teaching of emptiness of no short duration, which was not common to the heretics. It is said in the *Chandrapradipasamadhi:*

All entities are always empty in nature.
Thus also it is similarly said: here stated:

"Also, similarly for the subtle entity
One is not wise because one
Will not see the arising
Of objects through cause and conditions."
[Nagarjuna, *Yuktishastika*, #13]

"So, if even one object were to exist,
Would it not have intrinsic nature?
If so, it would contradict many of the scriptures,
And in itself, it would be incompatible with the world."
[Nagarjuna, *Precious Garland (Ratnamala)*]

[Kamalashila *Panjika* Derge Folio 130b]:
"Free from intrinsic nature of forms or non-forms."

[Kamalashila *Panjika*. Derge Folio 130b]:
"Having abandoned arising and perishing."
      Kamalasila identifies Brahman with "nature of self."
      [CF. Kamalashila, *Panjika*, 31a et al.]
      [CF. Mipham Rinpoche, Padmakara, p. 273]
Also: [Kamalashila *Panjika* Derge Folio 130b]:
"Free from intrinsic nature of forms or non-forms."

Three kinds of patience: (1) Accepting suffering, (2) Realizing the nature of dharma, and (3) Seeing the nature of things [that we are in samsara].

Madhyamaka

Successive pervasive (Skt. anvaya; Tib. *dogs khyab*):
"What is created, is impermanent."
Reversing pervasive (Skt. *vayavyapanti*; Tib. *rjes khyab*):
"What is impermanent is not created.

INDEX

Abhidharma, 51, 166, 172,

alaya, 44, 166

Dergey, 167

dewa chenpo, 167,

dharmakaya, 56, 93, 167, 170, 199,

emptiness, xvi, xviii, xix, 48, 49, 58, 63, 65, 71, 73, 75, 76, 86, 87, 90, 91, 164, 167, 169, 170, 174, 197, 198, 200, 202, 203, 204, 205, 206, 207, 211,

Great Ascetic, 169,

great vehicle, 84, 85, 163, 170, 209, 211,

Hinayana, 10, 91, 168, 207, 75

Kasyapa, 170,

Kapila, 25, 28, 27, 53, 68, 54, 64, 87, 90, 170, 190, 198, 203,

Mimamsa, 39, 169, 171, 195,

Manjushri, 1, 98, 171,

Madhyamaka, ix, x, xi, xiv, xvi, xviii, xx, xxi, 37, 59, 66, 69, 71, 77, 75, 79, 83, 86, 89, 96, 113, 162, 163, 164, 166, 170, 178, 179, 180, 184, 194, 201, 204, 207, 208, 211, 212, 219,

Mahamudra, 170,

Mahayana, xv, 73, 79, 84, 85, 94, 163, 169, 170, 174, 175, 176, 207, 210, 218, 220, 221,

mandala, xx, 167, 171, 179,

probandum, 45, 172,

probans, 45, 172,

rupakaya, 172,

rigpa, 172,

Rinchen Zangpo, 172,

Samkhya, 25, 27, 29, 30, 31, 49, 64, 87, 90, 170, 173, 190, 191, 192, 197,

Sautrantika, xx, 15, 16, 17, 18, 21, 23, 31, 39, 42, 66, 77, 79, 163, 173, 179, 185, 187, 195, 204, 208,

sems tsam pa, 173,
Sugata, 5, 55, 93, 95, 174,
Tathagata, 48, 49, 54, 85, 86, 87, 174, 210, 211,
tendrel, 174,
Vaisheshika, , 170, 171, 175,
Vaibhashika, xx, 28, 79, 91, 175, 179, 208,
Vajrasattva, 175,
Vajrayana, ix, xi, 218, 219, 175,
Vinaya, xx, xi, 172, 176, 179,

The Translation Committee:

Venerable Khenchen Palden Sherab Rinpoche

Venerable Khenchen Palden Sherab Rinpoche (1938-2010) was a renowned scholar and meditation master of the *Nyingma school of Tibetan Buddhism*. He was born in 1938 in the Doshul region of Kham, eastern Tibet. Around age four, before joining Gochen monastery, he began to read, write and lean chants and ritual ceremonies from his grandfather Lam Tharchok and his father Lama Chimed Namgyal. At the age of fourteen he entered the prestigious Riwoche monastic university where he excelled in Tibetan Medicine and literature, Sanskrit, and the Buddhist philosophy of all nine yanas.

In 1959, Khenchen Rinpoche and his family left their homeland in Tibet and made their way to India. After the tumultuous period following their exodus in 1967 he was appointed head of the *Nyingma* department of the Central Institute of Higher Tibetan Studies in Sarnath by H. H. Dudjom Rinpoche. He held this position of abbot for seventeen years, dedicating all his time and energy to ensure the survival and spread of the Buddha's teachings.

Ven. Khenchen Palden Sherab Rinpoche moved to the United States in 1984 to work closely with H. H. Dudjom Rinpoche. In 1985 he and his brother, Ven. Khenpos Tsewang Dongyal Rinpoche, founded Dharma Samudra Publishing. IN 1988, they founded the Padmasambhava Buddhist Center. Together the Khenpo Rinpoches founded Pema Samye Ling in New York, Padma Samye Chokhor Ling monastery and Orgyen Samye Chokhor Ling nunnery in Sarnath, India. They erected the Miracle Stupa in Shravasti, India, and rebuilt Gochen monastery in Tibet.

Khenchen Rinpoche has co-authored over twenty Dharma books in English with Venerable Khenpo Tsewang Dongyal Rinpoche and authored many other texts in Tibetan. He worked tirelessly his entire life to pass on the ancient and authentic practice traditions of Buddhism to inspire thousands of practitioners world-wide and to leave behind a community dedicated to peace, love and wisdom.

In June 2010, displaying profound signs of his realization, Rinpoche entered mahaparinivana peacefully at Padma Samye Ling. Truly; he was a warrior who conquered all negativities to fully accomplish the wishes of Buddha Shakyamuni and Guru Padmasambhava. We will honor and revere him and his legacy forever. A more extensive biography and full list of Rinpoche's works can be found at www.padmasambhava.org

Ven. Khenpo Tsewang Dongyal Rinpoche

Khenpo Tsewang Dongyal Rinpoche was born in the Dhoshul region of Kham in eastern Tibet on June 10, 1950. On that summer day in the family tent, Rinpoche's birth caused his mother no pain. The next day, his mother, Pema Lhadze, moved the bed where she had given birth. Beneath it she found growing a beautiful and fragrant flower which she plucked and offered to Chenrezig on the family altar.

Soon after his birth three head lamas from Jadchag monastery came to his home and recognized him as the reincarnation of Khenpo Sherab Khyentse. Khenpo Sherab Khyentse, who had been the former head abbot lama at Gochen Monastery, was a renowned scholar and practitioner who lived much of his life in retreat.

Rinpoche's first Dharma teacher was his father, Lama Chimed Namgyal. Beginning his schooling at the age of five, he entered Gochen Monastery. His studies were interrupted when his family had to escape to India. In India, his father and brother, Ven. Khenchen Palden Sherab Rinpoche (1932-2010), continued his education until he entered the Nyingmapa Monastic School of Northern India, where he studied until 1967.

He then entered the Central Institute of Higher Tibetan Studies, which was then a part of Sanskrit University in Varanasi, where he received his B.A. degree in 1975. He also attended Nyingmapa University in West Bengal, where he received another B.A. and an M.A. in 1977.

In 1978 Rinpoche was enthroned as the abbot of the Wish-fulfilling Nyingmapa Institute in Boudanath, Nepal by H.H. Dudjom Rinpoche Jigdral Yeshe Dorje, and later became the abbot of the Department of Dharma Studies, where he taught poetry, grammar, philosophy, and psychology. In 1981, H.H. Dudjom Rinpoche appointed Rinpoche as the abbot of the Dorje

Nyingpo Center in Paris, France. In 1982 he was asked to work with H.H. Dudjom Rinpoche at the Yeshe Nyingpo Center in New York. During the 1980s, until H.H. Dudjom Rinpoche's mahaparinirvana in 1987, Rinpoche continued working closely with him, often traveling as his translator and attendant.

In 1988, Ven. Khenchen Palden Sherab Rinpoche and Ven. Khenpo Tsewang Dongyal Rinpoche founded the Padmasambhava Buddhist Center (PBC) to preserve the authentic message of Buddha Shakyamuni and Guru Padmasambhava in its entirety, and in particular to teach the traditions of the *Nyingma* school and Vajrayana Buddhism. PBC includes over 20 centers in the U.S.A., India, Puerto Rico, Latvia, and Russia, as well as monastic institutions in India, the U.S.A., and Russia.

As a holder of the complete Nyingmapa lineage, Khenpo Tsewang Rinpoche is fully versed in the Theravada, Mahayana, and Vajrayana schools, and is a master of Dzogchen. He has co-authored over 35 Dharma books in English with Khenchen Palden Sherab Rinpoche, and has personally authored several books, including a biography on His Holiness Dudjom Rinpoche named *Light of Fearless Indestructible Wisdom*, two books of poetry on the life of Guru Rinpoche, including *Praise to the Lotus Born: A Verse Garland of Waves of Devotion*, and a unique two-volume cultural and religious history of Tibet entitled *"Expressing the Six Distinctive Greatnesses of the Ancient School by Recalling the Kind Legacy of the Great Masters, Translators, and Dharma Kings, Known as "Rejoicing Laughter of the Noble Beings,"* which details the historical bases of the Dharma in Tibet from the sixth through ninth centuries. At present, this is one of the only books written that conveys the Dharma activities of this historical period in such depth.

Ven. Khenpo Tsewang Rinpoche actively travels throughout the world giving teachings, empowerments, and personal guidance in fluent English at numerous retreats.

The main monastery and retreat center of the Padmasambhava Buddhist Center is Padma Samye Ling Monastery and Retreat Center, located in Delaware County in upstate New York. Located in the western region of the Catskill Mountains, the outstanding facilities are contained within 500 acres of forests, meadows, and natural springs. PSL hosts group and personal retreats throughout the year, as well as an annual philosophical Shedra, weekly Dharma Study, and a long-term residency volunteer program.

For more information about Khenpo Tsewang Rinpoche's activities, the Padmasambhava Buddhist Center, or to schedule coming to PSL for retreat or a visit, please contact:

Padma Samye Ling
618 Buddha Highway
Sidney Center, NY 13839
(607) 865-8068
w w w . p a d m a s a m b h a v a . o r g

PBC Schedule of Events: www.padmasambhava.org/events
PSL Resident Volunteer Program: www.padmasambhava.org/psl-dharma-skills-program

YouTube: www.padmasambhava.org/youtube
Facebook: Padmasambhava Buddhist Center
Twitter: KhenpoRinpoche
Instagram: www.instagram.com/khenporinpoche

To learn more about Ven. Khenpo Tsewang Dongyal Rinpoche:
www.padmasambhava.org/ven-khenpo-tsewang-dongyal-rinpoche

Marie Friquegnon

Marie Friquegnon is an emeritus professor of philosophy and of Asian studies at William Paterson University. She studied at Convent of the Sacred Heart 91st Street, Barnard College (BA 1965) and New York University (PhD in Philosophy 1974) She authored A Short Introduction to the Philosophy of Santaraksita and Reflections on Childhood. She edited with Noe Dinnerstein *Studies in the Yogacara Madhyamaka of Shantaraksita*, with Raziel Abelson and Ben Abelson *Clarity and Vision*, and with Raziel Abelson *Ethics for Modern Life*. She published with Khenchen Palden Sherab Rinpoche and Khenpo Tsewang Dongyal Rinpoche translations and commentaries of Santaraksita's Tattvasiddhi and Madhyamakalamkara. She is editing with Benjamin Abelson a collection of readings, *Great Disputes in Philosophy,* and is currently at work on a philosophical memoir about her intellectual journey from Thomistic philosophy to Vajrayana Buddhist philosophy, *Finding Santaraksita: A Philosopher's Journey on the Buddhist Path.* She was a student of His Holiness Dudjom Rinpoche, Khenchen Palden Sherab Rinpoche and currently is studying with the Buddhist teacher and scholar Khenpo Tsewang Gongyal Rinpoche.

Geshe Lozang Jamspal

Geshe Lozang Jamspal holds a Rigs-chen degree from Tashi Lhunpo Monastic University in Tibet, an Acharya degree in Sanskrit from Sanskrit University, Varanasi, and a PhD from Columbia University. Formerly Lecturer in Buddhist Sanskrit and Classical Tibetan in the Department of Religion at Columbia University, he is currently a professor at the International Buddhist College in Thailand. Geshe Jamspal has translated: *The Stages of Meditation* by Vimalamitra, *The Range of the Bodhisattva*—a Mahayana Sutra, with David Kittay, Nagarjuna's *Letter to King Gautamiputra* with explanatory notes based on Tibetan commentaries and with a preface by His Holiness Sakya Trizin, translated into English from the Tibetan with Venerable Ngawang Samten Chophel, and Peter Della Santina *The Treasury of Good Sayings of Saskya Pandita*, the eminent Tibetan Lama 1182-1251: *Development of Awareness and Conduct, The Universal Vehicle Discourse Literature (Mahayanasutralankara)* by Maitreyanātha/ Aryāsanga together with its commentary (Bhasya) by Vasubandhu (Translated from the Sanskrit, Tibetan, and Chinese by L. Jamspal, R. Clark, J. Wilson, L. Zwilling, M. Sweet, R. Thurman)
Geshe Jamspal has also translated *The Vajra Rosary Tantra*. In addition, he has translated sutras with his students for the foundation 84000: *Translating the Words of the Buddha*, as well as other texts from the Tibetan Buddhist canon.

Geshe Lozang Jamspal

Geshe Lozang Jamspal holds a Rigs-chen degree from Tashi Lhunpo Monastic University in Tibet, an Acharya degree in Sanskrit from Sanskrit University, Varanasi, and a PhD from Columbia University. Formerly Lecturer in Buddhist Sanskrit and Classical Tibetan in the Department of Religion at Columbia University, he is currently a professor at the International Buddhist College in Thailand. Geshe Jamspal has translated:

The Stages of Meditation by Vimalamitra, *The Range of the Bodhisattva*—a Mahayana Sutra, with David Kittay, Nagarjuna's *Letter to King Gautamiputra* with explanatory notes based on Tibetan commentaries and with a preface by His Holiness Sakya Trizin, translated into English from the Tibetan with Venerable Ngawang Samten Chophel, and Peter Della Santina *The Treasury of Good Sayings of Saskya Pandita*, the eminent Tibetan Lama 1182-1251: *Development of Awareness and Conduct, The Universal Vehicle Discourse Literature (Mahayanasutralankara)* by Maitreyanātha/ Aryāsanga together with its commentary (Bhasya) by Vasubandhu (Translated from the Sanskrit, Tibetan, and Chinese by L. Jamspal, R. Clark, J. Wilson, L. Zwilling, M. Sweet, R. Thurman)

Geshe Jamspal has also translated *The Vajra Rosary Tantra*. In addition, he has translated sutras with his students for the foundation 84000: *Translating the Words of the Buddha*, as well as other texts from the Tibetan Buddhist canon.

Made in the USA
Monee, IL
26 May 2023

33862034R00134